Humor and Laughter

HUMOR AND LAUGHTER

An Anthropological Approach

Mahadev L. Apte

CORNELL UNIVERSITY PRESS

ITHACA AND LONDON

Copyright © 1985 by Cornell University

All rights reserved. Except for brief quotations in a review, this book, or parts thereof, must not be reproduced in any form without permission in writing from the publisher. For information, address Cornell University Press, 124 Roberts Place, Ithaca, New York 14850.

First published 1985 by Cornell University Press.
Published in the United Kingdom by
Cornell University Press Ltd., London.

International Standard Book Number 0-8014-1720-1 (cloth)
International Standard Book Number 0-8014-9307-2 (paper)
Library of Congress Catalog Card Number 84-15618
Printed in the United States of America
Librarians: Library of Congress cataloging information
appears on the last page of the book.

The paper in this book is acid-free and meets the guidelines for permanence
and durability of the Committee on Production Guidelines for
Book Longevity of the Council on Library Resources.

To my favorite nutritionist
for humor, health,
and happiness

Contents

Preface

Three factors originally motivated me to undertake the research on humor that culminated in this book: my own growing interest in the phenomena of humor, my discovery that much research on humor in the social sciences had been carried out by psychologists and lacked a cross-cultural perspective, and my realization in the course of my reading that the anthropological literature included no single comprehensive treatment of the subject.

Anthropologists have generally ignored the topic of humor in their research. Although they are marginally interested in specific aspects of it in individual cultures, this interest has never prompted the attention paid to such other topics as kinship, religion, ecology, economic transactions, and political systems. Extensive analyses of the many characteristics of humor in individual cultures are rare, and cross-cultural studies of humor simply do not exist. I hope that my work will help stimulate some anthropological interest in humor, particularly among ethnographers.

In writing this book I have benefited from the help of more individuals than I can name. After learning of my research, colleagues, friends, relatives, and other people constantly brought to my attention publications in scholarly journals, newspaper articles, popular books, ethnographic data, and anthologies dealing with humor. The students in my seminars on the ethnography of humor helped me realize that I needed to explain concepts, arguments, theories, methods, and data that had always seemed perfectly clear to me, and they helped me find ways of doing so. Many friends and colleagues read drafts of individual chapters as well as the entire manuscript and provided constructive criticism. Although I

9

have not always accepted their advice, I have benefited from it: it helped me to see things from different viewpoints and to provide arguments and evidence to forestall some criticisms. In particular I thank the following people for their encouragement, help, advice, and constructive criticism: Paul Axelrod, Lorna Amarasingham Rhodes, Antony Chapman, Ernestine Friedl, Jerome Handler, Paul McGhee, Ellen Messer, Lawrence Mintz, John Morreall, Elliott Oring, D. P. Pattanayak, Naomi Quinn, Molly Schuchat, and Robert Weller, and my anonymous readers, who provided many useful suggestions.

During my research and writing, I lost my sense of humor on innumerable occasions, but my wife, Judit, and my children, Sharad and Sunita, helped me regain it by their understanding, cheerfulness, playful attitude, and, most of all, constant encouragement. Following the Indian tradition, however, I do not wish to thank them, for doing so would somehow break the bonds of intimacy among us.

MAHADEV L. APTE

Durham, North Carolina

Humor and Laughter

Introduction

A sense of humor and the ability to laugh and to speak make human beings unique in the animal kingdom; so goes our anthropocentric thinking. Yet few activities have remained as puzzling as humor and laughter. Scholars have tried to comprehend their nature since antiquity and have proposed many explanations for them.[1] Humor and laughter remain a major scholarly concern today, as witness, for instance, the international conferences held in recent years.[2] Researchers of humor come from diverse disciplinary backgrounds, ranging from the humanities to the social and natural sciences.

Some Definitions of Humor

Humor is perhaps one of the most difficult subjects to study. The extensive literature on humor repeatedly emphasizes the difficulties of defining the concept satisfactorily.[3] Goldstein and McGhee do not even attempt to define it "for the simple reason that there is no single definition of humor acceptable to all investigators in the area" (1972: xxi).

The problem of studying humor begins with its conceptualization. While there is general agreement that certain stimuli make individuals laugh or smile with pleasure, it has not been possible to determine with any precision what conspires cognitively between potential stimuli and the overt response of laughter or smiling. It appears that three elements need to be considered: (1) sources that act as potential stimuli; (2) the cognitive and intellectual activity responsible for the perception and evaluation of these sources leading to humor experience; and (3) behavioral responses that are expressed as smiling or laughter or both. These attributes of the conceptualization of humor generally occur sequentially as I have ordered them; however, it is the second phase, the mental activity experienced by an individual, that is most crucial.

The term "humor" and other expressions derived from it have been used to refer to all three phases or to any one of them. Events, actions, situations, and so forth are labeled "humorous" as if humor were an integral part of them, but they are external to the phenomenon, if the three-phase elaboration of the concept is to be accepted. Similarly, meanings of "humor" include the behavioral responses of smiling or laughter. For many scholars the term "laughter" is synonymous with the term "humor" (Bergler 1956:30ff.; Hertzler 1970), and the phrase "theories of laughter" often means theories of humor. While laughter and smiling are probably the most overt indicators of the humor experience and are therefore important in determining its occurrence, they differ from humor in being anatomically and physiologically observable overt activities. The "part for the whole" approach can be misleading unless the label "humor" clearly designates only a specific phase of the total conceptual configuration; various disciplinary backgrounds and interests predispose scholars to emphasize one phase of humor more than others. In meaning, the term "humor" overlaps with other terms, and the indiscriminate use of various related terms can create ambiguities. Despite an occasional attempt to determine and define their semantic boundaries (McGhee 1979:6–8), "wit," "comic," "incongruity," "amusement," "absurdity," "ludicrousness," "ridicule," "mirth," "funniness," and "playfulness" share at least some semantic properties with the term "humor" and are commonly used in scholarly discussions on the topic.

In this book "humor" refers, first, to a cognitive, often unconscious experience involving internal redefining of sociocultural reality and resulting in a mirthful state of mind; second, to external sociocultural factors that trigger this cognitive experience; third, to the pleasure derived from the cognitive experience labeled "humor"; and fourth, to the external manifestations of the cognitive experience and the resultant pleasure, expressed through mirthful laughter and smiling. Meaning 2 refers to the antecedents, and meaning 4 to the effects of the cognitive experience. I shall treat meaning 1 as a postulate, placing emphasis on the second and fourth meanings, since I shall focus on the nature of stimuli leading to the cognitive humor experience and its effects. The terms "laughter" and "smiling," or "smile," will be used to mean external manifestations of the humor experience. In essence, then, a basic tenet in this book is that humor, properly speaking, is a psychological and cognitive phenomenon[4] and that an anthropological perspective requires analysis of its antecedents and consequences with the goal of developing a comparative theoretical framework. I use the term "humorous" interchangeably with such other terms as "amusing" and "funny" to describe antecedents of the cognitive humor experience.

THE PURPOSE AND ORIENTATION OF THIS WORK

I shall pursue two broad objectives: (1) the exploration by cross-cultural comparison of the interdependence of humor and sociocultural factors in societies around the world, and the formulation of generalizations based on such an investigation; (2) the setting forth of theoretical propositions regarding the similar and different ways in which humor is linked to sociocultural factors. Clearly this study is comparative rather than ethnographic; there is a need for such an approach.

My two objectives can be achieved by providing answers to several types of questions. Are there cross-culturally shared ways in which humor stimuli are generated and humor is appreciated? Are there categories and types of humor that occur in many societies? The second question implies that conceptual categories of humor can be established on the basis of analyses of a few cultures or that they can be formulated as part of an etic framework,[5] after which process their distribution across cultures can be checked. The two approaches are not independent of each other but mutually reinforcing. Does humor serve similar purposes in many societies? Do similar behaviors, objects, institutions, and so forth across cultures serve as stimuli of humor? Do cultures share similar attitudes toward the need, desirability, occurrence, and use of humor in certain social events? In other words, are there indigenous explanations of humor phenomena that appear to be similar across cultures? Although the questions are framed in such a way as to develop generalizations, answers should also emphasize the nature of cross-cultural variation in the conceptualization, form, substance, and function of humor.

The orientation of this study is comparative, but its organization follows, with some exceptions, a holistic framework commonly

15

used in ethnographies of individual cultures. I analyze the interdependence of humor and sociocultural factors within the broad domains of social organization and expressive culture. Within social organization, I specifically emphasize the ways in which kinship, age, sex, role, status, and so on underlie the form, substance, and function of humor. Where expressive culture is concerned, I focus on the use of language, religion, and folklore as modalities for the initiation and expression of humor, although here, too, I direct my attention to form, substance, and function.

My discussion principally focuses on the external stimuli of humor and responses to it. Even if humor is a cognitive experience for an individual, it must have a cultural niche; it cannot occur in a vacuum. The stress on external humor stimuli is reflected in the consideration of their origin. I also explore the nature of sequential events of humor and its consequences at both individual and societal levels. I pursue both metatheoretical and prospective approaches, critically examining the theories of other scholars regarding the causes, facets, and effects of humor phenomena. In addition I formulate new theories and explanations by way of propositions and hypotheses after analyzing the interconnections between humor and other sociocultural dimensions to determine how they influence the nature and function of humor at the culture-specific and general levels.

I have emphasized the institutional development of humor for the most part, because sociocultural factors seem to influence the nature of humor considerably at the institutional level. By "institutional development of humor" I mean any set of culturally organized activity or behavior that results in a humorous experience (Malinowski 1944:52ff.). The institutional development of humor is easier to analyze because it is much more patterned than individualistic humor, which is often spontaneous, idiosyncratic, and dependent on the psychological moods of the individual.

As the first cross-cultural study of humor in general in anthropology, my book attempts to answer, however tentatively, the questions raised at the beginning of this section. Two axioms underlie my discussion, namely, that humor is by and large culture based and that humor can be a major conceptual and methodological tool for gaining insights into cultural systems. Humor is primarily the result of cultural perceptions, both individual and collective, of incongruity, exaggeration, distortion, and any unusual combinations of the cultural elements in external events. Humor is culture based in the sense that individual cultural systems significantly influence the mechanism that triggers the humor experience. Familiarity with a cultural code is a prerequisite for the spontaneous mental restructuring of elements that results in amusement and laughter or for the recognition of such restructuring in the sociocultural reality. Individuals are not conscious of this requirement, because they already possess the cultural knowledge to which they compare the humor-generating stimuli. An individual who is not a member of a specific culture and therefore has not internalized its behavioral patterns and value system may not experience humor, lacking the necessary standard for comparison.

My second axiom complements the first. If the foundation of most humor is cultural, then understanding how humorous experiences are cognitively formulated, either intentionally or accidentally, should lead us to better insights into the cultural system. The questions to be asked repeatedly are several. Why and how are certain combinations of cultural elements viewed as incongruent, exaggerated, inappropriate, distorted, and so on? What are the congruent, normal, standard, appropriate structures on which judgments of incongruity, exaggeration, and distortion are based? Are the combinations of disparate culturally cognitive categories seen as appropriate incongruities? Answers to such questions should make explicit the implicit patterned aspects of a cultural code so that they can be subjected to verification and confirmation.

Anthropologists and sociologists have occasionally expressed the view that humor is useful for analyzing and understanding sociocultural systems, although they have not yet systematically explored it. Note, for instance, the following remarks made by sociologist A. A. Berger: "Because humor is intimately connected to culture-codes, it is useful in providing insights into a society's values" (1976:115). Anthropologist Hall commented that "people laugh and tell jokes, and if you can learn the humor of a people and really control it, you know that you are also in control of nearly everything else" (1959/1968:56).

The Organization and Intended Readership

This book primarily addresses nonanthropologists interested in humor research. It discusses anthropological concepts, theories, and methodological issues, as well as anthropological contributions to humor by way of ethnographic data and analyses. Anthropologists interested in humor research may also find this work useful because of its emphasis on cross-cultural comparison. This introductory chapter outlines the general framework of the book and explains what an anthropological study of humor entails, describing criteria for selecting humor-related ethnographic data and the limitations of such a study. Chapters 1 through 4 explore the interconnections between humor and social structure. They focus on humor within the framework of kinship, sex roles, enculturation and socialization of children, and the ascriptive aspects of group identity.

Chapter 1 analyzes the phenomenon of joking relationship, examining the general scope and overall nature of relevant studies, including problems of terminology and definitions. There follows a cross-cultural analysis of joking relationships within a typological framework in which each category is discussed and is illustrated with relevant ethnographic examples. I briefly evaluate existing theories of the joking relationship and present theoretical propositions concerning its cross-cultural aspects.

Humor is examined in the context of sex roles in Chapter 2. It offers the thesis that humor fairly reliably indicates the inequality of the sexes. Although women are no less capable of developing and appreciating humor than men, women have been denied similar opportunities for publicly engaging in humor. Because modesty, passivity, and virtue are associated with ideal womanhood, women have been confined to the private domain, with many constraints imposed upon them. Only marriage, old age, and the greater freedom of behavior granted to women in groups to some extent alleviate this inequality between the sexes.

Chapter 3 examines the nature of children's humor across cultures. A fourfold classificatory scheme is presented, and each category of humor is analyzed in detail with illustrative ethnographic examples. Sexual differences in children's humor receive brief attention, as does psychological research on the relationship between humor and children's cognitive and personality development.

Chapter 4 analyzes ethnic humor to discover how its structure, substance, and function reflect the dynamics of intergroup interaction and the stereotypic images that specific groups hold of other groups both within and across cultures. To this end, I elaborate key concepts and critically examine both textual and contextual analyses of ethnic humor.

Part 2 examines humor in the context of such universal human attributes as language, religion, and folklore. Chapter 5 explores the nature and function of humor within the context of religion

18

across cultures. A major premise here is that religion, especially its ritualistic aspects in preliterate societies, permits institutionalized humor activity that has certain characteristics not found in other sociocultural contexts. Such humor appears to serve many psychological and sociological functions through the reversal of social roles, status, and behavioral patterns and by focusing on sexual and scatological activities.

Linguistic and sociolinguistic aspects of humor are considered in Chapter 6. I demonstrate how numerous universal categories of humor exploit the structural characteristics of language and probe the interdependence of language and other elements of culture as reflected in humor by focusing on cross-cultural differences and similarities.

Chapter 7 analyzes humor in folklore, with emphasis on the trickster figure. Folkloristic data on tricksters from different parts of the world show the widespread occurrence, popularity, and structural similarity of tricksters. Incongruity, the fundamental principle underlying trickster-related humor, finds biological, psychological, and sociocultural manifestations in the trickster's personality and action. I examine these manifestations from a cross-cultural perspective with the objective of developing some broad theoretical propositions.

Chapter 8 examines the evolutionary and biosocial attributes of laughter and smiling, starting with their anatomical and physiological bases and subsequently tracing their phylogenetic and ontogenetic developments. The phonetic aspects of laughter also receive attention, and I discuss the ways in which the actual occurrence of laughter and smiling is influenced by differential norms across cultures.

The Postscript considers some broad implications expressed as propositions concerning the relationship between humor and culture. Although speculative, these statements have their bases in the analysis of interconnections between humor and several diverse aspects of the sociocultural system viewed in a cross-cultural perspective.

An Anthropological Approach to the Study of Humor

Ideally, any anthropological consideration of humor should pursue a two-part approach involving ethnography and comparative study.[6]

At the culture-specific level, the examination of humor involves recording and describing events, actions, situations, and individuals perceived to be amusing by members of the culture being investigated. Because much humor is verbal, the ethnographer should describe humor-generating stimuli, especially speech acts, in terms of such components as time and place, formal and semantic properties of the utterance(s), participants' identities (sex, age, social status, role, and so forth), motives and expectations of participants, and cultural values underlying the humor experience. The ethnographer should also identify and record as many nonverbal humorous events as possible, using the natives' reactions of mirth and his or her own as the operational criteria.

In addition to recording and describing observed humorous events, the ethnographer should ask individuals to narrate events in the past that they, as either witnesses or participants, found humorous. Well-known storytellers in the culture being studied should be interviewed and their humorous stories recorded. Texts of all kinds considered amusing by the people—rhymes, riddles, tales, and proverbs—should be written down.

The analysis of data involves answering the following questions and others that are similar: In what kinds of social situations and interactions does humor occur? Are some social contexts more amenable to humor than others, and if so, why? How is humor initiated and developed in social situations? Are some patterned behaviors routinely considered amusing, and why? Are specific objects, roles, and individuals routinely recognized as humor-generating sources, and if so, why? For what specific purposes is humor used?

In addressing such questions, the analysis should indicate: the social-structural units of humorous events; the techniques used in humor; the accidental or intentional nature of humorous events; the motives and intentions of the individuals responsible for humor; the nature of responses to humorous events, as indicated by smiling, laughter, or other overt actions; the targets of humor events and their responses; and the cultural themes underlying amusing instances. The principal objective of the researcher is to discover as far as possible both the underlying patterns and the reasons for each amusing incident. The data should reveal recurrent themes pertaining to behavior, types of individuals, roles, status, institutions, and so on that constitute the stimuli for humor. Next the cultural values that give rise to humor should be identified. Explanations should expose the collective conceptualization of a cultural system's structure. It may be found that amusement is experienced when established patterns and structured social relationships are broken, distorted, or literally or liberally interpreted or when some unforeseen dimension is revealed. This last step in the analysis should disclose the way in which humor is linked to the value system of a culture.

The possible effects of amusing events on individuals and groups should be investigated—entertainment, ridicule, shame, a breach of etiquette, and so on. This kind of inquiry should assist the ethnographer in determining what functions humor serves in a culture. In short, the ultimate goal of the ethnographer-anthropologist is to analyze the formal and substantive aspects of humor, its sociocultural foundations and its determinants, the society's attitudes toward its nature and techniques in general and toward its appropriateness in specific social situations, and finally its functions.

Comparative Studies

Once some descriptive-analytical studies of humor in individual cultures become available, they should be compared in order to delineate the shared attributes of humor across cultures. It is possible to identify some general types of humor and the techniques used in its development. Generalizations based on comparisons of only a few cultures can be formulated as hypotheses or as propositions that can be validated, revised, or rejected on the basis of additional ethnographic data from many more cultures. The more diverse the cultures involved in cross-cultural comparisons, the greater the scope and validity of any proposed hypotheses. The types of hypotheses to be formulated can range from those dealing strictly with the formal nature, typologies, and functions of humor to those dealing with the interrelationship of humor with several aspects of sociocultural systems. Such hypotheses should also emphasize the nature of cross-cultural variation. Answers to questions such as the following should help manifest the range of cross-cultural variation: Why are certain forms of humor found in some cultures but not in others? Why do some cultures consider humor inappropriate in certain social situations, while others consider it appropriate in similar ones? Why is humor institutionalized in the context of some activities but not others? Why are certain roles prone to be targets of humor in some cultures more than in others?

Although I have discussed the two-part approach in sequential order, moving from culture-specific research to cross-cultural research, in practice it is often necessary to move back and forth between the two. As a broad comparative framework is developed, it can assist an ethnographer by providing an etic model of conceptual categories. In other words, the research methods of recording and observation, description, classification, analysis, conceptualization, hypothesis building, and theory formation are inextricably interwoven and mutually reinforcing.

The anthropological study of humor that I have outlined is idealistic. To judge from the existing data, humor has not been fully recorded, described, analyzed, and interpreted in even a single culture. I have sketched this ideal conceptualization of the anthropological approach to the study of humor so that it can be used as a model.

PREVIOUS ANTHROPOLOGICAL RESEARCH ON HUMOR

The literature on the topic of humor is simply enormous and is growing.[7] Humor has fascinated scholars of all disciplinary backgrounds since ancient times, as evidenced by the works of Greek, Hindu, and Chinese philosophers, literary critics, and others. In recent centuries, psychologists have made the most significant contribution to humor studies, whereas anthropological research on humor and laughter appears to have been sporadic and uneven. Descriptive accounts of laughter-evoking events, actions, situations, individuals, and folklore texts are occasionally found in ethnographies but occur marginally, only in connection with the description and analysis of aspects of cultural systems that anthropologists consider important and fundamental. A few overt manifestations of humor attracted anthropological attention primarily because they were closely linked to what were considered fundamental aspects of cultural systems. The phenomenon labeled "joking relationship," for example, has been studied extensively by anthropologists; joking relationships were a major attribute of kinship systems whose study has been a primary anthropological concern, and such relationships occur frequently in Africa and North America, traditionally the focus of much anthropological research. Similarly, "ritual clowning" has been studied extensively by anthropologists because it occurred within the context of "primitive" religions, which have also traditionally been subjected to anthropological investigations. Unlike joking relationships, however, studies of ritual clowning have been restricted by and large to the culture areas of North and Middle America.

The perceived significance of humor-related phenomena and their occurrence in many cultures have affected the development of anthropological theories regarding humor. Because joking relationships were identified in many areas of the world, anthropologists undertook comparative studies and proposed general theories. Similarly, ritual clowning occurred extensively in various forms among numerous tribes in North and Central America. As a consequence, general theories of ritual clowning were developed as early as the first decade of the twentieth century. In recent years anthropologists have begun to pay increasing attention to "play," another phenomenon closely associated with humor. The result has been much theoretical discussion about the cross-cultural nature and scope of play, as evidenced by the annual publications resulting from the meetings of the Association for the Anthropological Study of Play.

Beyond the areas that I have specified, there are only a couple of comprehensive anthropological studies of humor within the context of individual societies (Edmonson 1952; Hill 1943). While the many ethnographic accounts of cultures around the world during the past hundred years or so have occasionally mentioned joking, wit, humor, and so forth, anthropologists made no attempt to describe and analyze systematically the overall nature and function of humor in individual societies and its relevance to social structure, behavioral patterns, and value systems. Part of the problem lies in the difficulties of gathering humor data in other cultures by using the traditional methodological technique of participant observation used in fieldwork (Apte 1983:195–201). The gathering of humor data requires different skills and preparation.

The general neglect of humor as a topic of anthropological research is reflected in teaching practice. Most introductory textbooks do not even list humor as a significant characteristic of cultural systems together with kinship, social roles, behavioral patterns, religion, language, economic transactions, political institutions, values, and material culture. Jacobs (1964) alone emphasized the relevance of humor to ethnographic studies and anthropological theory in his introductory textbook and devoted a whole chapter to it.

THE NATURE OF ETHNOGRAPHIC DATA
USED IN THIS BOOK

Most of the ethnographic examples used for illustrative purposes throughout this book were gathered from published texts, while a few stem from my own observations and fieldwork. Because comparative studies have expressed theoretical concerns regarding the use of ethnographic data out of context (Ford 1967; Naroll and Cohen 1970), I have tried to develop theoretical propositions that compare some sociocultural factors as they relate to the occurrence, use, and function of humor. No propositions compare aspects of humor in isolation, nor do they assert that categories and types of humor are present or absent in specific cultures in isolation. As in all analyses of secondary data, the accuracy or contextual appropriateness of the ethnographic information cannot always be thoroughly verified. In this sense, the ethnographic data used in this study are anecdotal. They are, as Geertz has pointed out, "themselves interpretations, and second and third order ones to boot. (By definition, only a 'native' makes first order ones: it's *his* culture)" (1973:15). This limitation hardly detracts from the value of a study such as the present book or, more specifically, even from the generalizations reached following analysis of data. Investigators constantly attempt to negate theories and hypotheses with specific examples without simultaneously seeking to verify the "truthfulness" of ethnographic materials.

Another problem in using ethnographic examples involves determining their humorousness. I have used three criteria. I have accepted ethnographic accounts of events, actions, situations, and so forth as humorous if the reported response of participants is mirthful laughter, if the accounts are described by ethnographers as amusing, funny, witty, humorous, or ludicrous, and if I myself found the material funny in my reading of ethnographies. In citing instances from individual cultures, I have been primarily concerned with relevance to the theoretical arguments being pursued rather than with the quality (judged objectively or subjectively) of the humor. Examples of both "good" and "bad" humor are useful if they reflect or assist in the understanding of cultural systems. It is common knowledge that views concerning what is humorous and what is "good" humor differ not only interculturally but also intraculturally and often amount to interpersonal differences. My criteria for selecting ethnographic examples of humor offer a practical way of dodging, at least initially, the issue of determining what is humorous to whom and why. Any definitive attributes of the elusive concept of humor that can be extrapolated from the cross-cultural comparisons and theoretical discussions should help enhance our understanding of the phenomenon.

SOME CAVEATS

This book of course has limitations. As I have noted, my objective of providing a full-fledged treatment of humor in relation to human sociocultural systems at the culture-specific and comparative levels is somewhat hampered by lack of ethnographic data, problems of methodology, and difficulties in defining the phenomenon itself. I have not dealt with the symbolic and metaphorical aspects of humor, which are crucial in explaining its cultural bases and influences. I have also not included a cross-cultural comparison of humor based on the concept of obscenity. In much of my discussion I have relied almost exclusively on ethnographic and research material available in English. My aim is primarily to generate inductively derived theoretical propositions concerning the interconnections between humor and sociocultural systems. I do not develop hypothesis-testing strategies, nor do I test the hypotheses generated; my work is preliminary in nature. At the current stage of humor research in anthropology, a modest goal seems more realistic than an ambitious one.

I have taken a "middle-ground" approach in the sense that ethnographic data from only a limited number of cultures have been examined for comparative analyses leading to generalizations. The generalizations—not universal in any sense of the word—can lead us in two directions. Examination of many more societies and cultures can show that the generalizations are indeed "high order" or can emphasize cross-cultural variations, indicating the need either to improve existing theoretical propositions or to develop new ones explaining why such variations occur. Although it is cross-cultural in nature, this book is not statistically oriented. Statistical analyses are possible only when extensive ethnographic data have been gathered from several societies, using a common theoretical framework and similar methodological techniques. My cross-cultural approach is illustrative rather than analytically comparative, because the latter, though ideal, is impractical. Yet it is necessary for future anthropological research on humor that we develop preliminary typologies, tentative analyses, and theoretical propositions.

25

Finally, although I generally provide ethnographic examples in the "ethnographic present," the reader should not assume that the humor-generating activities cited are carried out at the present time. They were, however, presumably part of a specific cultural system at the time when the anthropologist gathered ethnographic data in the field.

PART I

HUMOR AND
SOCIAL STRUCTURE

1

Joking Relationships

Perhaps no other humor-related phenomenon within the framework of social organization has been as extensively studied by anthropologists as the "joking relationship," which is one of the major manifestations of kinship. The early anthropological interest in the joking relationship in preliterate societies led, initially, to detailed descriptions and subsequently, to analyses of this institutionalized form of behavior, which supposedly shows much joking, teasing, banter, horseplay, obscenity, and so forth. Recently anthropologists have turned their attention to investigating and describing comparable behaviors outside the domain of kinship in industrial societies as well.

The earliest mention of the "joking relationship" as a social phenomenon in anthropological literature dates to the last decade of the nineteenth century (Moreau 1943:386). It was not until the early twentieth century, however, that attention focused on the nature of joking relationships and that their significance in the social fabric of many societies was recognized. Since then, many ethnographic data on joking behavior among the indigenous populations of Africa, North America, Asia, and Melanesia have been gathered. Lowie (1920/1961) was one of the early anthropologists to discuss the nature of such a relationship in cross-cultural and functional terms. The phrase "joking relationship" itself gained acceptance and wide circulation in the anthropological literature by the 1930s and has retained its popularity in spite of the creation of many other terms.

Several reasons can be given for the anthropologists' fascination with the joking relationship and for their interest in describing and analyzing it. First, it appeared to be a novel but highly structured and institutionalized phenomenon in preliterate, small-scale societies. Most individuals in these societies knew of it, could describe it, and on several occasions displayed the often prescriptive joking behavior associated with it for the benefit of the ethnographers. Thus it was an observable phenomenon, and instances of joking behavior within the framework of social organization occurred regularly and with sufficient frequency for anthropologists to consider it patterned social behavior and not just individual whim or idiosyncrasy.

Second, the patterns of joking behavior manifested kinship-related roles within social organization. For most anthropologists, the study of kinship structure and the elaboration of its behavioral, ideological, and linguistic aspects constituted the single most important task, not only in ethnographic fieldwork and description, but also in the development of anthropological theory. Third, it was important in ethnographic accounts and analyses to show not only that joking behavior was an essential aspect of social interaction but also that joking relationships had a structural complementarity with, and functional relevance to, social structure and cultural values. Such an objective reflected the traditional holistic perspective of sociocultural anthropology. Because the joking relationship was relatively widespread, cross-cultural comparison was also a necessary aim to discern any universal trends and to develop global theories regarding its form and function.

Finally, the area orientation provided a major impetus to studies of the joking relationship. Although it had been observed in various parts of the world (Eggan 1937/1955; Lowie 1920/1961:100; Tax 1955), its most varied, extensive, and institutionalized forms were to be found among the various ethnic populations of East and Central Africa south of the Sahara. The British colonial administrators and the British social anthropologists who did most of their ethnographic fieldwork in Africa published significant studies dealing with various aspects of the joking relationship.[1]

In this chapter I shall briefly discuss the scope and nature of anthropological studies of the joking relationship, including the terminological and definitional problems; analyze the dimensions and structures of different types of joking relationships in a cross-cultural perspective; and examine and evaluate various theories regarding the joking relationship. Before I proceed with these goals, an operational definition is necessary. I shall treat the joking relationship as a patterned playful behavior that occurs between two individuals who recognize special kinship or other types of social bonds between them; it displays reciprocal or nonreciprocal verbal or action-based humor including joking, teasing, banter, ridicule, insult, horseplay, and other similar manifestations, usually in the presence of an audience.

THE SCOPE AND NATURE OF
THE ANTHROPOLOGICAL INQUIRY

In the early years since its discovery, the joking relationship was seen primarily as one of many manifestations of ties based on kinship and other similar social group relations in preliterate societies. Other manifestations included marriage, the exchange of goods and services, and reciprocal obligations and privileges. Thus for a long time attention focused primarily on studying the joking relationship in the context of kinship, and attempts to develop universal theories were limited to the ethnographic data from preliterate societies. In the 1950s, however, it gradually became clear that comparable social interactions occurred between individuals in large-scale, complex industrial societies who were not related either by kinship or by other similar structural ties but who nevertheless had established some social bonds. This awareness resulted in several new studies of comparable phenomena in such societies.[2]

In addition to studies of the joking relationship in industrial societies, ethnographic data indicated that, even in preliterate societies, all joking relationships were not kin based but existed in other types of social groups too. In many African societies, for instance, joking relationships exist among age mates (that is, members of the same age sets), among persons of different villages, or among persons of different occupational groups. These too have been described during the last several years.[3] It appears that the joking relationship based on kinship differs in some fundamental ways from that based on nonkin ties in both preliterate and industrial societies. The former seems more formalized, structured, and institutionalized than the latter; the former is kin category oriented, while the latter is person oriented; and finally, the former seems obligatory in nature, while the latter appears to be voluntary.

In societies with extensive kinship organization, much of an individual's social universe and the scope of his or her behavior are closely tied in with various consanguinal and affinal kins of descriptive and classificatory categories. Thus an individual is bound by kinship-based conventions to a considerable degree. A person's obligations, responsibilities, duties, rights and privileges, and potential marriage bonds are largely, if not totally, determined by the kinship network: the choice of marriage partners is limited, obligations cannot easily be shunned, and privileges cannot be ignored. Similarly, behavior toward all relatives cannot be the same. Joking behavior in this context, then, is not merely an independent phenomenon to be practiced at will but is structurally tied in with other manifestations of kinship by relations of either opposition or symmetry. No joking relationship, for instance, can be established with those toward whom avoidance behavior is expected. On the other hand, the joking relationship is expected toward potential marriage partners. The joking relationship is therefore one of the many important dimensions that characterize the nature of kinship and cannot be separated from it.

Not only the joking relationship but also the substance of joking is highly structured in many societies, so that joking behavior is not only prescribed but is also highly stylized. Rules can be formulated about what kinds of behaviors joking relationships do and do not permit. Outer limits of joking are easily determined, and obscenities and insults become stereotyped; parts of the body that can be touched in horseplay are predetermined (Sharman 1969). Thus the overall nature of joking becomes standardized (Goody 1956:80). Although all individuals may not necessarily conform to structured norms of joking, its very institutionalized nature brings the joking relationship under social control.

Such is not the case with the nonkin joking relationship, which is frequently a behavioral attribute of friendship or other similarly close associations and thus carries positive motives (Kennedy 1970:59). Beyond the general affirmation of these associations, there are few obligations, if any, and potential marital relations are rarely involved (Malefijt 1968a; Sykes 1966). In other words, the nonkin joking relationship is not tied to other aspects of social structure and does not have to be highly institutionalized. The outer limits of behavior involved in it are not readily determined; its nature is varied, and depends on the individual joking partner's creative abilities instead of being standardized. Thus two very different kinds of joking occur in kin-based and nonkin joking relationships. In the former the joking occurs "in a social setting where social relations are well determined," while in the latter it happens in a "social setting where relations are not highly determined, and where familiar and humorous exchanges are a means for interacting persons to alter, create and structure social relations" (J. Freedman 1977:155).

In determining the kin-based joking relationship, kinship categories in the abstract are more important than the individuals who fit into them. Thus members of certain kinship categories, whatever their age or sex, are potential joking partners. Even if one person does not want to play the designated role, he or she has to bear with such joking and other related behavior if a person in the appropriate kinship category decides to pursue it, as is clearly indicated by the numerous court cases in Africa during the colonial period. In some instances, the unwilling and aggrieved parties took matters to court, but the defendants in such cases justified their actions by saying that the plaintiffs belonged to the specific kinship category with which they were privileged to have a joking relationship. Traditions and other members of the cultures often confirmed such claims (J. C. Mitchell 1956:40–41; Pedler 1940). As will be seen later, relations such as cross-cousins,[4] grandparent/grandchild, and mother's brother/sister's son are well-defined kin-category-based dyads of joking relationship.

On the other hand, the nonkin joking relationship is person oriented in that it is established with a specific person. An individual chooses the person with whom to develop friendship and the joking relationship, although there may be other people of similar background and social position. A person working in a factory or an office has joking relationships not with all colleagues but only with a chosen few, and something similar is true in an individual's social circle outside the work domain.

The kin-based joking relationship is obligatory in the sense that individuals are under strong social pressure to bear without anger any joking, teasing, insult, or abuse imposed on them by their joking partners even if they are unwilling to reciprocate. Among the Ojibwa Indians, cross-cousins who decline to participate in a joking relationship are "considered boorish, as not playing the social game" (Landes 1937:103, as quoted in Howell 1973:6). Radcliffe-Brown even made this aspect a part of his definition of the joking relationship as "a relation between two persons in which one is by custom permitted, and in some instances required, to tease or make fun of the other, who in turn is required to take no offense" (1952/1965:90). The words "by custom" and "required" in this definition significantly illustrate the kin-rooted nature of this type of joking relationship, in contrast to the nonkin relationship,

33

in which *both* parties agree to participate in joking and either may choose to terminate it at any time.

The Lack of Research Emphasis on Humor

A major weakness in the existing studies of the joking relationship from the viewpoint of the student of humor is that much emphasis has been put on the relational aspects of the joking relationship and not enough on the phenomenon of joking itself. Relatively few ethnographic accounts describe in detail what actually happens by way of joking, irrespective of how the term is understood by the investigator. Detailed information about the verbal, gestural, and action-based manifestations of joking is often lacking; no explanations as to why various verbal exchanges are considered obscene, vulgar, crude, insulting, and so forth are given; the degree of freedom of action permitted in banter, horseplay, and practical jokes is not elaborated upon; and answers are not provided to questions regarding, for example, the elements of the phenomenon that are responsible for turning literal insults into symbolic gestures of friendship (J. Freedman 1977:158).

The existing ethnographic accounts are generally not helpful in understanding any symbolism underlying humor and joking, the nature of linguistic puns, the implications of suggestive gestures, the connotative aspects of banter and horseplay, or the visual effects of all such activities.[5] Initially, anthropologists were interested less in humor than in the significance of the joking relationship for social structure, particularly in the context of African societies (Sharman 1969:114). Relatively little about humor in African societies, or in general, was therefore known. The situation has altered little despite several new studies during the last two decades. Two factors have contributed to the state of affairs: the ethnographers' failure to understand the subtleties of many humorous acts involved in the realization of the joking relationship, due to their inadequate linguistic skills, and the inability of the members of the indigenous cultures to explain the innate symbolic aspects of such behavior, especially if it has been ritualized. The label "joking" may be inappropriate to the interaction because many of the actions and exchanges described by anthropologists as part of the joking relationship seem more in the nature of harassment, abuse, and insults.

In general, humor was not the primary focus of researchers who investigated the joking relationship. Rather it was analyzed as it was significant for the total kinship network and as it was relevant

34

to developing concepts of social alliance and solidarity, patterns of social interactions, social control, and finally social structure. Theoretical development of these concepts in individual societies and at the universal level has always been a major goal of anthropologists. Radcliffe-Brown, whose pioneering theoretical exposition of the joking relationship is still influential, deals only with its formalized or standardized types (1952/1965:104).[6]

Problems with Terminology and Definitions

The anthropological study of the joking relationship has changed fundamentally over the years. The object of inquiry has gradually acquired new meanings, making it less and less a singular phenomenon (J. Freedman 1977:155). What initially started as an investigation into a supposedly limited phenomenon—the joking relationship in some preliterate societies—has burgeoned into full-scale studies and global analyses of widely varied instances presumably illustrating the relationship's structural-functional principles. A plethora of terms and definitions have sprouted in the ever-growing literature on the subject.[7] As a result, many problems are evident in the existing descriptions and analyses of the joking relationship, especially with respect to definitions and the use of various concepts, categories, and terms. While the joking relationship itself is often defined, for example, the various terms used in its elaboration and categorization are neither adequately defined nor used rigorously and consistently. Identical instances and phenomena are described with different terms, while different ones are subsumed under a single term. Indigenous terms, used on rare occasions, are readily interchanged with the investigator's analytical categories without adequate explanations. No systematic efforts have been made to classify the semantic domain of the joking relationship in specific cultures by using the methodology and theory developed in ethnoscience. There is evident a tendency to create new terms just for the sake of novelty when existing terms and concepts seem quite adequate to describe the numerous aspects of the phenomenon.

The problems with defining the concept of the joking relationship are similar. Radcliffe-Brown's classic definition has remained in vogue despite many others proposed by different scholars, varying from the broadest (Bradney 1957; Lundberg 1969:22) to very specific ones (Brant 1948:160; Thomson 1935:460). Just as the joking relationship is variously described, so is the activity of joking. "Joking activity" has been used as a synonym for such other terms as

35

"teasing," "swearing," "taunting," "making fun of (another),"
"banter," "horseplay," "vulgar or obscene remarks," "playful insults," "sexual innuendos," "petting," "heavy petting," "rough
horseplay," "fondling," and "practical jokes." It has also been used
to refer to a wide range of activities as well as to varying degrees
of each. Radcliffe-Brown's definition led researchers to the problem
of separating joking from teasing. Some scholars (Girling 1957;
Loudon 1970; Nurge 1965; Sperling 1953) have suggested that teasing implies aggression, while joking does not. If such is the case,
then Radcliffe-Brown's theoretical framework for analyzing the
phenomenon suggests that the phrase "teasing relationship" is
preferable to "joking relationship," as Howell (1973) has suggested.

In view of the various difficulties that I have discussed, it is not
surprising that anthropologists on the whole have turned their
attention to describing and analyzing the *implications* of the joking
relationship and joking behavior rather than to their actual nature,
however the concepts are defined. The emphasis thus seems to be
on the reasons for the occurrence of the joking relationship and
joking and on their relevance to the wider context of kinship network, alliances, and reciprocity rather than on the substantive nature of the phenomena themselves. The explanation for such a
state of affairs seems to be, in summary: (1) the nature of activities
associated with the joking relationship, especially with its crucial
attribute, that is, joking, varies considerably across cultures; (2) the
relationship of the concept of joking to the wider concept of humor
remains ambiguous; (3) there is a lack of clarity and rigor in determining the precise attributes of the joking relationship and joking from the initiator's and the recipient's viewpoints within and
across cultures; (4) no conceptual framework has been developed
in which joking can be adequately related to teasing, banter, insults, horseplay, and obscenity. These concepts, together with joking, need to be incorporated in the domain of humor in such a
way as to make their structural relations explicit in a culture-free
theoretical model. Once such a model has been constructed, it can
be compared and contrasted with culture-specific models of the
joking relationship to produce a systematic comparison across
cultures.

THE DIMENSIONS AND STRUCTURE
OF THE JOKING RELATIONSHIP

The following typology is the basis for my analysis of the joking
relationship. Although the intertribal joking relationship cannot

36

technically be called kin based, it is included in that broad category because it has a more rigid structural nature than the nonkin joking relationship.

Kin-based Joking Relationships
   In the nuclear family
   In the extended kin group:
      Among individuals of the same generation
      Among individuals of adjacent generations
      Among individuals of alternate generations
   The interclan and intertribal joking relationship, including *utani*

Nonkin Joking Relationships
   Among age sets in preliterate societies
   Based on miscellaneous factors in preliterate societies
   In industrial societies

Kin-Based Joking Relationships

It is necessary to recognize within the domain of kinship in different societies which types of kin relations form the bases of the joking relationship and which do not. Such an approach helps us to extrapolate the most common kinship categories underpinning the joking relationship cross-culturally and to determine the nature of diversity regarding others. The discussion below starts from the smallest domain of kinship and proceeds toward the largest ones.

The Nuclear Family.   Relationships within a nuclear family do not seem conducive to the joking relationship. A person rarely has a joking relationship with his or her parents, children, siblings, or spouse(s). A survey of the joking relationship between primary, secondary, and tertiary kins of opposite sex by Murdock (1949:275ff.) clearly indicates that it rarely occurs between members of a nuclear family. In a sample of 250 societies, only 3 had the joking relationship between brother and sister from among the seven kin-based possible types of joking relationship between members of the opposite sex within the nuclear family, while 59 societies were found to have an avoidance or respect relationship between brother and sister. The joking relationship does not seem to occur between relatives of the same sex, for example, between father and son, brother and brother, mother and daughter, or sister and sister within a nuclear family.

The joking relationship apparently does not occur between members of the nuclear family because the kin ties are too close and

37

are imbued with strong feelings of authority, respect, love, sub-servience, and obligations, duties, and responsibilities, especially in preliterate societies. There is no room for "playful" interaction because the potential for infraction of the esteemed or authority relation is very real. The kinship roles and ensuing behavioral patterns are such that little leeway exists. One major factor responsible for the joking relationship between relatives of the opposite sex is the potential for sexual relations. It is absent, however, between primary kin because of the universally strong incest taboos. The fear of potentially destructive sexual relations between siblings of the opposite sex is quite strong, as indicated by a severe degree of avoidance behavior pattern between them in many of the societies included in Murdock's cross-cultural data.

Extended Kin Groups. Perhaps the most varied types of joking relationships occur between different secondary and tertiary relatives in extended kin groups. Depending on the aspects of kinship and marriage that are emphasized, the size of an extended kin group varies considerably across cultures. From an individual's point of view, such a kin group may include only lineal relatives of both ascending and descending generations or lineal and collateral relatives[8] on the father's side only, on the mother's side only, or on both sides. An extended kin group may also include relatives acquired by marriage. Thus in a society, an individual's extended kin group may maximally include relatives of both sexes of his own generation and of ascending and descending generations on his father's and mother's side. The criterion of generation has been used to classify such an extended kin group further in order to discuss various types of joking relationships within it.

The Same Generation. Among the various types of joking relationship in this category, that between cross-cousins of the opposite sex seems to occur most frequently. Murdock's presentation of comparative data (1949:277ff.) shows that the joking relationship between cross-cousins of the opposite sex on the father's side as well as on the mother's side constitutes the second most frequent type, topped only by the joking relationship between a man and his wife's younger sisters and that between a woman and her husband's younger brothers.

Interestingly enough, an equal number of cases of avoidance between cross-cousins of the opposite sex also seems to occur. There is reason to suspect that these behavioral patterns are closely associated with prescribed and prohibited marriage practices, respectively. In societies where cross-cousin marriage is either pre-scribed or preferred, the individuals involved are potential marriage partners and hence are permitted to joke with each other. Whether maternal or paternal cross-cousin is the preferred marriage partner depends on whether the principle of patrilineality or matrilineality applies. Where descent from both father and mother is recognized, either or both cross-cousins may be involved in the joking relationship.

Whether the individuals involved in such a relationship are actual or classificatory[9] cross-cousins and whether they are close or distant relatives is often important (Howell 1973:14). Among the Australian tribes of New Queensland, the actual versus classificatory distinc-tion is applied to all relatives, and restraint must be observed in interactions with all consanguinal relatives. Among the Koko Ya'o tribe of Australia, marriage between actual cross-cousins is even prohibited, though it is permitted between classificatory cross-cou-sins (Thomson 1935:475). The situation is similar among the Gogo (Rigby 1968) and the Ndembu tribes of Africa (Turner 1957:253). Thus the degree of close kinship is obviously a significant factor in determining the joking relationship. The interaction between actual cross-cousins is likely to be close and involved, often similar to that between siblings in a nuclear family. Therefore, the higher the degree of close kinship, the lesser the possibility of developing a joking relationship. The earlier generalization about the lack of a joking relationship among primary relatives in a nuclear family is extended in some cases to collateral blood relatives also.

The rationale in such situations appears to be the following. Relatives within a nuclear family do not marry each other, hence no joking relationship exists. Collateral relatives on the other hand can and often do marry: therefore there is a joking relationship. The greater the distance between such collateral relatives, the higher the possibility of marriage and therefore also of the joking rela-tionship. As we move from the close biological sibling relations to distant biological ones, especially to cross-cousins and beyond to classificatory cross-cousins, the possibility of both the joking re-lationship and marriage increases. It appears, then, that ideas of incest are inversely related to practices of marriage and the joking relationship, not only within the nuclear family, but also within the network of secondary and tertiary collateral and affinal relatives in the extended kin group. Where incest taboos are strong, the development of sexual involvement and of a joking relationship based on it is nonexistent.

39

Occasionally the notion of incest is sufficiently broad to exclude not only actual sexual relations but also the discussion of sexual topics and obscene verbal exchanges between male and female siblings. Such activities with persons outside the kin network are also prohibited in front of a person's sibling of the opposite sex. Males are especially restricted from saying anything of a sexual nature directly to or in front of their sisters. Among the Rapans of Polynesia, males never discuss sexual matters either directly with their sisters and female cousins or in their presence. This constraint may lead to unexpected teasing situations in which a "brother" is made a butt of joking. "The youths take advantage of this [restriction] in their banter, mercilessly kidding a young man about his sex life when his 'sister' is present. The poor fellow is unable to retort in kind and must take the ribbing in embarrassed silence" (Hanson 1970:117–18). Similar social restrictions exist in other traditional societies, especially those where there is strong segregation of the sexes. Among the high castes in Hindu society in India, for example, males generally do not practice sexual joking and teasing in the presence of their female siblings or any other female relatives.

Occasionally, however, sexual joking may be allowed between brothers and sisters, provided that a nonrelative is the object. While doing fieldwork among the Abron people of Ivory Coast, anthropologist Alland became the object of a joke. A young girl was teased by her brothers that she and Alland were having sexual relations, and when she protested, her brothers said that she was afraid of the anthropologist's penis (Alland 1975:75). Alland does not specify, however, whether the "brothers" were biological or classificatory siblings. After Alland started calling the girl "sister," the joking stopped, which suggests that incest taboos restricting sexual joking among close siblings may extend to even fictive siblings.

The joking relationship does not *always* occur between cross-cousins who are potential marriage partners. On the basis of a cross-cultural study, Brant concluded that a "potential sexual relationship is not a *sufficient* cause of the joking pattern, or that unknown contravening factors are operative" (1948:162). In other instances, even if the joking relationship, including sexual license, exists among cross-cousins who are potential marriage partners, it is not permitted after the marriage of the girl either to her joking partner or to another person (White 1958).

In some societies the potential for marriage is the basis of the joking relationship among siblings-in-law of the opposite sex as well. A man may have a joking relationship with his wife's younger sisters or with his elder brother's wife. Conversely, a woman may have a joking relationship with her elder sister's husband or with her husband's younger brothers. The joking relationship toward siblings-in-law of the opposite sex "appears to depend almost exclusively upon whether or not preferential mating with such relatives is prescribed." True license "is confined almost exclusively to siblings-in-law who are potential secondary spouses" (Murdock 1949:281–82). The cross-cultural data of Murdock indicate that the highest number of joking relationships occur between a man and either his wife's younger sister or his elder brother's wife and is indicative of preference for junior sororate and junior levirate, respectively. The data also indicate the importance of both marital status and relative age in the development of a joking relationship, because it exists between a man and his wife's unmarried younger sisters just as it exists between a woman and her husband's unmarried younger brothers. A Thonga man, for example, shuns his wife's elder sisters who are not among his possible mates but treats her younger sisters with utmost freedom because they may become subsidiary wives (Lowie 1920/1961:103).

The nature of "joking" behavior is varied in the joking relationships between both collateral and affinal relatives of the opposite sex. It often involves physical contact and horseplay, obscene exchange, sexual suggestions, and teasing of a sexual nature. Sometimes joking exchanges may be more in the nature of playful insults and can be used to criticize one's spouse indirectly, as a channel for expressing anger and resentment, and for communicating the cause of displeasure when no other culturally acceptable way perhaps exists (Hammond 1964:265).

The joking relationship between cross-cousins and between siblings-in-law of the same sex also occurs. Murdock (1949:279) has stated that relations between brothers-in-law are usually marked by reserve or respect, but he does not support his position with any ethnographic data. His major point is that the two men have totally different sexual relations with the same woman. While a brother must observe the strictest taboo, a husband has unrestrained sexual freedom. Any allusion to sex by the husband may therefore arouse unconscious anxiety in the brother, while similar allusions by the later may arouse suspicions of incest. Murdock's argument merely suggests that the joking relationship between brothers-in-law may be devoid of any sexual banter and verbal exchanges, although joking of a nonsexual nature may take place.

The relation between brothers-in-law is the result of mutual co-

41

operation and friendship, especially if a person wants to make sure that his sister is well treated and is taken care of by her husband. The husband, on the other hand, may depend on the assistance of his brother-in-law because of the competition with his classificatory brothers. Such is the case among the Yanomamo Indians of Brazil. Among them, agnates of the same generations are "brothers." They compete for women from the same category of "potential wives," however, because women are generally in short supply. On the other hand, affinal relatives are allies, and the relationship between brothers-in-law grows more intimate as they grow older. They play and joke with each other, exchange possessions, protect each other, and give mutual assistance. Thus the ties of marriage are in some instances stronger than ties of blood (Chagnon 1968:58ff.). Among the Tarahumara Indians in Mexico, the most intense joking behavior is noticed between true or classificatory brothers-in-law (Kennedy 1970).

In societies with patrilineal kinship and strong male dominance, an asymmetrical joking relationship may exist between a person and his wife's brothers. Wife givers are generally inferior to wife takers in such societies, so that a man can make fun of his wife's brother with impunity, knowing full well that his brother-in-law cannot and will not respond in kind. Among the Hindus in North India, a wife's brother is always regarded as someone to be made the butt of joking. The term *sālā*, meaning "brother-in-law" in Hindi and other North Indian languages, has even acquired the connotation of mild abuse. This attitude also extends to a person's mother's brother who, in such kinship systems, is lower in status than a person's father's brother. Among the Marathi speakers on the west coast of India, there is a proverb "to make a maternal uncle out of someone," meaning to make someone the butt of a practical joke.

Little has been said about the joking relationship between male parallel or cross-cousins, although it probably occurs in some societies. In such relations, however, individually formed friendships may be more influential than the specific kin ties. In rare instances, the joking relationship and homosexuality among male cross-cousins have been reported (Lévi-Strauss 1943, as quoted in Howell 1973). Unfortunately, no account exists narrating actual joking among such partners, and in general, anthropologists have little elaborated actual joking among secondary consanguinal or affinal male kinsmen. Kennedy (1970:40) states that joking behavior between male siblings-in-law among the Tarahumara Indians often appears to outsiders to have a strongly homosexual content.

The existing ethnographic literature also indicates that institutionalized joking rarely occurs between females of the same generation. On the whole, women in traditional and preliterate societies appear not to engage actively in establishing a joking relationship with other female relatives. I have found very few examples in my survey of the relevant literature. Among the Tallensi and Lowiili tribes of Africa, women who are related to each other in the capacity of brother's wife and husband's sister joke with each other (Fortes 1949:120; Goody 1956:51). Interestingly, a woman calls her brother's wife by the term "wife," thus developing an intersex fictive relationship. In other words, the joking relationship among these women is established only when one of them fictitiously changes her sex, creating an "as if" relationship, which perhaps suggests that the sexual potential is important for establishing it. The women themselves give this explanation; a woman who calls any of her brother's wives by the term "wife," and has a joking relationship remarks, "If I'd been a male wouldn't she then have been my wife?" (Goody 1969:77). The only other ethnographic example of joking between females is described by Kennedy (1970:42) among the Tarahumara Indians in Mexico and involved grandmothers and granddaughters.

Adjacent Generations. Among the many types reported, the much emphasized and discussed joking relationship is that between mother's brother and sister's son. In a paper specifically devoted to this topic, Radcliffe-Brown (1952/1965:15–31) theorized about its common occurrence. He argued that this relationship reflects the underlying principles of privileged familiarity and of special rights of property that a sister's son has with respect to his mother's brother in African and Polynesian patrilineal societies. Radcliffe-Brown's major thesis is that a considerable degree of familiarity is possible only between persons of the same sex, and although in patrilineal societies a mother is likely to be more loving than distant, a high degree of familiarity cannot be established because of sex differences. Hence there is a need to transfer such familiarity onto the mother's closest sibling of the opposite sex, namely her brother. Respect must be shown to all of the father's siblings, including his sisters, and all must be obeyed. On the mother's side, however, the relationship is marked with affection and familiarity, resulting in indulgence and a relative freedom of behavior that develops into an asymmetrical joking relationship. A sister's son may tease and behave disrespectfully toward his mother's brother, but the latter is expected not to reciprocate. If the nephew, using one of his many prerogatives, steals the uncle's property, for example, a fine beast from his herd, the uncle is not supposed to protest.

Radcliffe-Brown (1952/1965:98–99) later improved upon his original theory by changing the "indulgent" aspect of the mother's brother's role to an "ambivalent" one and by emphasizing the conjunctive and disjunctive aspects of the relationship between the mother's brother and the sister's son to explain the "familiar" behavior. Tax (1955) uses both the sex principle and the extension-of-sentiment principle to explain why the brother respects his sister and hence her child and thus does not reciprocate the indulgent behavior of his sister's son.

Goody has criticized the analysis and explanation of Tax by arguing that, by manipulating the "principles," other results can also be obtained. In this context he says: "Why, for example, should the 'sex principle' be operative in the relationships between brother and sister rather than the 'equivalence of siblings' as Radcliffe-Brown had originally maintained? Moreover, once having introduced a supplementary explanatory principle of 'female dominance', the way is open to the introduction of other such external factors, such as the structure of unilineal descent group, mode of transmitting property, etc." (1969:49).

Not only is Goody's criticism sound, but there is also a fundamenal difference between relations of familiarity and relations of joking, if we are to take Radcliffe-Brown's later position. Lowie had already emphasized that a familiarity relationship "differs fundamentally from the phenomenon of the joking relationship with its blending of serious and comic elements" (1920/1961:101). In other words, a familiarity relation need not and does not always develop into a joking relationship, although Murdock (1949:277) seems to use the terms "joking" and "familiarity" synonymously. Many factors are necessary for such a development. If the degree of familiarity becomes intense, the chances of developing a joking relationship are even less, because the relationship then becomes too involved and too fragile. According to another theory (Howell 1973), the very potential for close familiarity is often the basis for establishing joking. Once such potential is realized, however, joking is reduced and may disappear altogether.

Because an element of violence is involved in the ritual stealing of the property of mother's brother by sister's son in some societies, perhaps the term "privileged aggression" is as appropriate (Goody 1969:41) as Radcliffe-Brown's earlier phrase "privileged familiarity," which in his later writings becomes a "joking relationship." Thus the "sentiment hypothesis" of Radcliffe-Brown is not necessarily a positive one leading only to affection and indulgence but may lead to resentment and antagonistic attitudes. The joking relationship between father's sister and brother's son seems much less common than that just discussed. Rather this relationship seems marked by respect and reserved behavior, as indicated by Murdock's (1949:277) inclusion of thirty cases in the respect category ar.d only nine in the category of joking.

A joking relationship between a man and his mother's brother's wife also occurs in some societies, for instance, among the Mossi of West Africa. It is asymmetrical, however, and the mother's brother's wife takes the more aggressive role (Hammond 1964:200). A joking relationship between a man and his father's brothers or his mother's sisters seems rarely to occur. It has been reported, however, between a man and his father's sister's husband; a "Banks Islander . . . may heap almost any indignity on his father's sister's husband, threatening him, and mocking him continually" (Hocart 1915, as reported in Lowie 1920/1961:101). A similar situation exists among the Cherokee Indians (Gilbert 1937/1955:326). A joking relationship between a person and his or her parents-in-law is generally absent, the reason being that relations and behavior patterns associated with such consanguineal ties as child and parent are extended to structurally parallel affinal ties.

Alternate Generations. By far the most common type in this category is the joking relationship between biological and classificatory grandparents and grandchildren, as reported for many societies.[10] The ethnographic descriptions of this type of joking relationship show a wide range of behavior, including strictly verbal joking, name calling, pretending to be husband and wife, some mild horseplay, and horseplay leading to even sexual acting. This variation is closely related to differences, such as whether relatives are of the same or the opposite sex, whether kin ties are biological or classificatory, and whether the nature of the relationship is close or distant. Among the Jopadhola, for example, joking with grandparents should be only verbal, must not include horseplay, and must not refer explicitly to sexual relations between the wives and husbands (Sharman 1969:109). The nature of joking among the Gusii is more of "playful insulting," including the mutual use of the term *yaa*, suggesting a mild insult. Mayer (1951:38) reports one

45

such instance he observed when "an elder sitting under the eaves of the hut where I visited him one sweltering day called out to his six year old grandson, 'come, you dog, get me some water' to which the child promptly replied, '*yaa*, you are a dog yourself, go get me a drinking cup, I am thirsty!' "

Despite the variety of joking in this category of joking relationship, analyses of individual cases clearly suggest that it develops primarily because of the easygoing, relaxed, and friendly relations between the parties involved, which are marked by a lack of authority. Grandparents in most societies are not responsible for raising their grandchildren in a proper way; child rearing is primarily the obligation of parents. Grandparents enjoy socializing with their grandchildren without feeling burdened by responsibilities. The bond is even further strengthened "by the fact that each can expect from the other an unconscious sympathy for his own dissatisfaction with the intervening relative" (Murdock 1949:278). The tolerant and natural affection of a grandparent for a grandchild is reciprocated by the latter's love, deriving to some extent from the knowledge that the grandparent may allow the grandchild to do as he or she pleases and will demonstrate affection. Thus "the total relationship between grandparent and grandchild, actual or classificatory, often requires consideration of social bonds that go far beyond the simple identity relationship" (Howell 1973:13). Such a consideration may involve marriage obligations with respect to grandparents' clans, as is the case among the Cherokee Indians (Radcliffe-Brown 1952/1965:100).

Grandparents and grandchildren are united not only by kinship but also by social bonds extending beyond kinship. They are "separated by age and by the social difference that results from the fact that as the grandchildren are in the process of entering into full participation in the social life of the community the grandparents are gradually retiring from it" (Radcliffe-Brown 1952/1965:96). There is thus no possibility of competition or of the development of tension. Relative age is also a significant factor in this category of joking relationship. As the grandchildren grow older and are ready to enter adulthood, joking seems to be replaced by the respect that grandchildren show grandparents. A joking relationship of this type changes its nature over a period of time, in other words, or may become inoperative altogether as the life cycle advances.

On the whole, then, joking relationships based on kinship have many common attributes, of which the following seem significant: a patrilineal or matrilineal emphasis on descent and inheritance;

the descriptive versus classificatory nature of the relatives involved; the authority of the various relatives; segregation of the sexes; avoidance and respect patterns based on a fear of potential incest, leading to incest taboo; and asymmetrical relations leading to deference and/or subservience.

Clans and Tribes. From an individual's point of view, the interclan and intertribal joking relationship is the most outward extension of institutionalized joking. It has been reported extensively for many African cultures, and in no other part of the world have such joking relationships developed between ethnically and sociopolitically defined large groups.[11] The interclan joking relationship is varied in nature. Among the Ambo of Northern Rhodesia, for example, it is determined by the mutual relation of either hostility or dependence of the clan totems. "[A] member of the Goat clan may enter into a funeral friendship which involves joking relationship with any member, male or female, of the Iron clan, because the clan objects of Iron and Goat are considered antagonistic—a goat being killed with an iron tool" (Stefaniszyn 1950:290). On the other hand, the Snake and Grass clans have a dependence relationship because the snake hides in grass.

In addition, an interclan or intertribal joking relationship only partially manifests the more important institution of friendship among clans or tribal members, with its significant function of assistance in the funeral of a friend. Many reciprocal services are also performed by clans that have such a relationship. Colson (1953) therefore suggested that it is better to use a broad term such as "clan reciprocity," to indicate such relationships than to specify either the funerary or the joking aspect. The suggested label puts the joking relationship in a better perspective by emphasizing that it is indeed only one aspect of the various modes by which alliances are formed.

Occasionally interclan joking differs in nature from that permitted in other social-structural relations, as reflected in the kinds of insults, obscenities, and other practical jokes that are either permitted or taboo. Among the Plateau Tonga, for example, clan joking involves not only play on the presumed antagonism between the clan animals, and obscenities or rough words, but also accusations of sorcery. Such sorcery accusations used even in joking by persons not standing in an interclan joking relationship would be considered a real insult, and the accuser would be called to account for it and would be made to pay damages (Colson 1953:49).

47

Members of numerous clans and tribes in Africa offer historical explanation of the interclan and intertribal joking relationship by referring to antagonistic relations among them in the past. In contrast, few indigenous explanations are provided for the joking relationship within a kinship system. According to Moreau (1941:3), there is a fair degree of unanimity in expressing the way in which previous inimical relations between clans or tribes develop into joking ones. Not all anthropologists seem satisfied with this explanation, however, because the tribes do not all refer to a historical origin (Christensen 1963; Wilson 1957). One view is that such relationships develop as tribes work together and that previous conflicts leading to joking relationships must have been of a sporadic nature and not very severe (Wilson 1957:112). In addition even tribes that were hostile in the past had to have mutual respect as enemies in order to develop such a relationship. Thus mutual respect also seems to be an important criterion for establishing the joking relationship between clans and tribes.

The intertribal and interclan joking relationship is a relatively recent phenomenon (Christensen 1963; Gulliver 1957). It started after tribal warfare had been discouraged by the European colonists and after European law and government had been established, resulting in some degree of political unification. Persons from formerly hostile tribes encountered each other while working together in urban administrative centers, and the contact led to the development of a joking relationship. Hence the word chosen to describe the bond is from Swahili, a new lingua franca of East and Central Africa (J. C. Mitchell 1956:37). Another investigator contends that the interclan and intertribal joking relationship seems too ingrained in some populations to be a recent phenomenon; in some tribes there are even elaborate folktales to explain its existence between clans that are assumed to be of equal status (Colson 1953:51).

It is also plausible that the interclan joking relationship is much older than the intertribal one and that the practice was extended from the former to the latter. Once this type of joking relationship had spread over a wide area of East and Central Africa, it acquired local characteristics, indigenous linguistic labels, and other associated practices. The underlying structural principles appear to be the same, however, namely, mutual cooperation, close friendship, and willingness to exhibit these relations through joking. The joking relationship was probably further strengthened when members of various indigenous tribes, and clans within them, began to migrate to distant areas for work and desired friendship and assist-

48

ance from people of different clans within their own tribes or from neighboring tribes. Thus the colonial rule, urbanization, and distant migration helped to strengthen the existing joking relationship further and to encourage further active cooperation. For this reason, perhaps, the interclan and intertribal joking relationship is a well-established and wide-spread phenomenon among the Bantu-speaking people of East and Central Africa.

The culmination of the interclan and intertribal joking relationship is seen in the widely known institution of *utani*, of which many detailed accounts and analyses are available.[12] The word *utani* appears to have been derived from an Arabic root, *watan*, meaning "home." The verb *tania* in Swahili means "to be familiar with, chaff, treat as very near kin or a great friend" (Moreau 1943:386–87). The terms *watani* (plural) and *mtani* (singular) are used to refer to a person with whom someone else has an utani relationship. The term *utani*, with slight linguistic variations, occurs in many tribes in East Africa, while in others comparable indigenous terms exist. Even in the latter cases, however, the Swahili term is preferred (Christensen 1963:1315), which suggests that the utani institution had its origin among the Bantu-speaking people in East Africa and diffused over a wide area.

Utani implies not only a joking relationship but also social obligations, and the phenomenon occurs both between tribes and between clans within individual tribes. It is observed not only by people of indigenous religious faiths but also by Muslims and Christians. Joking behavior associated with utani includes all kinds of horseplay and sexual playacting between individuals of the same or the opposite sex. Forfeiture of personal property by the joking partners, if carried out in a specific, well-established fashion, is sanctioned. Practical jokes comparable to the "April fool" type of deception in Euro-American cultures are quite common (Moreau 1943:392–93). At the same time individuals from different clans or tribes who stand in utani relationships are also obliged to provide mutual help and hospitality and are expected to be generous toward their watani. They are expected to help in funeral arrangements if a mtani dies. There are also sanitary and magical aspects of utani (Beidelman 1966; Christensen 1963).

Despite the established social relevance of utani, not everyone participates in it. Rather participation is left to the discretion of the individual. Occasionally an individual may become an unwilling partner in acts of practical joking or snatching. Instances reported by ethnographers in which such one-sided behavior resulted in court cases (Gibbs 1969:195; J. C. Mitchell 1956:40; Pedler 1940:170–71) suggest that responses of those who were unwillingly involved in the manifestation of utani often reflected the situational contexts and the participants' social and marital positions.

Nonkin Joking Relationships

The ethnographic literature on the nonkin joking relationship in preliterate societies seems primarily devoted to joking behavior among age mates. A few studies mention other types, but their description is often cursory (Hammond 1964; Stevens 1978).

Age Sets in Preliterate Societies. Institutionalized joking in many African societies occurs in social groups that parallel groups based on kinship. One such group is that of age sets. Joking among age mates occurs in many African societies with a preponderance of age grades and age sets.[13] Although the existence of sodalities of different kinds among the Indians of North America has been reported (Driver 1969:345ff.), they do not seem comparable to age sets in Africa, and no special joking relationships among their members have been reported.

An age set is essentially a group of peers who pass together through the successive age grades, which are specified periods within the life cycle, the transition from one period to the next being marked by some formal ceremony. Individuals in an age set share many life cycle rites. As a result, a feeling of solidarity, close friendship, and mutual cooperation develops among members of the group. Age sets vary in nature cross-culturally, however. Among the Gusii, for instance, age sets are structurally unimportant (Mayer 1951:28) and have no internal organization, corporate interests, or solidarity, unlike age sets among the Kipsigis and Masai.

In some respects joking relationships among members of age sets are comparable to those between kin of the same generation but lack the ensuing obligatory responsibilities. "It is a privilege to be exercised at will, not a compulsive or obligatory pattern of behavior" (Mayer 1951:33). In other words, the structural factors of age grades provide opportunities for individuals to develop a joking relationship if they so desire, and personal and situational factors influence its development or its absence. The reported instances of a joking relationship among members of age sets seem primarily limited to men. On the whole, age-set relationships are much less prevalent among women, and hence the potential for developing a joking relationship is not so strong.

The joking of the "pals" among the age sets constitutes a relationship quite different from all other kinship and residential relationships. It is unique because it is based on "true" personal friendship, is not obligatory, and is therefore free of tension. By the same token, "brothers," "parents and children," and even close neighbors are not suitable choices as pals. They are too close, the relationships abound with restraints, and proper behavior is characterized by obligatory respect, avoidance, and so forth, so that "extreme closeness, no less than extreme distance, is incompatible with the relationship of pals" (Mayer 1951:35). And yet close contact and intimate knowledge of one another form the basis of a joking relationship once it is established, so that former pals who become separated when one moves away cannot be pals unless they continue to see each other frequently.

In some ways, then, a joking relationship among pals in age sets is comparable to close friendships that individuals form because they share some unique life experiences together, are not inhibited by social structural constraints of kinship, and develop a genuine mutual affection. As in all friendships, if the dyad is broken for any reason, the friendship may not survive unless special attempts are made to preserve it. Situations and relations comparable to those of the Gusii pals can be found in Western societies. Wars produced many "war buddies," and young people going through college or university together form comparable bonds.

Miscellaneous Factors in Preliterate Societies. Joking relationships based on factors other than kinship or friendship have also been reported, although they are not as widespread. Among the Luvale in East Africa, for instance, persons born on the same day can establish a joking relationship. So can persons with the same name, provided there is not a considerable age difference between them (White 1958:32). Intervillage institutionalized joking occurs among the Mossi, as it also does between members of the Mossi tribe and an indigenous blacksmith caste (Hammond 1964). Joking among localized residence groups such as ward members, and between those who live near a river and those located inland from it, has been reported for the Bachama in Nigeria (Stevens 1978). The joking relationship is reported between the Tuareg nobles and the Inadan artisans who live together in the Air region of Niger in North Africa and are mutually dependent. The Inadans are considered low in

51

status by the Tuaregs, who seem more privileged to make fun of the Inadans (Kirtley and Kirtley 1979).

Industrial Societies. The joking relationship in industrial societies is voluntary, informal, and basically person oriented. Whether or not joking patterns in industrial societies are institutionalized and can be considered "true" joking relationships has been a controversial issue. The answer depends on how we define the nature of institutionalization. It has been argued (J. Freedman 1977; Kennedy 1970:59) that joking patterns in industrial societies are not the same as those in preliterate soceties. Why and how they differ, however, is not always explained.

The joking relationship in industrial societies seems less given to the kinds of extreme forms of joking behavior that are found in preliterate societies. Rather it is often mild and broad-based. Joking behavior in a modern department store, for example, is not confined to teasing and being teased, but has a "slightly wider variety of method and a very much wider variety of subject matter" and "is altogether less formalized than that of primitive societies" (Bradney 1957:183). Such joking includes telling funny stories about members of the store, commenting on weather and on other similar topics of mutual interests in a jovial fashion, and telling jokes in some way relevant to the subject of conversation. The situation is similar in offices, factories, and mines (Handelman and Kapferer 1972; Lundberg 1969).

Joking relationships with sexual overtones demonstrate patterns that differ from those in preliterate societies. Existing accounts of such joking relationships (Malefijt 1968a; Sykes 1966) suggest that the audience is an essential aspect of their manifestations. It is worthwhile to summarize Sykes's study to understand the implications of this point. He described the joking relationship among men and women in a Glasgow factory where four types of dyads existed: old men and old women; old men and young women; young men and old women; and young men and young women. The most public obscene banter and horseplay occurred between old men and young women. These were frequently initiated by the old men, who "were permitted gross obscenity in their relations with young women, [and] almost anything could be said as a joke without causing offence." They "were permitted a great deal of license in publicly touching, kissing and petting the young women who rarely objected and if anything encouraged the men" (Sykes 1966:190). These same old men, however, were not allowed to behave in such a fashion in private, and if they tried heavy petting, the women protested strongly and refused to deal with them. On the other hand, interaction between young men and young women was considerably free of sexual banter and horseplay. It was perhaps mildly suggestive on the part of men, but the women always responded with insulting comments, and there was nothing like the open obscene banter that took place between old men and young women. Yet it was common knowledge that these young men and young women frequently carried on heavy petting privately in various places in the factory.

Sykes concluded that gross obscenity and horseplay in public were found only between men and women who were not potential sexual partners. On the other hand, those who could be potential sexual partners did not engage in sexual banter, horseplay, and obscenity in public. Sykes's observations suggest a striking contrast between preliterate and industrial societies in the "public" aspects of a joking relationship with sexual potential. In preliterate societies potential sexual partners, especially cross-cousins, openly engage in obscene horseplay, banter, and so forth. The reserve seems to be the case, however, in industrial societies. Sykes's conclusions are also supported by additional evidence of a somewhat different nature (Malefijt 1968a). Among the Dutch people, the joking relationship with sexual overtones can occur between a married man and a woman who may be a friend of his wife. She may be married or single. Although joking is sexually suggestive, no horseplay or physical contact takes place. It is important, however, that such joking usually occurs in front of the wife, who, if anything, approves it and is pleased with it. The suggested explanation is that this "public" display between her husband and her female friend quite assures the wife that no sexual affair is going on between them in private and that "their presumed sexual relationship is indeed nothing but a joke and thus without factual reality" (Malefijt 1968a:1182).

In preliterate societies, siblings-in-law who are potential secondary spouses may engage in public sexual joking. Murdock (1949:282) reports that, in the majority of tribes among whom sexual joking or license toward a wife's sister or brother's wife commonly occurs, both premarital and extramarital relations are fully or conditionally permitted, especially between a man and his sister-in-law.

Another way in which the joking relationship in industrial societies differs from that elsewhere is that an individual may choose the sort of social situation in which to manifest the relationship.

53

In order to carry on joking, both parties have to agree that a social situation is suitable. If a person indicates negative reaction to inadvertent joking by someone else in a given social situation, such joking is not likely to occur again in similar circumstances. In the joking relationship among five female office workers described by Howell (1973), for instance, one participant made it clear that she was not interested in joking in the "work" situation, and although she had a joking relationship with her colleagues, joking took place only outside the office, especially during lunch.

A comparable example involves the joking among the long-shoremen of Portland, Oregon (Pilcher 1972). The longshoremen clearly separate the "work" domain from the "private" and "family" one. Although well-established joking relationships exist, what is permitted in one social situation is not allowed in another. In the work situation, for instance, extreme obscene swearing, nicknaming, vulgarities, and crude joking take place and are easily tolerated. Even a hint of such joking in family surroundings, however, and especially the use of the nicknames commonly used in the work situation, may lead to serious physical fights, and the initiator of such crude joking and nicknaming may be severely punished (p. 105).

Joking relationships in industrial societies occur not only among men but also among women (Bradney 1957; Howell 1973); they are absent among women in preliterate societies. Such joking relationships occur in industrial societies because women find themselves in social situations outside the family and kinship domain and have essentially the same need to relieve work tensions or to have congenial relations with their colleagues. We might expect, however, that in preliterate societies too women would need such relief, because they are also engaged in a variety of activities. To what extent joking relationships among women in industrial societies involve obscene banter and teasing and so forth is not clear; ethnographic data are lacking.

The joking relationship in industrial societies is used for group identity; this is not its significant aspect in preliterate societies. Acceptance of a person's joking is an indication that he or she is part of the social group. When any new person is introduced to a social group, the members generally maintain some distance and evaluate the new individual. Joking may be carried on among the members without the newcomer. A newcomer may be only gradually accepted in the group, and an individual who makes an attempt to join in by self-deprecatory joking has better chances of

54

being included. On the other hand, the exclusion of newcomers despite their persistent attempts to participate in the joking behavior may indicate that they are being denied entry into the group and the group identity that comes with it. In other words, joking relationships and joking itself serve as screening procedures for membership, especially in small groups, and also help define and redefine the boundaries of differentiated social groups.

Studies of Howell (1973), Loudon (1970), Lundberg (1969), and Malefijt (1968a) clearly support these observations. Although there were differences of status among the five female employees of a small insurance company studied by Howell, joking behavior showed a well-established pattern among only three of them. No joking relationship was established with the remaining two for a variety of reasons, one of which was the deliberate attempt by the threesome to deny membership to one person in the informal joking group; all her attempts were rebuffed by the others. Discouragement from participation in joking signaled exclusion. When Lundberg (1969) began his research in a small business firm, he was considered an outsider, and it was only after ten days or so that he could venture to add something to the accepted joking in the electric motor repair shop. Nearly two months later, he actively participated in a practical joke that was being played by the repair crew on the female secretaries in the office, who, of course, formed a separate group. During Loudon's (1970) study of the public teasing that was quite common among the members of a community from the island of Tristan da Cunha who were living in England, he was made to understand that it was not appropriate for him to join in because he was an outsider.

Depending on the work situation in industrial societies, the nature of joking may vary. Joking was relatively light and included many innocuous activities among the employees of a department store (Bradney 1957), because the work was probably not strenuous or dangerous. When work among the longshoremen (Pilcher 1972:110–11) involved hard physical labor and was hazardous, however, joking encounters were harsh, sustained, and marked by many obscenities and vulgarities.

The group-identity and group-inclusion functions of joking and joking relationships as well as the situational variation in joking do not appear to be significant in preliterate societies. The reasons may be that, first, all social relations are already defined by other factors, notably kinship; and second, joking among appropriate kin, age mates, clan members, and so forth can occur in any situation where the individuals meet or interact. The studies of joking relationships in industrial societies suggest that joking relationships seem to develop primarily in work-related or goal-oriented contexts, to which such joking is confined. When such joking is extended to nonwork situations on a few special occasions such as Christmas, retirement parties, and so forth, attempts are made to create a non-work-related social atmosphere, and individuals may assume their "private" social role and behave in quite a different manner. Once the special occasion is over, however, and the usual "public" and "work" nature of the social setting has been reestablished, individuals who revealed their private personalities may be embarrassed and are prone to regret the "error."

In general, then, joking relationships in industrial societies seem quite different in nature from those in preliterate societies with regard to social-structural dimensions, to substantive nature, and to functions. In industrial societies such relationships are developed primarily to ease social interactions and contacts forced upon individuals because of working conditions. The establishment of a joking relationship with someone else is still mostly voluntary, however, if group identity and demarcation are not involved. Where joking relationships mark group identity and signal the inclusion or exclusion of a new individual, group consensus is important. The nature of joking itself is often related to the nature of the work. The more dangerous the work, the higher the degree of coarse and obscene joking. Similarly, the greater the degree of cooperation among individuals, the more extensive the nature of the joking. Yet each potential setting for joking needs to be constantly verified in order to avoid "offending" or embarrassing the other person involved. Joking in such relationships is not predetermined by a recognition of the license to joke and is not routine but is setting-specific and must be dealt with anew for each situation, despite the broad base of similar social settings for many such joking occurrences (Handelman and Kapferer 1972:497). Social relations are constantly checked and rechecked to confirm that the joking frame is maintained and that individuals are not hurt by such interaction. Any feelings of jealousy, aggression, resentment, and so forth are expressed only with close friends in social situations other than stable work settings.

THEORETICAL CONSIDERATIONS

The extensive, diverse, and complex nature of the phenomenon labeled "joking relationship" and its existence in many cultures have posed a real challenge to anthropologists, especially those who believe in global theories. Although early accounts of the joking relationship were primarily ethnographic, there soon emerged a theoretical interest about the possible causes of its development and its potential functions. Not until Radcliffe-Brown's famous essay on the subject was published in 1940, however, did scholars attempt a systematic analysis of the joking relationship. Radcliffe-Brown's theory evoked some criticism (Griaule 1948), and he wrote another article in 1949 in response to it. Later, anthropologists studying the kin-based joking relationship generally accepted Radcliffe-Brown's theory with only minor modifications. Only in the last ten years or so have there been substantive criticisms of his theoretical position and the development of alternate theories.[14]

Radcliffe-Brown was primarily interested in explaining what he called "formalised or standardised joking relations" (p. 104) in preliterate societies "in which the basic social structure is provided by kinship" (p. 101). He was looking for common elements in all instances of joking relationship that made "this type of behavior appropriate, meaningful and functional" (p. 106). He believed that the interpersonal joking relationship between various consanguinal and affinal relatives and its counterpart between clans and tribes exhibited the same structural features (pp. 94–95). Both were "modes of organizing a definite and stable system of social behavior in which conjunctive and disjunctive components . . . are maintained and combined" (p. 95). To Radcliffe-Brown, social disjunction "implies divergence of interests and, therefore, the possibility of conflict and hostility while conjunction requires the avoidance of strife" (p. 92).

Radcliffe-Brown's reasoning appears to have been the following. Relations of alliance exist only in those societies where contractual relations do not exist; that is, kinship and other obligations are not contractual but are based on social bonds. The joking relationship is one of the four modes of such an alliance or consociation, the others being marriage, the exchange of goods and services, and the exchange of names or sacra. Each mode may exist independently of the others or may combine with the others in several different ways. The maintenance of social order demands social conjunction, yet "social structure separates [relatives] in such a way as to make many of their interests divergent, so that conflict or hostility might result" (p. 103). There are two ways to resolve these ambivalent and potentially dangerous situations. One is by showing respect and avoiding social interaction, and the other is by joking, which involves "mutual disrespect," license, and teasing, "which is always a compound of friendliness and antagonism" (p. 104).

The notion of friendship is obviously crucial to Radcliffe-Brown's theoretical discussion. Yet his treatment of it not only is unsatisfactory but also leads to some contradictions in his arguments. First, he defines friendship in a negative fashion when he states that it "means an obligation for the two persons not to enter into open quarrel or conflict with each other" (p. 107). Second, he argues that friendship underlies both polar types of behavior, that of respect and avoidance (pp. 92, 96) and that of joking, license, and teasing (pp. 97, 106). Third, he affirms that there is a clear distinction between friendship relations and those of solidarity established by kinship or by membership in a group such as a lineage or clan (p. 112). This last assertion, however, leads to a contradiction, because both respect avoidance and joking behavior based on friendship occur among various relatives. Thus on the one hand they are considered relations of friendship, while on the other they cannot be so because they involve alliance and solidarity based on kinship. To add to the confusion, Radcliffe-Brown speaks of the social relations of "friendly rivalry" as being of considerable theoretical importance (p. 112). It is only to be regretted that he did not find the satisfactory general theory for "relations of friendship" for which he and Marcel Mauss searched over many years (p. 113). Radcliffe-Brown's theory is primarily functional in nature: the purpose of joking is seen to be the maintenance of social order and is rooted in teleological and psychological explanations, the latter based on the assumption that friendly or playful disrespect and teasing are a cathartic device that reduces real hostility and develops solidarity.

Since Radcliffe-Brown's seminal contribution, numerous ethnographic studies of the joking relationship in quite diverse societies have been carried out. Some scholars have analyzed the joking relationship in specific cultures within Radcliffe-Brown's theoretical framework, while others have criticized him and have proposed theories of their own based on their analysis of specific ethnographic material. Both textually and contextually oriented theories have been proposed to explain the existence of the joking relationship and to analyze its nature. Because of their cross-cultural perspective, the contextually oriented theories seem to focus on delineating social-structural elements and their ordered relations. By and large, they pay little attention to the interconnections of the culture-specific factors involved in the joking interactions themselves, such as topics or themes of joking, settings of joking activities (time and place), the kinds of verbal codes and the nonverbal behavior that accompanies them, the subtle nuances and the symbolic and metaphorical nature of cultural and linguistic materials used, and the implicit cultural expectations regarding their outcomes.

In general, the joking relationship has been analyzed and explained within a structural-functional theoretical framework. The functional explanations are often psychological in nature and have been much influenced by the theory and interpretation of Radcliffe-Brown, which have been applied to specific ethnographic examples of the joking relationship with few modifications. A major reason for the popularity of the structural-functional approach is the belief that it leads to universalistic statements. In other words, individuals who propose such theories can claim that they are suitable for analyzing and explaining joking relationships in many cultures. The proponents of the structural-functional theoretical approach believe that joking relationships in different cultures share some common social-structural elements that are interrelated in an orderly fashion and fall into a small number of patterns that can be abstracted for cross-cultural comparisons and for global theorizing. Thus such variables as sex, generation, relative age, and different types of consanguinal and affinal relations constitute the structural elements within the domain of kinship. The extrapolation of these structural elements from the numerous ethnographic examples of the joking relationship for cross-cultural studies has been relatively easy. In contrast, extrapolation of the substantive and culture-specific elements of the joking activities themselves and of the ideologies and value systems behind them is not feasible because they are not amenable to such a process. In addition, contextual variations in verbal and nonverbal joking behavior are specific to individual cultures and cannot easily be fitted into general patterns for the development of global theories. Whether or not the contextual variations relate to and affect structural patterns has been a controversial issue. Malefijt (1968a:1182) has argued that they do not, while Brukman (1975) has attempted to demonstrate that they do.

There is a major difference of emphasis between the analyses of joking relationships on the one hand and their explanations and interpretations on the other. In analyses of joking relationships, joking is used merely as a criterion to separate certain social relationships from others. Relationships are then categorized and contrasted on the basis of various key attributes. In other words, the structural approach emphasizes social relationships rather than actual joking activities and interactions, because the latter are not amenable to broad cross-cultural generalizations to the same extent that the former are. On the other hand, in interpretations of joking relationships, especially in functional terms, the emphasis falls primarily on the purposes joking serves and on the ways in which it links social structure to life processes.

Whether in analyzing joking relationships we should consider only the social-structural factors or the conceptual systems believed to underlie such relationships is a controversial issue. The former approach may lead to theoretical emphasis with cross-cultural orientation, as it did for Radcliffe-Brown, while the latter may result in culture-specific theories that may be quite insightful but may be of little use in developing general theories. In his analysis of the utani institution among the Kaguru, for example, Beidelman (1966) examines the Kaguru abstract systems of values pertaining to pollution due to death, prohibited sexual relations, and misconduct. He argues that the institution of utani represents a medial zone between two strongly contrasted conceptual distinctions relating to morality as reflected in acts, states, and things.

Despite the difficulties that I have mentioned, the structural approach has generally been more fruitful than the functional one for analyzing the joking relationship, the main reason being that analyses are based on observable empirical data from which structural elements can be abstracted. When it comes to interpretations and explanations of joking relationships, however, the situation is different. While the structural analyses of the joking relationship are post facto, the various explanations, especially those couched in functional terms, are not subject to the same rigor as empirical observations.

Numerous functional explanations of the joking relationship have been proposed. Radcliffe-Brown (1952/1965) proposed several microfunctions, such as the reduction of hostility, the release of tension, and the avoidance of conflict, leading to the macrofunctional explanation of the joking relationship in terms of social harmony and stability. Lowie (1920/1961) was one of the earliest anthropologists to suggest that joking serves the function of social control. Other proposed functional explanations indicate that the joking relationship makes possible emotional catharsis and communication (Hammond 1964); releases sexual and aggressive impulses (Murdock 1949:282); offers pure entertainment and drama (Kennedy 1970); establishes social etiquette and a screening procedure for group membership (Malefijt 1968a); releases strenuous and dangerous work-related tension (Pilcher 1972:109ff.); serves as a symbolic indicator of strong affinal ties (J. Freedman 1977); demonstrates "exclusiveness of association" (Stevens 1978) or supplies a badge of group identity (Lundberg 1969); and permits the exploration of potential closeness in social relations (Howell 1973). This list of functions is by no means complete.

Theories and functional explanations proposed by scholars seem applicable to either the kin-based joking relationship in preliterate societies or the nonkin ones in industrial societies. It is clear that Radcliffe-Brown's theory, for instance, is primarily relevant to kin-based joking relationships among preliterate societies, as is Murdock's (1949). On the other hand, theories proposed by Handelman and Kapferer (1972) and Lundberg (1969) seem applicable to nonkin joking relationships in industrial societies. Investigators who propose the so-called global theories, however, fail to acknowledge that their validity seems limited.

Researchers who propose functional theories seem to differ in their perspective and emphasis. Some prefer to focus on positive functions, others on negative ones. Thus Kennedy believes that patterns of joking behavior are institutionalized because they "provide joy and euphoria so common in comedy and laughter" (1970:52). Radcliffe-Brown, on the other hand, credits joking relationships with the avoidance of conflict and the reduction of hostility (1952/1965:104). Functional theories also vary in their emphasis on individuals or groups. Many functions are considered to be universal by the individuals who propose them. Some authors have proposed a single functional explanation (J. Freedman 1977; Kennedy 1970; Stevens 1978), while others (Hammond 1964; Malefijt 1968a; Radcliffe-Brown 1952/1965) have proposed several. In some cases different functions are attributed to different types of joking relationship (Malefijt 1968a). Few writers, however, have systematically listed different types of joking relationships and joking activities with the functions they are supposed to serve, although Murdock (1949:276) observed that different explanations were probable for joking relationships among different relatives. The functional explanations proposed by anthropologists have only occasionally been acknowledged or accepted by members of the cultures in which joking relationships exist.

A major problem with functional theories of the joking relationship is that they are educated guesses at best. It is not difficult to demonstrate either that joking is intended to achieve all the goals claimed for it by both the participants and the ethnographers or that both joking and the joking relationship are seen by the members of a culture as achieving these goals. It is much more difficult to show that joking actually serves these functions. The effectiveness of joking is not measured. This drawback applies especially to psychological explanations, none of which has been validated by systematic experimentation. Many functional explanations, therefore, are merely hypotheses that cannot be tested. All such theories, however, seem to imply some quantitatively measureable degree of effectiveness or seem to suggest that there is a demonstrable cause-and-effect relationship between joking and the desired results, whatever they may be. Such relationships have not been proven beyond doubt. They can merely be inferred because of consistent association as in the case of joking among longshoremen in Portland, Oregon (Pilcher 1972), where obscenity and joking increase in intensity and content as the work becomes hazardous but decrease when the individuals are not in such potentially dangerous situations and rarely occur beyond the work setting.

If theories of the joking relationship are to be based on interactional and behavioral aspects of joking, then it is necessary to verify that these aspects are actually manifested. Doing so is not a problem if the theories and explanations are based on several actually observed instances of joking. If they are based only on the statements of the informants, however, they may explain only the ideal or presumed (C. E. Richards 1969) behavioral patterns rather than those that are manifest. Informants may have a tendency to state what they think members of their society ideally do or are presumed to do, without basing their information on their actual observations of joking behavior. Some types of joking relationship in a culture are possibly idealized or obsolete despite informants' assertions. Although ethnographers are increasingly careful in verifying their data, it is probable that the joking relationships being analyzed exist only ideally or only in the past, as one anthropologist noted (W. W. Simmons 1971:81).

Anthropologists often tend to generalize inductively from the analysis of the joking relationship in a single culture and propose global theories to explain it universally. Such an approach is unsatisfactory. Joking relationships are quite diverse in nature. They involve verbal and nonverbal behavior based on interpersonal and intergroup relations; they occur in numerous social settings; they involve participants with different motives; and they lead to consequences that the participants may or may not expect. It is therefore unrealistic and somewhat naive to assume that a single global theory could adequately explain the joking relationship.

A few authors (J. Freedman 1977; Kennedy 1970; Stevens 1978) take a more cautious approach in theorizing about the joking relationship. Kennedy and Freedman both note that a major distinction needs to be made between joking relationships in traditional, homogeneous, small-scale societies and those in industrial, heterogeneous, and complex societies. Kennedy in particular argues, and quite rightly in my opinion, that a general classification of the various types of joking relationship needs to be undertaken before any theories for all such activities and the social relations on which they are based can be proposed. Such a classification has been a major objective of this chapter. Stevens (1978) rightly suggests that various explanations are equally relevant and that taken together they are useful for understanding the complex nature of the joking relationship. This change in approach is indeed welcome; some scholars earlier insisted on presenting global theories, as if joking relationships in many cultures were very similar (Hammond 1964; Radcliffe-Brown 1952/1965).

One reason for the persistence of global theories of the joking relationship concerns the discipline of anthropology as it seeks to develop universally valid statements about human existence and about the contributions of social and cultural systems. A single theory sufficient both to analyze and to explain all types of joking relationship in human cultures everywhere, however, may be much less insightful than theories tailored specifically to individual cultures. A single broad theory would also be contrary to the holistic principle inherent in the understanding of individual societies and cultures and emphasized by the disciplinary perspective.

Pursuing this train of thought, I would argue that many minitheories are preferable to a single global theory in understanding the complex and diverse nature of joking relationships. Only after many minitheories have been developed to account for more specific and limited aspects of the joking relationship will the development of a global theory be feasible. Minitheories may complement each other in that some may explain aspects of the joking relationship that are not explained by others. Thus in the process of understanding the complex nature of the joking relationship in a cross-cultural comparative perspective, scholarly goals would be better served by considering all plausible explanations than by evaluating the superiority or inferiority of individual theories. Minitheories not only should explain different types of joking relationship but also should provide explanations as to why particular types develop in some societies and not in others. In other words, attempts should be made to correlate the joking relationship with other aspects of cultural systems.

If global theories are to be developed at all, the classificatory framework presented in this chapter is the first step in that direction. It should also be recognized that the distinction between kin-based and nonkin joking relationships is fundamental and cannot be eliminated. Kin-based joking, rooted in kinship relations that cannot be rejected or negated, manifests the consequences of those relationships, whether positive or negative. Nonkin joking, on the other hand, most often forms an integral part of social relations and cannot be separated from them. Within the domain of kin-based joking relationships, it is possible to develop some theoretical explanations that may have cross-cultural validity. These too, however, must be restricted to each broad category within the classificatory framework. The hypothesis that the joking relationship is not found among members of a nuclear family because of their very close interdependence and because of incest taboos, for example, should be applicable cross-culturally.

The development of general theories to explain the nonkin joking relationship is more difficult because of that relationship's complex nature. Many factors determine its form and substance—for instance, the social setting, the participants' role, age, sex, and social status, their conscious and unconscious motivations and expectations regarding the outcomes of joking encounters, the presence or absence of an audience, the collective goals of social groups such as group solidarity and social differentiation, and so forth. The social relations and situations of which joking patterns form a part are much more fluid than kinship relations, making it difficult to develop a single global theory applicable to all types of nonkin joking relationship.

Radcliffe-Brown was quite aware of the problems inherent in developing global theories that may not satisfactorily explain all instances of joking relationship, as the following remark indicates: "It is not a question of whether my theory, or any other general theory, of joking relationships is or is not satisfactory. It is the different question of whether such a general theory is possible, or whether attempts to arrive at one should be abandoned in favour of resting content with particularistic explanations" (Radcliffe-Brown 1952/1965:114).

64

A major weakness of the various theoretical contributions to the joking relationship is their failure to develop the concept of friendship sufficiently at the culture-specific and universal levels. It should be obvious from the discussion so far that the notion of friendship is very crucial to understanding the nature of the joking relationship, especially in industrial societies, where it appears to replace many secondary kinship relations in social milieu. Only recently have attempts been made to consider friendship in a cross-cultural perspective (Leyton 1974), however, or to discuss its significance for social relations in individual cultures (Bell 1981; Kiefer 1968). This literature does not, however, explore the interconnections between friendship and the joking relationship. Even Radcliffe-Brown, who recognized the significance of the notion of friendship for the joking relationship, defined it in a rather cursory, narrow, and negative fashion and did not elaborate on its varied nature or on its multitudinous interconnections with joking relationships. One major goal of any future studies should be to explore the nature of friendship cross-culturally in considerable depth as well as to probe the interdependence of friendship and the joking relationship within the broad framework of social organization and the cultural system.

THEORETICAL PROPOSITIONS

Several theoretical propositions may be formulated on the basis of my overall discussion of the joking relationship in this chapter.

There is a fundamental dichotomy between kin and nonkin joking relationships in sociocultural systems.

Kin-based joking relationships are category oriented, generally obligatory, normative, and both reciprocal and nonreciprocal, in contrast to nonkin joking relationships, which are person oriented, voluntary, and generally reciprocal.

Positive encouragement from potential joking partners is a necessary precondition for establishing and maintaining joking relationships in industrial societies; in preliterate societies, however, such relationships are not voluntary.

While kin-based joking relationships between women are generally absent in preliterate societies, nonkin joking relationships do occur between women in industrial societies.

Within the domain of kinship, the joking relationship is generally absent among members of nuclear families.

Ideas of incest are inversely related to joking relationships of a sexual nature, hence the absence of joking relationships in those kinship relations where incest taboos are strong.

The occurrence and nature of kin-based sexual joking relationships are determined by marriage customs as well as by sexual taboos. Such relationships are quite common between individuals who are prescribed or preferred marriage partners, for example, between men and their wives' younger sisters in societies that practice sororate marriage and between cross-cousins in societies where cross-cousin marriage is preferred.

An asymmetrical joking relationship is likely to occur between a man and his wife's brother(s) in patrilineal societies with strong male dominance.

Joking relationships between grandparents and grandchildren of both sexes are widespread across cultures.

Friendship is a significant prerequisite for nonkin joking relationships in industrial societies.

Joking relationships among members of specific professional groups and other types of social groups in industrial societies manifest a consciousness of group identity and group solidarity.

2

Sexual Inequality in Humor

In this chapter I aim to study the sex-related differences in the nature, dissemination, use, and appreciation of humor across cultures and to explore and generalize regarding the many factors likely to be responsible for these differences. Such an endeavor is timely and significant in view of social scientists' growing interest in exploring similarities and differences between the sexes in both human and nonhuman social groups. Anthropologists interested in humor should also find useful the opportunity to develop a better general understanding of humor's relationship to social organization.

Social scientists interested in sex roles have investigated anatomical and physiological differences between the sexes, sexual division of labor, role models available to children in the enculturation and socialization process, and social-structural variables responsible for differential status and behavior. Anthropologists have contributed substantially to this research by providing ethnographic material, thus adding a cross-cultural perspective.[1] There are, however, no anthropological analyses of humor as it relates to sexual differences. The discussion of humor, when it occurs in the context of sexual differences, is brief, cursory, and often marginal with respect to other empirical and analytical issues. On the other hand, psychologists have begun to study sex-related humor in earnest, as indicated by recent experimental research and publications.[2] Although the psychological studies, based on empirical data and rigorous methodology, are interesting, their samples are mostly limited to Western societies, especially Anglo-American ones. Such studies are also primarily oriented toward exploring sexual differences in the appreciation and evaluation of humor and lack analyses of its content and techniques. Such studies are important, however, not only because of their methodological contributions but also because of their attempts to relate their findings to sociocultural phenomena. In this respect the psychological research complements anthropological investigations.

Keeping this background in mind, we should ask the following crucial questions. Are there differences between men's and women's humor? If so, then what is the nature of these differences? To what extent are these differences related to societal attitudes toward sex-role models and to normative behavioral patterns concerning women? And finally, under what circumstances and in what manner are these differences minimized, if at all? The extent to which biological differences between the sexes influence the personality development of men and women is a complex issue that remains unresolved. It is readily apparent from ethnographic data that generally, but not universally, men and women have different social status, and women on the whole seem to have lower social status than men, especially in the public domain. The anthropological observation that there are no truly matriarchal societies in the world but many patriarchal ones (Keesing 1975:63; Schneider 1961; Schusky 1972:9) indicates men's greater authority and higher status (Evans-Pritchard 1965:50). Even in matrilineal societies women tend to exhibit a deferential attitude toward men, as noted by Schlegel (1972:84) in a cross-cultural study of domestic authority. In a sample of matrilineal societies for which data on female deference exist, Schlegel found that 64.2 percent of the women exhibited deference toward either husband or brother.

The factors that might be responsible for women's low social status, real or perceived, vis-à-vis men, and its perpetuation, have been much discussed in the current literature on women's studies. Explanations range from sociobiological to psychological determinants. Such sociocultural factors as differential socialization, lack of economic and political power, lack of a contribution to the production of necessary goods and services, dominant cultural values concerning ideal womanhood, and a general dependence on males for security have been variously considered as the causes for the existing inequality between men and women (Martin and Voorhies 1975; Quinn 1977; Rosaldo and Lamphere 1974). It has also been argued (Rogers 1975) that, even when women are independent of men because of their own, separate economic resources, are free to participate in various activities without regard for the sexual di-

68

vision of labor, and have equal control in the distribution of ancestral or personal property, they seem to accept the myth of social superiority of men.

BASIC PREMISES

I wish to put forward three basic premises concerning sex-related aspects of humor. First, women's humor reflects the existing inequality between the sexes not so much in its substance as in the constraints imposed on its occurrence, on the techniques used, on the social settings in which it occurs, and on the kind of audience that appreciates it. Second, these constraints generally, but not necessarily universally, stem from the prevalent cultural values that emphasize male superiority and dominance together with female passivity and create role models for women in keeping with such values and attitudes. Finally, certain social factors such as marriage, advanced age, and the greater freedom enjoyed by women in groups remove some of the constraints ordinarily imposed on them and reduce the differences between men's and women's humor. These hypotheses primarily indicate existing cross-cultural trends suggested by available ethnographic data and should not be considered absolutely universal. It is also important to realize that men's capacity for humor is not superior to women's. Rather, both the prevalent cultural values and the resultant constraints prevent women from fully using their talents.

ATTRIBUTES AND VARIETIES ABSENT FROM WOMEN'S
HUMOR IN THE PUBLIC DOMAIN

A major consequence of the behavioral, expressive, and other sociocultural constraints imposed on women is that many common attributes of men's humor seem to be much less evident or even absent in women's humor. In public domains women seem generally not to engage in: verbal duels, ritual insults, practical jokes, and pranks, all of which reflect the competitive spirit, and the aggressive and hostile quality, of men's humor; slapstick; institutionalized clowning; and institutionalized joking relationships with female kin.

Verbal Duels, Ritual Insults, and Practical Jokes

Women's humor generally lacks the aggressive and hostile quality of men's humor. The use of humor to compete with or to belittle others, thereby enhancing a person's own status, or to humiliate others either psychologically or physically, seems generally absent among women. Thus the most commonly institutionalized ways of engaging in such humor, namely, verbal duels, ritual insults, and practical jokes and pranks, are rarely reported for women. Ethnographic data from many cultures show, for example, that adolescent boys and men engage in ritual insults.[3] In such verbal duels the participants hurl all sorts of obscenities and insults at each other—often at the expense of their female relatives—to the amusement of the audience. These verbal duels and ritual insults are well institutionalized, the rules of performance are known to contestants and spectators alike, and the goal is one-upmanship on the basis of quick repartee until one contestant either gives up or resorts to physical violence. Such accounts of verbal dueling and ritual insults among women contestants have generally not been reported. The only example I found is that of Mitchell-Kernan (1972), who reported her own participation in such a contest with a male opponent. Although in some cultures it is believed that women play their own verbal duels, neither female nor male ethnographers have substantiated the report. Gossen (1976:127–28) claims that such is the case among the Chamula Indians in Mexico but also states that young girls are not supposed to hear men's verbal duels and that girls who do cannot giggle or otherwise acknowledge the exchanges because to do so would suggest that they are sexually available.

Ethnographic accounts of women playing practical jokes or pranks on each other or on men in everyday social interactions seem almost nonexistent. On the other hand, men seem to play practical jokes not only on other men but also on women. Among the Hupa Indians of North America, men prefer playing practical jokes, while women show a lack of interest in this type of humor (W. J. Wallace 1953). The Trumai Indians of Central Brazil often frightened women by playing practical jokes on them. Interestingly, women played an active role, pretending fright when they were the victims of such pranks (Murphy and Quain 1955:92–93). The folklore and mythologies of many cultures present additional evidence that aggressiveness and pranks are absent from women's humor. While no female trickster or clown figures are to be found in the prose narratives of any culture, there is a preponderance of male tricksters and clowns.[4] Even when the trickster figures are animals, they are either specifically identified as males, as in the case of the Raven in the Tlingit Indian myths (Radin 1956/1969), and Ture, the spider, in Zande tales (Evans-Pritchard 1967), or references to their physical features, especially the penis, leave no doubt about their male identity. Sometimes the events in the various episodes of the trickster cycles of myth clearly suggest the maleness of the character, as evidenced by the Assiniboine trickster myths (Radin 1956/1969:97–103).

Occasionally, oral literature indicates that a society prefers men to be tricky and clever in their humor. While examining humorous situations in the myths of Clackamas Chinook Indians for the purpose of classifying fun-generating stimuli, for instance, Jacobs (1960) found that trickery and cleverness in men and children, but not in women, was a stimulus for humor and laughter. "In their myths Chinook did not indicate that a woman before menopause would ever display so masculine a virtue as canniness"(p. 186).

Slapstick

Just as verbal aggressive humor and practical jokes seem much less prevalent among women, there is little ethnographic evidence to suggest that women individually participate in slapstick or in other similar kinds of humor in which physical roughhousing or horseplay are involved. In a cross-cultural study of sex differences in the behavior of children aged three through eleven (Whiting and Edwards 1973), it was found that boys engaged in more rough-and-tumble play and verbal aggression than girls. Boys were also more likely to counterattack physically or verbally if someone took aggression against them. Girls showed an overall tendency to withdraw in the face of aggression. Aversion to physical and aggressive action thus appears to be inculcated quite early in women, and this perhaps explains the near absence among them of humor that involves slapstick, physical roughhousing, and horseplay. Almost no account of rough physical games among women in non-Western cultures is to be found. Even in Western societies women have generally not participated in the rougher physical games, and although women in recent years have increasingly done so, they are still quite few compared with men. In this connection Tiger remarks that "a cursory survey of the world's major sports must lead to the conclusion that they are very much male-dominated—almost en-

tirely so for sports involving teams of more than two persons"
(1969/1970:149).

Institutionalized Clowning

In general, women individually do not clown for humorous effect, especially in social situations that are public. Ethnographic
accounts of secular and ritual clowning indicate that in very few
cultures are there female clowns. Court jesters and clowns, whether
they appear in classical Sanskrit plays of ancient India (Bhat 1959)
or in Shakespearean plays, are generally males. Historical and analytical studies of the development of court jesters, clowns, buffoons, and fools (Swain 1932; Towsen 1976; Welsford 1935; Willeford
1969) show that women rarely, if ever, played such roles. Ethnographic accounts of festivals and/or rituals indicate that women
rarely act as clowns, either by themselves or in cooperation with
men, and some scholars (King 1979; Makarius 1970) have offered
explanations. In Western societies, the occasional woman clown in
theaters and circuses, the most conventional arenas for clowning,
merits feature stories in newspapers and magazines. Even in ordinary social relationships and interpersonal interactions, especially in the public domain, women develop humor by clowning
much less frequently than men.

One possible explanation for the relative absence of clowning
among women is that norms of propriety in many societies do not
permit women to be totally uninhibited. Fox wrote of a "normative
restriction" applied to women, and a kind of "social control over
women's social behavior is embodied in such value constructs as
'good girl,' 'lady,' or 'nice girl.' As a value construct the latter term
connotes chaste, gentle, gracious, ingenuous, good, clean, kind,
virtuous, noncontroversial, and above suspicion and reproach"
(1977:807). Yet freedom of behavior and freedom from social sanctions are a major aspect of any kind of clowning. Thus women feel
more constrained in social interactions in the public domain that
involve individuals of both sexes and of diverse ages and occupations. In social interactions involving only women, however,
clowning does occur, as I shall show later.

In cultures where institutionalized clowning is an integral part
of rituals, women often either are excluded from participation in
the ritual or may function only on the periphery and therefore
cannot be clowns. In societies where ritual clowning is a well-
established institution, clowns have a high social status and im-

portant duties to perform (Spicer 1940:125). In some American Indian communities in the southwestern United States and Mexico, men must be apprentices for some time before they can act as clowns (Bricker 1973:70, 155–56). The leaders of the ritual clowns usually acquire extensive experience over a long period of time (Spicer 1954:91). The longer a person acts as a clown at a religious function, the higher his prestige. Within the framework of the ritual itself, clowns can burlesque and mock with total impunity anybody and everybody, including the priests and the officials at the ceremonies (Crumrine 1969; Parsons and Beals 1934; Spicer 1954:173–74). Among the Rio Grande Pueblos, clown societies exist, but only males become members (Dozier 1961:115–16). In religious contexts clowning manifests high social status. The absence of women clowns therefore suggests that their status relative to that of men in community rituals and ceremonials is inferior overall.

Institutionalized Joking Relationships

Also absent from women's humor is an institutionalized joking relationship between female kin. Although many societies have well-established joking relationships among various kin, these appear to be primarily between males or between a male and a female. I found only two examples of structured joking involving female relatives in my survey of the extensive ethnographic literature on the subject, which I discussed in Chapter 1. Among the Tallensi there is a mutual joking relationship between a woman and her brother's wife (Fortes 1949:94, 120), and grandmothers and granddaughters have a joking relationship among the Tarahumara Indians of Mexico (Kennedy 1970).

My discussion suggests that several points should be noted. Women seem not to engage in the development of certain categories of humor because they do not have the same degree of freedom that men do. Sociocultural reality in many societies means in part that men's activities usually take place in public arenas, while women's activities occur in more private ones (Farrer 1975:ix). Women's relative lack of freedom to engage in certain types of activities in the public domain seems closely related to their socially inferior status in that domain (Sanday 1974:205) and to the emphasis that many societies place on such cultural values as modesty, politeness, and passivity in the context of female sex roles.

It could be argued that the lack of ethnographic data on humor as part of women's expressive behavior is due to difficulties in obtaining such data. Male ethnographers may not have easy access to women's activities that provide a setting for humor (Farrer 1975:ix). This view, however, does not take into account the fact that it is in the public domain of social interaction, which is generally accessible to ethnographers of both sexes, that certain humor-generating activities are not undertaken by women individually. A more plausible argument may be that bias on the part of anthropologists and folklorists may result either in a lack of interest in women's activities, especially their expressive behavior, or in attempts to force women's verbal creations into preexisting categories and genres developed from men's expressive culture (Farrer 1975:viff.). Such a lack of interest in women's activities may reflect the belief that they are insignificant, a view that seems to have been accepted until recently even by women scholars. A greater awareness of the relevance of women's roles and activities to cultural systems should lead to extensive research on women's humor in the future. Such research may indicate that the varieties of humor discussed above do occur among women, and possibly women have developed certain types and attributes of humor generally not found among men.

The cultural values of modesty and passivity for females that are found in many societies mean that girls receive differential treatment. The purpose of such treatment is to inculcate in girls from early childhood the value of ideal female sex roles. There is generally stricter control over girls than over boys with respect to overall behavior, but especially sexual conduct, personal attire, appearance and posture, work load, expressive behavior, and the appropriate share of responsibilities. While the degree of control over girls may vary cross-culturally, in almost no societies is boys' overall behavior regulated more strictly than girls. Whiting and Edwards (1973) found cross-culturally that girls from ages seven to eleven were significantly more compliant with respect to their mother's demands than were boys, a finding that echoes the results of an earlier cross-cultural study (Barry, Bacon, and Child 1957), which concluded that girls were under more pressure than boys to be nurturant, obedient, and responsible, while boys were under more pressure, to achieve and to be self-reliant.

Girls are instructed from an early age to sit so as not to expose themselves, and they generally start wearing clothes sooner than boys. Girls are also given household tasks earlier than boys, so that their play activities are restricted sooner. In their cross-cultural study of sexual patterns, Ford and Beach (1951) found that, in societies that treat boys and girls differently, the sexual activities of girls are more carefully controlled. Similarly, Ford and Beach concluded that, in societies that practiced segregation and chaperonage to control the sexual behavior of adolescents, boys were less carefully watched than girls. The restrictions on women's behavior are manifested in other ways as well. In many cultures norms of modesty cause women who laugh freely and openly in public to be viewed as loose, sexually promiscuous, and lacking in self-discipline. Such restrictions are found among the Mundurucú Indians in South America, the Sarakatsani shepherds of Greece, people in rural India and the Middle East, and other groups.

Another reason for the absence of certain varieties in women's humor is their lack of opportunities for "performance" in public. It is commonly recognized by folklorists that performance is a crucial and indispensable factor in the realization of humor in prose narratives and other genres, especially in preindustrial societies (Bascom 1955; Finnegan 1970:2–7, 319–32). In many societies boys are actively encouraged from an early age to develop rhetorical and linguistic skills, because good orators and storytellers acquire public recognition; storytelling is a significant event for amusement and entertainment. Women, however, are not encouraged to develop the linguistic skills necessary for such performances. Among the Limba in Africa, for instance, women generally do not tell stories because it is believed that speaking well, using rhetoric, parable, or illustration effectively, is a specifically masculine activity: women are mostly expected to listen (Finnegan 1967:69–70).[5]

Such differential attitudes and consequent behavior with respect to linguistic skills are by no means characteristic of only preindustrial societies. In discussing the characteristic features of American women's language, Lakoff (1975:56) claims that women generally do not tell jokes in social situations because such behavior is not in keeping with the politeness expected of them. According to a folk belief in American culture that is shared by both men and women, women cannot tell stories or jokes correctly. The persistence of such beliefs and the resulting attitudes may explain why a woman folklorist (Kalčik 1975:5,7) found that, even in women's rap sessions, women "consistently began and ended with apologies: for speaking, for the content of their speech, for speaking too long," and so forth. Such behavior indicates that middle-class American women do not feel that they have the same freedom and choice of speech that men do.

75

FACTORS THAT REDUCE SEX-RELATED DIFFERENCES

I do not mean to create the impression that women's humor and other modes of expressive behavior are totally constrained. First, constraints are viewed as necessary for an ideal female sex role, and not all women necessarily conform to such expectations. When the norms are broken, the nature of sanctions varies across cultures, from the strongest (such as a gang rape among the Mundurucú Indians in South America) to mere whispered gossip. Several factors also alleviate the sociocultural restraints on women, allowing them to engage occasionally in humorous activities comparable to those of men. In addition, women use certain strategies to circumvent the sociocultural restraints.

Women's Humor among Women

Some varieties of humor that are usually absent from women's expressive behavior in the public domain are present in the private domain, where the audience generally includes only women. In many preindustrial societies humor created by women individually seems confined to social situations in which only women are present; in an all-female audience women behave more freely and creatively. Common topics for humor development in such gatherings include men's physical appearance, their social behavior, their idiosyncrasies, their sexuality, their status-seeking activities, and their religious rites. These characteristics are generally presented in an exaggerated and mocking fashion.

Elizabeth Fernea (1965/1969) reports that the chief entertainment among women of the Iraqi village where she lived consisted of mock imitation of men. The women felt free to do these mock imitations because the audience was exclusively female. The men never knew about the activities, because there was almost total segregation of the sexes; few social interactions involved participation of both men and women, even within kinship and household groups. The situation is somewhat similar among French peasant women, as described by Rogers.

> One gets a very different impression of women when they are observed in a room of men, on one hand, and with a group of women, on the other. The woman in the corner is a sharp observer; what she sees is later reported to other women admidst clicking tongues, shaking heads, or gales of laughter. Women are not particularly awestruck

by men despite the impression they give when publicly in their presence. If a man happens on a group of women in the street or in a barn, they invariably disperse, fall silent, or change their conversation, losing their feminine ambiance. [1975:741]

In Sicily, ribaldry as a form of humor occurs frequently among women's groups. "There are women who function in the role of comedians or social satirists, always in an explicitly sexual context" (Cronin 1977:85–86). Such women become famous for their expertise in satire, teasing, joking, ridicule, and impersonation. Men are never permitted to participate in the humor-creating activities of these women but know of them and are afraid of becoming the subject of such "female dramas" (ibid.).

Mock imitations of men by women may occasionally become obscene. It appears, however, that obscene elements are introduced only by married women, and unmarried women and young girls generally do not participate. Among the Magars, a tribe in Nepal, weddings provide opportunities for mock imitations. In a groom's village, when all adult men leave to accompany the groom, the married women gather at the groom's house. Some dress in their husbands' clothing, especially military uniforms, and one or two tie large phalli to themselves. These women sing erotic songs. Some dance, and those with phalli chase the dancers and pretend to force them to have sexual intercourse. "The women who take the part of the men are the focal figures, and their rendition of the sexually aroused male is satirical and immensely amusing to the group" (Hitchcock 1966:46).

The case of the Magars and similar practices among other groups[6] suggest that standards of modesty, which is considered an essential aspect of women's behavior and personality in many cultures, are observed more stringently for single women than for married women. In many societies, especially those in which segregation of the sexes in quite rigid and those in which notions of honor and shame are intimately related to women's sexuality (Fox 1977:807–808; Peristiany 1966), unmarried women are strictly guarded, are expected to behave passively, and are not supposed even indirectly to encourage males in any form of sexual encounter. In some cultures, unmarried women are not supposed to have a knowledge of sexual activity. Married women, on the other hand, have a somewhat higher status than unmarried ones. Because they are supposed to have had sexual experiences, they are considered knowledgeable about male sexuality. Nevertheless, married women are more likely to imitate male sexuality for an all-female audience than for a mixed audience except on special ceremonial occasions when such imitation may be carried out by women collectively.

Women's Collective Engagement in Humor

When women act collectively, many of the behavioral constraints that they must observe as individuals can be disregarded. This is especially the case in rituals involving female rites of passage, especially women's puberty rites (B.B. Whiting 1963:189). Marriage also seems to be a rite of passage that frees women from social restraints with respect to humor. One collective humorous activity of women involves singing songs that ridicule male sexual activity, especially at rites of passage. Women seem to derive much amusement from such songs, and in some cases the practice has developed into a social institution. The mock imitations of men by Magar and Gusii women are also often accompanied by singing activities. In North India women from the bride's side collectively sing obscene songs at weddings, deriding and ridiculing the bridegroom about his lack of sexual powers (E.O. Henry 1975; Jacobson 1977). Jacobson reports having seen women from a bride's party dashing potfuls of scarlet and indigo dye into the faces of the men who accompanied the groom. The women smeared the bright goo into the ears and noses of their unprotesting victims and, after tying a cowbell around the neck of the groom's father, began to sing "raucous and risqué" songs.

The burlesquing and ridiculing of men's ritual and status-seeking activities form another collective humorous activity of women. Among the Kwakiutl Indians of the northwestern United States, the potlatch ceremony was very important to men, because the prestige and status of chiefs depended on their generosity at such events. Yet Kwakiutl women have reportedly performed mock potlatch ceremonies (Codere 1956:343). Gusii women seem to treat men's rituals lightly and occasionally try to be amusing by mocking various acts or by creating a recreational atmosphere inconsistent with the seriousness of such ceremonies (B. B. Whiting 1963:82). Hopi Indian women mock men's kachina dances and sing obscene and humorous songs about men during the Marau ceremony (Schlegel 1977:257).

Among the people of Alor, boys around the age of sixteen grow their hair long and start to borrow male accoutrements such as a sword, front and back shields, a bow, a wide belt of woven rattan, and other similar objects. Boys rarely succeed in acquiring all of them but try to get as many as possible. The boys walk about, wearing the emblems to show off and to proclaim adulthood. On such occasions, they are often subjected to the half-admiring, half-derisive comments of old women and girls. There is even a special expression for the type of laughter women direct toward such young men, which anthropologist DuBois translates by the word "hoot." The character of this laughter "is as unmistakable as the laughter that accompanies the telling of smutty jokes in our culture" (DuBois 1944/1960:81). A boy among the Blackfoot and Cree Indians setting out on his first war party—an important event—is given a derogatory name, which sticks with him until he has won honor in war by stealing a horse, killing an enemy, or performing some other heroic deed. Women, including the fiancees of such young men, take a special part in ridiculing and making fun of them (Driver 1969:384).

The Effects of Advanced Age and Altered Body State

Age and the resultant changes in a woman's body seem to be other important variables affecting humor. Ethnographic evidence suggests that as women age and reach menopause, they seem to grow bolder, start competing with men openly and freely in all types of humor, and often prove their equals. In many societies men seem to accept this change status in elderly women, perhaps because such women no longer bear children and the sex-specific norms of behavior are relaxed for them. Even in societies with strict segregation of the sexes and the practice of purdah, elderly women are much less restrained than younger ones (Fox 1977).

Elderly women's relative freedom of speech and behavior has been noted in many ethnographies. Osgood (1951:114) reports that, among the Koreans, a women beyond menopause is considered to be sexless in the eyes of the people and can therefore do pretty well as she pleases. In Bali, where "modesty of speech and action is enjoined on women, such behavior may be no longer asked from the older women, who may use obscene language as freely as or more freely than any man" (Mead 1949:180).[7] Elderly women participate in supposedly exclusive male activities such as political deliberations, drinking and smoking, and decision making. Their freedom to indulge in obscene speech also offers them opportunities to compete with men in humor. Devereux reported of his old female informant thus: "My aged informant, Tcatc, because of her age, felt free to speak up in the tribal council. 'Because of her age' she was also quite ready to engage in sexual banter, obscene even by the standards of the Mohave man" (1947:532).

In Chinese villages old women, in addition to smoking and attending meetings normally reserved for males, also talk "dirty" and act as teasers. When an old woman in a social group clears her throat, preparing to speak, other people stop talking and listen intently, expecting to be amused. Barnett (1970), who made these observations, narrates the following incident, in which he himself became the target of their teasing: "I was sitting in front of the village store in a group one day while four married girls were washing clothes across the street in a bent-over position. A woman of eighty nudged me and in a loud voice exclaimed 'That girl over there is waving it at you. Go over and stick her!' She and the other older women laughed loudly as several men smiled" (Barnett 1970:450).

In Okinawan villages men and women are entertained at festivals by drinking, dancing, and joking. While young women do not drink sake at these celebrations and show much inhibition and restrained behavior, old women consume sake as men do and have few inhibitions. Dances simulating sexual behavior performed by an old woman and young man appear to be funnier and more humorous than similar dances performed by other pairs (B. B. Whiting 1963:452).

The relaxation of sociocultural norms for older women and their active participation in humor in the public domain characterize not only preindustrial but also industrial societies. In a study of joking relationships among male and female workers in a Glasgow factory by Sykes (1966), it was observed that old women often initiated sexual banter when interacting with young men in front of other people. Young women rarely initiated such encounters, either with old men or with young men. Although sexual encounters occurred between young men and women in isolated areas of the factory, the convention that young women should be modest in their behavior and speech in public was retained, and hence they did not take the initiative in joking exchanges.

THEORETICAL PROPOSITIONS

The general discussion in this chapter permits the formulation of several theoretical propositions.

Sexual Inequality in Humor

Men and women appear to have unequal status across cultures. By restricting the freedom of women to engage in and to respond to humor in the public domain, men emphasize their need for superiority. Men justify such restrictions by creating ideal role models for women that emphasize modesty, virtue, and passivity.

Restrictions on the kinds of humor in which women can engage offer an important avenue to social control that has been generally ignored in anthropological research.

A sexual distinction that transcends gender constitutes the basis of competition and tension between men and women for sociocultural dominance. This distinction emphasizes women's ability to engage in sexual intercourse, to conceive, and to give birth, while the gender aspects imply merely the anatomical differences. Men seem intimidated by the idea of sexual freedom for women because they fear that it might make women more like men: aggressive and promiscuous. They also fear that such freedom may disrupt social order, hence their desire to control women's sexuality at least in the public domain.

Women's relative freedom to engage in humor in the public domain is related to their position in the life cycle. As they advance through it, the restrictions are relaxed, and women publicly engage in humor to greater degrees, eventually competing with men.

3

Children's Humor

The formation and recognition of social groups based on the criterion of age seem fundamental to all human societies. While the division of humans into adults and children seems fairly widespread, the composition and boundaries of these two primary groups are complex and difficult to define. It may be possible to describe the division using a purely physiological criterion: adults are sexually mature and are capable of procreation, while children are not. This criterion is not satisfactory, however, because sociocultural attributes are superimposed on physiological ones, leading to considerable cross-cultural variation.

The discussion of humor in the context of age groups is problematic for a number of reasons. First, several age groups are recognized within the broad categories of adults and children. In Anglo-American cultures, for example, children are described by such terms as "infant," "toddler," "preschooler," "preteenager," "teenager," and "adolescent." Such labels and the divisions they indicate within the two primary groups vary cross-culturally. In the investigation of child-rearing practices in six cultures made by the Whitings and their associates (B. B. Whiting 1963), it was observed that in the broad category labeled "children," further divisions based on age as recognized in each of the six cultures under study varied considerably. Second, even when children reach puberty, they are not often treated as adults. Thus the biological and sociocultural identities are not coterminous. Third, not only age categories but also the transition periods between them are important in most cultures, and there is cross-cultural variation in this respect too. In some societies transitions from one age state to another in the life cycle are only minimally recognized, if at all, while in others they are of considerable significance. All these caveats should be kept in mind in connection with the use of the term "children" in the remainder of this chapter.

The anthropological investigation of children's humor is important for a variety of reasons. The nature of the socialization process is often reflected in children's humor. It is therefore an index of the processes whereby children develop into socially acceptable persons and acquire many sociocultural skills, such as language, body control, profession, and role playing. A comparison of children's humor in their different developmental stages in individual cultures provide insights into their mental processes, cognitive developments, emotional anxieties, and preoccupations. A fundamental assumption among scholars of the "cultural and personality" school in anthropology has been that behavioral norms, cognitive skills, value systems, and attitudes are internalized by children primarily as a result of socialization and enculturation. Humor is no exception to this process. The Whitings and their associates undertook their extensive ethnographic studies of child-rearing practices to verify the hypothesis that differential patterns of child rearing will lead to differences in the personality of children and thus to differences in adult personality (B. B. Whiting 1963:5). Although the six ethnographic studies emphasized behavioral systems of feeding, toilet training, dependence, aggression, competition, and identification, children's humor unfortunately did not receive attention as a critical variable.

Children's humor is often modeled on adult patterns of social interaction and humor. Some of the same techniques of humor are used, and the same genres and categories are emphasized. Therefore investigation of children's humor helps to confirm analyses of adult humor and its dominant patterns. Middle-class American children, for example, start telling jokes at an early age, which suggests that joke telling is a major cultural activity in most social situations. Kanuri children in Nigeria engage in telling and creating riddles; their culture emphasizes this activity (Peshkin 1972). Young boys among Chamula Indians memorize many set phrases and engage in verbal duels with their age mates and with older boys, indicating the adult preoccupation with this genre of humor and its popularity in various social activities (Gossen 1976). The prevalence and range of humor among children is also an indicator of a society's positive or negative attitudes toward humor in general. That adults encourage children to participate in humor and to appreciate it suggests a society's positive attitude toward it. On the other hand, the relative paucity of children's humor reflects a society's negative attitudes toward it.

Mere observation of behavior is often not sufficient for understanding cultural norms, and studying children's humor along with that of adults helps in discerning the implicit values. Children's humor is especially relevant in this context, because children tend to be less inhibited than adults in mocking and ridiculing peers for deviant behavior. I shall discuss in this chapter the various salient features of children's humor in a topical fashion. My overall goal is to demonstrate how children's humor, while being an essential component of a cultural system and sharing many features of adult humor, differs from it in some fundamental ways.

CLASSIFICATION

Children's humor can be broadly classified into four categories: linguistic humor, humor in play, scatological and sexual humor, and humor of socialization. The fourfold classification is based both on the subject matter of children's humor and on the techniques for its development. The main purpose of the typology is to provide an analytic framework within which children's humor can meaningfully be discussed. In culture-specific contexts the categories may overlap, and the boundaries between them may be subject to frequent shifting. Some categories are more wide-ranging than others, and further subtypes within them can be recognized. Within the "humor in play" category, for instance, further subtypes— games, practical jokes, trickery, clowning, and so forth—can be made.

Socialization and sexual differences in children's humor will be discussed to determine whether the sexual inequality in adult humor has its roots in the differential patterns of socialization used in many cultures in raising male and female children. I shall also explore the relationship between children's ability to create, to comprehend, and to appreciate humor and their overall cognitive and personality development.

Linguistic Humor

The notion that certain types of verbal activities are playful and humorous has been widely accepted by scholars. In recent years playful speech has attracted the attention of many scholars, and many ethnographic descriptions and linguistic analyses of children's speech play have resulted. Linguists, folklorists, anthropologists, and psychologists have extensively discussed the linguistic aspects of children's humor.[1] Because many aspects of linguistic humor found among both adults and children are discussed in the chapter on linguistic aspects of humor, the following discussion will be brief.

In the process of language acquisition, children have great fun manipulating the structural elements of language. They frequently take apart and put together in a myriad ways various units of language. They create words, sentences, rhymes, riddles, puns, and other compositions that are novel, nonsensical, and funny. All such activity seems to amuse children and continues even after they have mastered the basic structural features of the language of their social group. Repetitions and tongue twisters, simple and chain rhymes, grammatical anomalies, talking backward, nonsense creations, secret languages; punning riddles in which ludicrous literal meanings override the metaphorical meanings; jumprope songs; linguistic games; and songs that employ various rhythms, metrical patterns, and beats are all part of children's repertoire.

Children's linguistic humor is likely to become more complex as they grow up. What amuses children up to the age of four or five years may be quite uninteresting to older children. Similarly, what adolescents find linguistically humorous may seem trivial and even banal to adults. Simple repetition of words and sentences, which young children find most amusing—note the popularity of "The House That Jack Built" and other similar stories in children's storybooks in Anglo-American cultures—often leads to the later development of tongue twisters using phonetically similar sounds that are repeated rapidly, creating ludicrous utterances. Children seem universally to challenge playmates to recite tongue twisters accurately, deriving great amusement and laughter when hilarious mistakes are made. The creation of nonesense words and the attachment of some meaning to them seems particularly prevalent in the early stages of language learning up to the age of four or five, when children seem much aware of the phonological and grammatical characteristics of language. It is not uncommon for children at this age to speak with each other in what they consider to be a new language, which may be totally nonsensical from the adult viewpoint. Such make-believe development, which provides children with total freedom of play and creativity, also becomes a major source of humor.

During the next developmental stage, especially between the ages of six and eleven, children use secret languages either for sheer amusement or for secrecy. Pig Latin is the best-known example, but similar instances of both play and secret languages have been described for other languages.[2] Although the pleasure of keeping secrets from adults as well as from other companions is sometimes a motive, play languages are often used for sheer fun and amusement. At the same stage children start enjoying nursery rhymes and seem to become involved with riddles (Wolfenstein 1954:93) in which punning plays a large part. Punning emphasizes differences between literal and metaphorical, or denotative and connotative, meanings. Some riddles involving puns may indeed appear ludicrous from the adult viewpoint, and as children grow, their punning and riddles become more complex and subtle.

It can be hypothesized that, in those preliterate societies where verbal performance is valued and where linguistic play is an important part of it, the degree of encouragement given to children to engage in verbal games is greater than in societies that lack such positive orientation toward verbal performance. Similarly, the higher the attention given to verbal performance, speech making, and rhetorical skills in a society, the greater the inclination of children to play linguistic games and to develop linguistic humor. In such societies adults are likely to emphasize that expertise in language is desirable and to encourage children who show signs of linguistic creativity. Among the Kanuri of Nigeria, for instance, oratory is considered prestigious, and knowledge of proverbs, sayings, and riddles is valued. Creating new riddles and trying them on peers is a favorite pastime of Kanuri children of all ages. Those who come up with difficult but interesting riddles are publicly praised by teachers and other adults (Peshkin 1972).[3] A systematic cross-cultural analysis needs to be undertaken to verify the hypothesized correlation. It would also be worthwhile to determine whether the degree of children's speech play and linguistic humor is greater in those traditional societies that have a very positive value orientation toward political language, oratory, and linguistic virtuosity (Albert 1972; Bloch 1975) than in societies—for example, among the Gbeya of the Central African Republic (Samarin 1969)—in which such a value orientation does not exist, in which no emphasis is placed on public demonstration of linguistic skills, and in which no attention is paid to how well children acquire language.

Linguistic humor is very much part of the overall process by which both language and the rest of the culture are acquired (Gossen 1976:146; Sherzer 1970:352). The increase in complexity of linguistic humor, which parallels progress through developmental stages, makes children aware of the structural and lexical subtleties of language, motivates them to learn the fine nuances, and challenges them to be creative. It also helps them learn patterns of language usage that are appropriate in numerous social situations, thus increasing their overall mastery of the cultural system.

Humor in Play

Any discussion of humor in play is problematic both because play itself is complex and diverse and because it is closely associated with humor. Considerable literature exists on the play element in human and animal societies. The study of play has received new impetus among social scientists since the establishment of the Association for the Anthropological Study of Play in 1974. Several volumes of papers read at the association's annual meetings have been published.[4] Interest in play as a subject of investigation and research is not restricted to any one discipline but rather has involved scholars from the humanities, social sciences, and natural sciences.

Scholars are divided in their assessment of the importance of play in human culture. The major difficulty lies in defining play. It has been defined in numerous ways, ranging from the very narrow to the very broad. Biological, sociocultural, or psychological aspects of play have been emphasized, depending on the individual scholar's disciplinary interests. Formal properties and diagnostic attributes of play have been extensively listed by many scholars.[5] Yet difficulties remain in clearly delineating crucial properties. Stevens's remarks in this connection are noteworthy: "Our association [The Association for the Anthropological Study of Play] is entering its fourth year of existence without having satisfactorily delineated the parameters of what it is we are talking about" (1977a:239).

For the purpose of discussing humor in play, the following definition by Edwards seems suitable: "Play is a voluntary and distinct activity carried out within arbitrary boundaries in space and time, separate from daily roles, concerns, and influences and having no seriousness, purpose, meaning, or goals for the actor beyond those emerging within the boundaries and context of the play act itself" (1973:49). A great deal of the existing literature on the subject is devoted to children's play, especially games. Anthropologists, folklorists, and social psychologists have been interested in describing

87

and analyzing children's games in many societies for nearly a hundred years, and there is considerable ethnographic data on the subject (see the extensive bibliography in Schwartzman 1976).

Anthropologists generally agree that play is universal among both humans and other animals. The formal and substantive nature of human play is culturally determined, and there is much cross-cultural variation. One anthropologist (Norbeck 1971:48) has argued, however, that human play is unique because it is molded by culture and is conditioned by learned attitudes and values that have no counterpart among nonhuman species. Such a view tends to take the rather extreme position that humans are unique because they possess culture. The considerable research on play in other animals, however, especially among primates in recent years (Baldwin and Baldwin 1977; Smith 1978) indicates that there are many similarities in the play-learning processes of young primates and human children. Both explore their environment and go through the processes of familiarization and habituation that eventually lead to pleasurable stimulation and arousal by play (Baldwin and Baldwin 1978).

A major aspect of human culture is learned behavior. Research on primate play clearly indicates that it too is a learned behavior (Baldwin and Baldwin 1978; Smith 1978), a conclusion suggesting, contrary to the views of Norbeck, that human play is not unique, although its degree of complexity and cross-cultural variation is probably greater among humans than among primates. Whether or not play among primates is conditioned by learned attitudes is a question still to be satisfactorily answered. In their review of ethnographic studies of children's play in Africa and South America, Schwartzman and Barbera (1976) observe that anthropologists have described and interpreted children's play in four ways: (1) as an imitation of and/or preparation for adult life (thus play is regarded as functional for enculturation and socialization of children); (2) as purely sports activity given to ethnographic reporting, with emphasis on its structured nature (thus games are meticulously and carefully described, but no information is provided on unstructured play activity, and there is no discussion of the sociocultural relevance of games); (3) as a projective or expressive activity that reveals children's anxieties and hostilities, which are assumed to result from the socialization or child-training practices of a society; (4) as an essentially trivial and unimportant pastime. Despite the extensive ethnographic literature on children's play, until recently little attention was paid to its cross-cultural and comparative aspects. The first major attempt in this direction is that of Roberts, Arth, and Bush (1959).

The domain of play seems to divide into two major types: the organized and the unorganized. Most sports and games fall into the former category, while all other activity is relegated to the latter. Organized play suggests the existence of certain rules about how the activity is to proceed, what is permitted, what is not, and so forth. The issue of whether or not rule-governed activity constitutes play has been controversial. Both Huizinga (1944/1955:11) and Caillois (1961:9–10), the leading theorists on the subject, argue that play is governed by rules, while Edwards, whose definition I quoted above, rejects the proposition that rules are a necessary element of play activity (1973:48). To complicate matters further, Stevens (1977a:240–46) suggests that human play is both a biological and a cultural phenomenon and is governed by rules (by which he means cultural conditions).

To what extent is humor an integral part of play? The question is complex and controversial. Humor is just as elusive and difficult to define, and just as culturally conditioned, as play. Both are considered pleasurable activities, however, and both can generate the responses of smiling and laughter. Thus the dividing line between humor and play is very thin indeed. It is difficult to provide uniformly applicable criteria to separate the two because of the considerable cross-cultural and intraculturally contextual variations in their behavioral and cognitive aspects. Scholars are therefore divided in their view about the relationship between play and humor.

Huizinga, while arguing that play is the opposite of seriousness, nevertheless says that "in itself play is not comical either for player or public" (1944/1955:6). He further observes that the "mimic and laughter-provoking art of the clown is comic as well as ludicrous, but it can scarcely be termed genuine play" (p. 6). The qualifying "genuine" in this context is noteworthy. Most tellingly Huizinga comments, "All the terms in this loosely connected group of ideas—play, laughter, folly, wit, jest, joke, the comic, etc.—share the characteristic which we had to attribute to play, namely, that of resisting any attempt to reduce it to other terms. Their rationale and their mutual relationship must lie in a very deep layer of our mental being" (p.6). Norbeck emphasizes that play is "often related to wit and humor but not synonymous with them" (1976:7). Because the attributes associated with the concept of humor as elaborated in the Introduction include stimuli leading to a cognitive experience that either is accompanied by or produces mirthful laughter or smiling, I view as humor any play that is accompanied by or results in smiling or laughter. From this perspective humor is very much a part of unstructured play and of games that do not involve competition.

To what extent is competition in different cultures emphasized and encouraged or looked down upon and discouraged? The answer depends on numerous factors, including a society's value system and ideology, the nature of socialization, or simply the number of age mates for the development of serious competition in games (Draper 1976). Simple societies marked by a high degree of egalitarian social structure and lack of political authority apparently either do not have games involving competition or have games of physical skills only.[6] On the other hand, complex, stratified societies with extensive political structure emphasize competition and winning. The ancient Romans, for example, did so during the classical period, and in the contemporary world all Western societies emphasize competition. In American culture "winning is everything."

On the whole, then, competitive play and humor show an inverse relationship. Too much emphasis on competition leads to considerable seriousness, which is not conducive to humor. Occasionally, the very notion of competition may itself become a stimulus for humor. Among Eskimo children, games almost always lack competition and opposition. If competition occurs at all, it is not taken seriously. Serious cheating practiced surreptitiously to win games is therefore absent. Blatant cheating, however, is frequently introduced for humor, amusement, and laughter. Its major purpose is to make everyone notice it and to evoke a response of mock anger, which may amuse and humor everyone (Ager 1976:83).

There are few available ethnographic accounts of games devoted exclusively to the development of laughter. A notable example, involving games among the Kumongo children of central New Guinea, was reported by Aufenanger (1958:578). These children play one game of making faces with the goal of causing everyone to laugh. Ears, eyes, mouth, tongue, nose, and hands—all are brought into play. The children also engage in tickling as an activity in itself. Other activities that Kumongo children pursue to stimulate laughter are getting wet, muddy, dirty, and so forth, and all are thought to be funny. The same may apply to children in many other societies.

It appears, then, that children everywhere derive great fun and amusement from many types of unstructured play activity in which competition is absent or is only minimally stressed. Blurton-Jones in comparing British and Bushman children states: "Laughter in children is most strongly associated with chasing and fleeing, hitting and wrestling" (1972:69). Similarly, Navaho children enjoy chasing each other, and there is "much good-humoured scuffling. In occasional quarrels, they will jeer and make faces at each other" (Leighton and Kluckhohn 1974:60). Observations in ethnographies of various cultures suggest that the following statement, made with respect to American children, has universal applications.

> There are the *stunts*, the tricks one learns to do with one's own body, control of which becomes so important and which has so many peculiar and unsuspected potentialities. School-age children learn to make themselves cross-eyed, to see double, to contort their faces into horrendous shapes, to rub their stomachs while patting their heads, to perform exercises in double-jointedness, to cross their arms and clasp their hands and be perplexed as to which finger is which—late in this period, a fortunate few will even be able to wiggle their ears. [Stone and Church 1957:212]

One important attribute of play included in the definition given earlier is that it must be voluntary. Many activities are amusing to children only when they are undertaken voluntarily. Adults are not always sensitive to this significant point. In an Okinawan village, children of ten to twelve years are required to collect giant African snails after a heavy rainfall and to hunt frogs, dragonflies, grasshoppers, and so forth. The adults know that children amuse themselves by pursuing these activities on their own and assume that such collecting is *always* fun. Children consider it a chore, however, because they are scolded if the animals, which are used for chicken feed, are not gathered in sufficient quantities (B. B. Whiting 1963:518).

In addition to unstructured play, children often engage in tricks, pranks, practical jokes, clowning, and so forth. In some instances such activities may become the major objectives of children's play groups. The aim is to embarrass one of the playmates so that he or she is laughed at. Pushing a child over something, making loud noises unexpectedly behind a child engaged in some activity, pulling away clothes to expose sexual organs, and generally annoying the victim or catching him (or her) unaware seem to be widespread practices among children. Practical jokes are often aimed at destroying poise and control over any one or more of the five elements of self and situation—spaces, props, equipment, clothing, and the body—giving rise to considerable embarrassment on the part of the victim (Gross and Stone 1964). One function of such deliberate embarrassment is socialization; by perpetrating and enduring such practical jokes, children learn how to be poised in potentially embarrassing social situations in adult life. Occasionally even adults become the victims of such pranks by children. Despite the extensive ethnographic literature on children's play (Schwartzman 1976), practical jokes, pranks, tricks and so forth have not received as much attention as they deserve.

Sexual and Scatological Humor

The subject of sexual and scatological humor among children has generally been neglected by anthropologists. Wolfenstein's (1954) detailed analysis of sexual and scatological jokes among American children and Legman's (1968:49–112; 1975) anthologies of various categories of children's sexual and scatological humor in the Anglo-Saxon world are major contributions by nonanthropologists to this topic. There is a widespread belief, however, that children enjoy scatological and sexual humor of both the verbal and nonverbal varieties (Greenway 1965:57–58; Legman 1975:812; Wolfenstein 1954). Legman and Wolfenstein explain this phenomenon on the basis of the Freudian view that all children go through periods of orality and anality, later followed by the phallic, latency, and genital stages.

Children are generally curious about their bodies and the elimination of waste. This curiosity, which is a part of overall self-awareness and the sense of identity, is strongest in the early stages of childhood. As children grow up, they also become increasingly curious about sexual intercourse and procreation. While interest in the scatological aspects of the body may diminish with age, inquisitiveness regarding sexual activity remains strong through adolescence and adulthood. Depending on a society's attitudes, children's curiosity regarding body waste and sex may be repressed, encouraged, or satisfied in a casual way. The prevalence of scatological and sexual humor among children in any society may be closely related to that society's attitudes and to the resulting child-rearing practices.

Societies around the world vary considerably with regard to their attitudes toward body wastes and elimination processes, toilet training practices, and sexual activities. Cultures can be plotted along a continuum in this respect; at one extreme are those with the most casual attitudes, and at the other those with many restrictions. Similarly, societies range in their tendency to encourage early sexual activities and knowledge. In many societies toilet training is usually achieved with a minimum of fuss, and attitudes toward the control of defecation, urination, farting, belching, and so forth are casual. Sexual intercourse and procreation may be similarly treated. Children may have opportunities to observe sexual activities among adults, including their parents, as well as among animals. Youngsters may occasionally observe the birth of an animal. Restraints on adult sexual behavior in semipublic places may be minimal, and adults may openly discuss various aspects of sexual acts or may refer to sexual organs or intercourse. Such seems to be the case among the Siriono Indians of Bolivia (Holmberg 1950/ 1969) and among the Pilaga Indians (J. Henry 1949; Henry and Henry (1944), to name just a few examples.

On the other hand, in some societies considerable emphasis is put on early toilet training, and attitudes toward waste elimination may be anything but casual, causing children to develop repressive tendencies and anxieties about elimination processes. A restrictive attitude usually also prevails with regard to sexual intercourse and procreation. Children may have few opportunities to satisfy their curiosity, because discussion of these matters may be taboo and they may have few opportunities to observe sexual acts. Such seems to be the case among the Japanese (Gorer 1949), the Ulithians (Lessa 1966), and midwestern middle-class Americans during the 1940s (West 1945).

In the 1940s and 1950s anthropologists and psychologists of the culture and personality school emphasized a high degree of association between certain adult personality traits and early restrictive discipline concerning excretary processes and sexual instincts.[7] Using the theoretical framework of the culture and personality school in anthropology, I suggest that considerable interest in scatological and sexual humor among children and adolescents in a society may be associated with strict toilet training and restrictive discipline or attitudes. Conversely, relative disinterest in scatological and sexual humor among children of all ages may be associated with more casual attitudes. The lack of ethnographic data on scatological and sexual humor among children in many societies may make it difficult to test such a hypothesis. It is borne out, however, by a folklorist's study of scatological humor of children in North India (Vatuk 1968).

93

In discussing scatological and sexual humor among children, we may make a primary distinction between verbal humor and humor based on playacting. Both can be overtly aggressive or nonaggressive. Aggressive verbal humor involves teasing or ridicule in which a child is disparaged in some way for failure of bowel or bladder control or for deviant sexual activities. Sometimes a child may be ridiculed on account of his parents' or siblings' sexual activities. Nonaggressive verbal humor involves the narration of jokes and stories that have scatological and sexual content or merely use words that refer to sexual intercourse, sexual organs, the process of elimination, and the waste itself, especially feces. Aggressive nonverbal humor consists of practical jokes that expose the victims in some act of a sexual nature or force the victim to be at the receiving end of sexual and scatological actions. Nonaggressive nonverbal humor involves playacting in which imitation, most often of sexual intercourse but occasionally also of defecation, urination, or farting, takes place.

Some ethnographic data present children's narrative humor of a scatological and sexual nature. American children of all ages quite commonly tell scatological and sexual jokes and riddles. The major themes of this humor are exposure of sexual organs, excretary activities, and feces (Wolfenstein 1954). On the basis of a study of humor among boys playing little league baseball, Fine (1976) concludes that, in American culture, preadolescent boys regularly pass through a stage in which it is considered very masculine to tell sexual jokes dealing with penis length, homosexuality, and standards of sexual performance. These matters are the subject of curiosity as well as sexual anxiety. Fine claims that, by exchanging jokes, boys acquire additional knowledge about sex. Humor in this context serves an informative function as well.

Vatuk's (1968) analysis of sexual and scatological humor in the folklore of Hindi-speaking children of North India suggests that Indian children of all ages use in their play many riddles with the feces motif. They tell each other stories in which excrement and defecation play a major part. Games and rhymes involving references to urine, feces, farting, and defecation, including sound symbolisms, are quite popular and are used to achieve a humorous effect. Note, for instance, the following rhyme:

a:da: pa:da: kisne pa:da:
ra:ja:ji:ka ghori ne pa:da:

thim tha:m thus
[Vatuk 1968:275]

This verse can be translated as "Someone farted. Who farted? The king's horse farted!" The last line appears to be an onomatopoetic imitation of the noise of farting. Vatuk gives several other examples of rhymes, stories, riddles, and games of a similar nature.

Scatological and sexual humor is very much a part of verbal exchanges that take place among children in their games. The object is to tease, ridicule, or insult the opponent and to outsmart him or her generally, and the label "verbal dueling" (sometimes "ritual insults") is commonly used in the literature describing such exchanges. Verbal exchanges of this type generally involve accusations of incest; of strong sexuality or impropriety on the part of the opponent's parents, especially the mother; of the consumption of excrement or urine; of lack of control over the bodily processes of elimination; and of passive submission to anal intercourse. Detailed ethnographic accounts and analyses of such verbal exchanges among children of varied ages in many cultures have been carried out.[8]

Verbal dueling is quite diverse in nature. It varies from one-word or single-sentence utterances to couplets. Exchanges occur between two individuals in a continuing fashion, developing a sequence, or they may occur among a group of children, each taking a turn and trying to outdo the previous speaker while teasing someone else. In some instances these verbal exchanges have sexual and scatological overtones only in a metaphoric sense that the literal meanings of the words used may not make plain. In other cases the dueling may be more direct in nature. Direct exchanges appear to be more common among young children up to eight or nine years of age. These children also tend to memorize the sequences and are not very good at improvisation. Whenever they are challenged by older children, they lose, because they seldom succeed in going beyond a memorized sequence (Gossen 1976:143). Although young children of both sexes may participate in such verbal duels, beyond a certain age girls in many cultures seem not to continue playing them. As boys grow older, they try to be more creative, using numerous devices to outdo their opponents, and they also become better at improvising.

If any conventions and rules of verbal dueling exist, participants must observe them. In the verbal dueling of Turkish boys, for instance, a retort should generally end-rhyme with the initial insult, just as the text should force the opponent into a female or passive role. This feature is important, because in Turkish society men decidedly dominate women. Publicly women are subordinate to men and are supposed to be passive in sexual intercourse. Similarly, in Turkish culture it is shameful and demeaning to take a passive role in homosexual relations. Insults that force an opponent into a female or passive role therefore definitely establish the masculinity and superiority of the winning player (Dundes, Leach, and Özkök 1972:135–36, 156). Rhyming a response to an opponent's initial challenge is also a rule of Chamula verbal dueling (Gossen 1976). Scatological insults occur among white adolescents in American culture (Ayoub and Barnett 1965), but American black, Turkish, and Chamula adolescent boys seem to have a considerably richer repertoire of verbal exchanges than white adolescents, whose material "is limited in content as well as form and quantity. *Shit* is the most common topic, and in general the insults are based on taboo words rather than taboo activities" (Labov 1972a: 322).

Scatological and sexual humor based on playacting involves simulating sexual intercourse or waste elimination and engaging in horseplay or tricks that expose a child's sexual organs as well as the posterior. Available ethnographic data suggest that boys engage in these activities more often than girls. Boys among the Kwoma people in New Guinea frequently play a game in which "one boy chases another, throws him down, and simulates copulation with him. Other boys in the group then take advantage of the aggressor and pretend to copulate with him until four or five boys line up in this way all laughing and yelling with enjoyment." When they break away, each boys calls another his wife and claims to have impregnated "her" (J. M. Whiting 1941:50–51).[9] Sexual and scatological humor among children, whether verbal or nonverbal, generally provides a channel for satisfying their curiosity about their bodies, bodily functions, and sexual intercourse. Verbal sexual humor is not only informative but also helpful in alleviating anxiety stemming from lack of knowledge in sexual matters. At the same time, such humor channels aggressive tendencies in a competitive fashion while providing opportunities for creativity and for establishing prestige among peers. This latter function seems particularly relevant in the case of adolescent boys, as reflected in ritual insults and verbal duels. Among American black adolescents, for instance, a person who excels at ritual insults is much admired by his peer group (Labov 1972a).

A major source of children's humor is the socialization process itself. Children consciously and unconsciously imitate adult behavior, and adults often encourage them to do so by offering rewards, praise, or a temporary "make-believe" adult status. Children's attitudes toward adult activities, language, emotional displays, and values and beliefs, however, are rarely uniform. For children, socialization, especially its behavioral aspects, is pleasant as well as discomforting. Although much behavior may be easy for children to imitate, they find it often incomprehensible in terms of the cultural values and beliefs. Explicit directions and explanations may often be lacking, so that children's curiosity is not always satisfied.

Much depends on the adults' attitudes toward children's personality development, and these vary across cultures. Even within a single society, opinions regarding the "proper" ways of raising children may differ considerably, depending on the socioeconomic and religious backgrounds of adult family members. Despite these differences, children acquire a bewildering array of norms, and humor and play activities have a major part in the enculturation process. The category of socialization humor is somewhat different from those discussed earlier, in which only the humor developed and enjoyed by children was examined. In studying socialization humor we must recognize two major types: (1) humor enjoyed by children in which either other children or adults are targets and (2) humor enjoyed by adults in which only children are the targets. The first type is almost always based on some socially unacceptable behavior or event, while the second type may be based on both socially acceptable and unacceptable traits.

Other Children or Adults as Targets. Children use various techniques in socialization humor. They may playfully imitate adult behavior, employing exaggeration and caricature as the major techniques. Or they may ridicule and embarrass one of their peers by making him or her the butt of their humor primarily for failure to master socially acceptable role-specific behavior. Children may deliberately play a role incongruent with their age and sex, or they may engage in humor by reversing the social role relationships, either between adults or between adults and themselves.

Humor that involves mimicking certain adult behaviors is widespread among children of most cultures. Such imitation takes place for fun or for the purpose of ridiculing adult behavior. A favorite mime of Kwakiutl Indian children of Blackfish village in Oregon was acting drunk (Wolcott 1967:29). Among Jamaican boys and girls who spoke creole and who were taught standard English, girls adopted the standard form more than boys did. It was also noticed, however, that boys amused themselves by a somewhat exaggerated mimicry of girlish voices, conveying bits of standard speech when they were not aware that they were being observed by teachers (Craig 1971:381). Such mimicry suggested that Jamaican boys associated the acquisition of standard English with femininity and lack of toughness. They made fun of the behavioral traits that they probably considered incongruent with masculinity.

It is often difficult to predict which aspects of adult behavior children may find humorous. Occasionally the events they imitate may be quite serious. Yet without understanding the substance and the nature of such events and their associational emotional involvement, children seem to imitate them merely for amusement. In their play activity Tiwi children of Australia imitate even the occasions of death and wailing. They form two groups and use the names of living adults as if they were dead (Goodale 1971:40). Among the Ijaw of Nigeria, children play a game in which they imitate a dance to appease the spirits of supernatural elements (Leis 1972:61ff.).

Ridiculing and embarrassing another child by making him or her the butt of humor is a common tactic among children. Often they engage in such humor because of the victim's failure to behave in a socially acceptable manner or according to role-related expectations. Among the Kwoma tribe of New Guinea, adults expect nude boys to control penile erection in public. Once a young boy's playmates and his elder brother found him with an erect penis. They not only teased him, but his brother told the story in a joking manner to the victim's older sisters by putting a stick between his legs; the sisters laughed at their younger brother (J. M. Whiting 1941:49).

In the Egyptian village of Silva, children made fun of behavior that in their observation was unacceptable in their community. Filial love, for instance, was generally not expressed in sentimental terms. Therefore, it was a great joke among the children of one neighborhood to repeat statements of an urban child whom they heard saying, "I love my father, I love my mother" (Ammar 1970:233–34).[10] Children sometimes engage in humor by reversing

98

the social-structural relations among adults. They make the dominant roles subservient and vice versa. In villages in North India, husbands are always stereotyped as dominant, while wives are perceived as submissive in husband-wife relations. Indian children seem to derive much amusement from reversing these and other social relationships: children's songs make fun of the traditional authority figures of husband, father, and mother-in-law (Vatuk 1968). In their songs, husbands are portrayed as weak and cowardly or are beaten up by their wives.

Children as the Targets of Adult Humor. A major aspect of socialization is the interest shown by adults in their children's personality development. Most adults are in a biologically and socioculturally superior position vis-à-vis their children and are therefore able to manipulate and control them. Occasionally, adults take advantage of their superior position and amuse themselves at the expense of children, teasing, ridiculing, and laughing at them or just refusing to take them seriously. In other social contexts, however, adults are amused because they see an incongruity in the children's acts between outward appearance and implications that are beyond children's comprehension. Adults also find humor in children's efforts to imitate adults in carrying out certain responsibilities. Children are often viewed by adults in such contexts as behaving like monkeys, which mimic what they see.

In societies where verbal insults are a major means of aggressive behavior and social ridicule, children learn the formal aspects of insults without understanding why they are insults. Thus it is not uncommon to find children producing "insults" with the proper linguistic markers and paralinguistic features but with not quite suitable cultural content. A Samoan child, for instance, attempted to insult another child by saying, "Your father sleeps with your mother" (Mitchell-Kernan and Kernan 1975:313). Children from three to five years of age among the Ijaw of Nigeria try to insult each other but in this early stage say the insults incorrectly. Older children and adults find such situations amusing (Leis 1972:47).

In cultures where storytelling is a major pastime or where there is an emphasis on verbal accomplishments, children imitate some of the relevant speech acts without understanding that the contents are equally important. A favorite preoccupation of Ijaw children from age five to eight is storytelling. "Before a child reaches his eighth year he can make up a story by fitting together short epi-

99

sodes from tales he has heard from adults or older children. The discontinuity of narrative and the misuse of words greatly amuse adults since the errors indicate that children lack an understanding of what they are repeating" (Leis 1972:56). Such behavior is widespread. In American middle-class society, in many social situations a child is readily observed telling a joke that he either has not understood or has only partially understood, as shown by changes made in repeating it and by the botching of the punch line. In American culture "a child acquires the joke-telling style and the notion of the function of a joke before he understands that jokes also imply certain content. He can, thus, be seen to imitate joke-telling styles and to laugh at the end of a joke when the content of his joke makes no sense at all" (Mitchell-Kernan and Kernan 1975:314).[11] Anecdotes recounting children's remarks that adults, but not the child, found amusing abound in popular magazines such as *Reader's Digest* and *Family Weekly*.

What is true of verbal imitations is also true of imitations of nonverbal behavior, especially sexual behavior. In societies where children can observe the sexual behavior of adults or animals, they may imitate it without really understanding the implications. Little boys and girls among the Siuai of the Solomon Islands in New Guinea, for example, sometimes enlivened their game of "house" by pretending to copulate. In such activities they were obviously imitating either parents or dogs, both of whom they could readily observe in and around the house. Their elders, though enjoying the display as a great joke, generally stopped it (Oliver 1955/1967:141).[12]

Both role-deviant behavior, if the breach is not too serious, and role-appropriate behavior by children are amusing to adults. In the former case ridicule is the technique used to make the children feel shame and behave properly in the future. In the latter case, however, the reaction of adults involves not only laughter and smiling but also pride and satisfaction, as the behavior shows that a proper job of socialization has been done. Therefore, occasionally, role-appropriate behavior on children's part is deliberately evoked by adults, and when children respond as they are expected to, adults are humored, especially when the social significance of such behavior is beyond the children's grasp. Among the Sharanahua Indians of Peru, for example, sex-differentiated behavior is inculcated in children quite early. Little boys are trained to be sexually aggressive, while little girls are taught not only to provoke boys but also to protect themselves. In this context Siskind (1973) narrates the following incident.

> Three-year-old Comafo was brought to my house by one of the women who take care of him. Old Baido laughingly pretended to grab the woman and Comafo stood up fiercely and aimed the conventional Sharanahua "fuck you" gesture at Baido. Comafo's grandfather pounded his chest and beamed proudly at his small grandson. Everyone else laughed, and Comafo cried. Comafo has learned a basic social fact that other men are his competitors over women, and this is why Basta, his grandfather, was proud. Comafo has not yet learned to conceal his anger, but adult laughter will soon teach him. [P. 108]

Similar examples can be readily found in other cultures.[13]

There is often a tendency among adults to laugh mockingly at children's emotions. Occasionally, adults either do not believe that children are capable of serious and genuine emotional response or feel that taking children's emotional responses seriously is like treating them as adults. Adults also tend to tease children deliberately in response to distress or anger, believing that teasing will teach the youngsters self-control, especially if society emphasizes emotional self-control in social encounters. Children often find such teasing disturbing and respond in a socially unacceptable way, however, as the incident described by Siskind illustrates. Although Comafo had learned the appropriate male role behavior of aggressiveness, he had not learned to control his anger when he was teased. In many societies children are treated in a similar fashion. Among the Siriono Indians of Bolivia, children's anger and aggression are treated with amusement and elicit mocking laughter from adults. Parents often tease their children and thus provoke them to some act of physical aggression, which is then laughed off. "A young child in a temper tantrum may ordinarily beat his father and mother as hard as he can, and they will just laugh" (Holmberg 1950/1969:205).

Occasionally a dilemma is created because the situation evokes ambivalence, namely, the desire to treat a child's emotional behavior at the adult level, on the one hand, and on the other, the feeling that such a response is inappropriate because the person involved is not an adult. Such ambivalence often causes the adults to smile and to laugh. It confuses children, however, because they are no longer in a position to predict the boundaries within which they can operate, and this uncertainty in turn may affect their socialization. The following case is illustrative. Mothers among the Ijaw of Nigeria often have difficulties in teaching five- to eight-year-old children the importance of both respect and retaliation behavior and the importance of being able to separate the two. According to anthropologist Leis (1972:58), one reason for the confusion among children regarding the appropriate use of such behavior responses is that mothers often laugh at infantile displays of aggression, for example, when children hit them or throw mud at them. But when children provoke their mothers repeatedly in this fashion, the mothers tend to punish them severely. The inconsistent adult response confuses children as they try to interpret the limits of appropriate aggressive behavior.

SOCIALIZATION AND SEXUAL DIFFERENCES

Sexual differences in the development, comprehension, and appreciation of humor among children have been investigated primarily by psychologists interested in child development. Anthropologists have contributed little by way of ethnographic observations and cross-cultural research on this topic. The extensive anthropological literature on socialization in general, however, is relevant here because the findings of psychologists regarding such sexual differences support the conclusions of anthropologists studying cross-cultural aspects of socialization, namely, that boys on the whole are subject to less social control and pressure to conform than girls.

Psychologist McGhee draws the following tentative conclusions on the basis of research primarily among Anglo-American children: (1) boys are likely to respond to humor by laughter and girls by smiling; (2) girls' responsiveness to humor, especially their smiling or laughter, is more susceptible to the reactions of other people than is boys'; (3) boys appear to be more responsive to hostile-aggressive forms of humor than girls; (4) the "limited evidence suggests that boys may be better at gaining insight into the nature of certain types of humor and at creating their own examples of humorous responses" (1976b:178); (5) boys try to make others laugh by clowning and by other behavioral stimuli more than girls do; (6) sexual differences in the development of, and responsiveness to, humor are operative during the middle childhood years, between the ages of six and eleven.

These tentative conclusions suggest that perhaps the humor-related behavior of boys and girls may be a part of the overall sexual differences, as indicated in many cross-cultural studies of children's socialization[14] that have identified clear patterns of sexual differences in physical activities. Boys generally engage in more rough-and-tumble play and verbal aggression than girls. Boys are also likely to counterattack physically or verbally in response to aggression. On the other hand, girls show an overall tendency to withdraw in the face of aggression more frequently than boys (Whiting and Edwards 1973). The survey data in the cross-cultural study of games confirm "the preference of women for games of strategy and of chance and the preference of men for games of physical skill" (Roberts and Sutton-Smith 1962:177). Such preferences may have their roots in early childhood, as Sutton-Smith and Roberts noted in another study of games. They claim that "boys played games of physical skill because this is the power form that they can most easily command; and that girls showed a preference for games of strategy and chance because these are the lesser power forms available to them" (1972:339). The differential treatment given to boys and girls in the socialization process in many societies primarily underlies these differences. The basis for such treatment is the emphasis on notions such as modesty, passivity, and obedience, which I discussed in the previous chapter in relation to cultural values of ideal female role models. These notions are applied to girls' behavior from an early age, with the result that more restraints are imposed on their behavior than on that of boys.

HUMOR AND PERSONALITY DEVELOPMENT

Exploring various aspects of the relationship between humor and the overall personality development of children has primarily been the concern of psychologists. They have shown much interest in studying children's humor from the decade of the twenties. Until recently, however, few attempts were made to delineate developmental changes in children's responses to humor stimuli. The findings of many earlier studies were not related to any type of theoretical framework (McGhee 1971a:33).

Psychologists have been concerned to study children's humor comprehension and appreciation primarily in relation to personality characteristics. While experimental techniques were used in studying school-age children's humor, observational techniques were primarily used in studying preschool children's humor. Cognitive aspects of children's humor have received much attention in these studies. Early efforts in this direction were primarily concerned with correlating humor comprehension and appreciation with cognitive mastery, operationally defined in terms of IQ scores and age. It has been argued, however, that age in itself is not an explanatory variable (McGhee 1974a:722). Among psychological studies based on interviews, Wolfenstein's work (1954) stands out, because it dealt not only with humor comprehension and appreciation but also with the content of humor.

During the last fifteen years, psychological research on children's humor has increased significantly[15] and has highlighted some theoretical emphases and methodological problems. In general, much of this recent research has been influenced by Piaget's work on children and has consequently stressed numerous aspects of children's humor as they relate to different preoperational and operational stages of growth within Piaget's theoretical framework. As a result, cognitive development and its association with the comprehension and appreciation of humor have received considerable attention. On the other hand, the nature of the association between children's humor and their personalities, the creative aspects of their humor, and humor as it can facilitate learning among children have not received adequate attention (McGhee 1977a).

In current research, attention generally focuses on verbal and pictorial humor. The usual experimental technique is as follows: preselected cartoons or jokes are shown to individual boys and girls within and across certain age categories, and their responses to the samples, as evidenced by the degree of laughter or smiling, are recorded. Clowning and other situational humor have not received adequate attention, perhaps because they would be more difficult to fit into experimental designs. There has also been a greater focus on studying humor comprehension and appreciation than on studying creation of humor-generating stimuli; the methodological techniques and experimental designs do not readily permit observations of natural events in which humor is either deliberately generated or occurs unintentionally.

Even in studies of humor comprehension and appreciation as they relate to cognitive development, the theme of incongruity and its resolution have been emphasized much more than other aspects of humor. Thus in many studies of humor comprehension and appreciation, jokes are presented to children in two versions, one with the incongruity alone and the other with the resolution of this incongruity. The subjects are then asked to rate the funniness of both versions on a five-point scale. In the following riddle-joke, for instance, the question raises incongruity, while the answer provides its resolution: Q: "Why did the cookie cry?" A: "Because its mother had been a wafer [away for] so long." A version of this joke with incongruity alone would be: Q: "Why did the cookie cry?" A: "Because its mother was a wafer."

Much of the current psychological research is limited in the sense that little attention has been given to children's humor in non-Western societies. Although cross-cultural studies are known to be essential, the major problems in undertaking them seem to be methodological, involving translation difficulties in preparing pre-set humor samples or in choosing the culturally appropriate material to elicit responses from children in specific cultures. Adequate cultural knowledge of a particular society is also necessary for a psychologist to plan an experiment design appropriately (McGhee 1972). Only one study has come to my attention (Kreitler and Kreitler 1970) in which Israeli children of both European and Asian or African origins were used as subjects to test a hypothesis concerning humor appreciation.

The quantification of humor appreciation is a major methodological problem in the current psychological research on children's humor; reliable measures have not been adequately developed. Similar problems exist regarding the measurement of humor comprehension, especially in the case of children who are unable to "explain" why the material presented to them is humorous because they lack fully developed language. On the whole, scholars do not seem to agree regarding the importance of determining the extent of humor comprehension and regarding the ways in which it affects the appreciation of humor. Until humor comprehension can be measured, it is difficult to use laughter in response to humor as an index of appreciation (McGhee 1977a).

In spite of such problems, the extensive psychological literature on children's humor has led to many significant insights concerning the relationship between the developmental changes that occur in children and the degree and extent of children's humor creation, comprehension, and appreciation. It is now generally agreed that a certain degree of linguistic skills is a prerequisite for appreciating puns, especially riddles based on puns. Similarly, a minimum level of memory retention is essential for joke appreciation (Pien and Rothbart 1977). Appreciation of humor based on particular concepts appears to be greatest soon after these concepts are acquired. On the other hand, there is reduced appreciation on the part of children who do not possess these concepts and also on the part of children who mastered them much earlier. Thus maximal appreciation of humor appears closely associated with a certain degree of cognitive challenge (McGhee 1976a). It also appears that only some cognitive strategies, such as identification of the absurd with criticism, wonder, or mockery, facilitate appreciation of humor, resulting in laughter or smiling (Kreitler and Kreitler 1970).

Physical incongruences constitute major physical stimuli of humor in early childhood. Although these are remembered, they are gradually reinforced with stimuli from conceptual discrepancies as logic and "rational" thinking develop and are used. The increase in overall linguistic skills and the growing ability to see new relationships between various objects, events, or conceptual categories are also responsible for the perception of new humor stimuli (Abrams 1977). Although there appears to be general agreement that smiling and laughter develop quite early in infancy, opinions vary concerning the age at which infants are capable of experiencing humor. Shultz (1976) and McGhee (1977b), the two leading scholars in the field, seem to disagree. In general, the findings of one researcher are not necessarily confirmed by the results of other scholars. Much depends on how hypotheses are formulated and which theoretical model is emphasized. Models emphasizing the "pleasure principle," the "arousal principle," the "cognitive mastery principle," the "cognitive congruency principle," and other principles have been used by different scholars to determine how children experience humor and how they react to it.

THEORETICAL PROPOSITIONS

The following cross-culturally significant theoretical propositions emerge from the discussion of children's humor.

The prevalence and range of humor among children indicates a society's positive or negative attitudes toward humor in general.

Linguistic humor provides children with positive reinforcement in language acquisition, because it is based on manipulation of the structural elements of language. By the same token, children's linguistic humor becomes more complex as they increase their mastery of the language.

Children are more encouraged to play verbal games in those cultures that positively value and emphasize rhetorical skills than in those that do not.

Because of its serious nature, competitive play reduces the occurrence of humor except when it involves competition in humor itself, as in ritual insults. On the other hand, unstructured play and humor reinforce each other.

A relatively high occurrence of scatological and sexual humor among children in a culture may suggest repressive and strict attitudes toward sex and body waste. Conversely, a relatively low occurrence of sexual and scatological humor among children in a culture may suggest casual attitudes toward sex and body waste.

Children's humor plays a major role in the enculturation and socialization processes because it involves mimicking adult behavior and making fun of individuals who fail to master role-appropriate and socially acceptable behavior.

Adults deliberately induce children to imitate adult role-appropriate behavior because they enjoy the incongruence between such behavior and the children's lack of understanding of its inappropriateness for them.

Sex-related differences in the nature, techniques, and appreciation of children's humor have their bases in the socialization process, which puts greater constraints on girls than on boys.

4

Humor, Ethnicity, and Intergroup Relations

Human societies have come in contact with each other on account of war, trade, migration, and so forth or because of curiosity about their fellow beings. Knowledge of other societies accumulates through such contacts, becomes a part of the cultural heritage of all societies, and is passed from generation to generation. Intercultural contacts and interactions have led societies to formulate opinions, beliefs, and attitudes about peoples who are culturally "different." The "images" developed in turn become the bases of "ethnic humor," which has been much discussed in recent years.

The concept of ethnic humor is operationally defined in this chapter as a type of humor in which fun is made of the perceived behavior, customs, personality, or any other traits of a group or its members by virtue of their specific sociocultural identity. I shall expand this definition further in a later section. Although the phrase "ethnic humor" may be of recent origin, humor disparaging other groups is probably as old as contact between cultures. The tendency to ridicule and to mock groups other than one's own is widespread in human societies (Birnbaum 1971; Dundes 1975; Roback 1944). Until World War II, however, ethnic humor did not receive much attention as a topic of research even in the multi-ethnic American society, perhaps because of the considerable emphasis on cultural assimilation. As many former European colonies in Asia and Africa began to gain independence in the post–World War II era, pride in nationality and ethnic identity increased worldwide (Emerson 1960). This phenomenon, along with similar developments in Europe and America, accelerated social science research on ethnicity in general, and scholars have been engaged in exploring many aspects of ethnic identity and its effects on intergroup interaction.

One outcome of this emphasis has been extensive research on ethnic humor, especially in American society. Scholars have investigated the sources, forms, types, contents, and functions of ethnic humor and responses to it in intragroup and intergroup interaction as well as its relevance to ethnic identity.[1]

Different disciplinary backgrounds have led researchers to formulate diverse goals, methodologies, and perspectives. Psychologists, for example, on the whole are interested in developing theoretical models that predict the factors that motivate individuals to engage in ethnic humor or the variables that determine their differential responses to it. Such models are then validated through controlled experimental studies.[2] Sociologists, folklorists, and anthropologists, on the other hand, have been generally concerned with content analyses and with typologies of themes extracted from ethnic jokes.[3] The research on ethnic humor in the United States in the 1940s and 1950s was primarily concerned with white-Negro or Jewish-Gentile interaction and with the images these groups had of each other as reflected in their respective humor. More specifically, the studies included content analyses of intergroup humor to discover attitudes (Barron 1950); investigations of racial humor in relation to ethnic and social class background (R. Middleton 1959; D. C. Simmons 1963); research into the use of humor to establish dominance in interethnic relations (Burma 1946); and analyses of the self-image that minority ethnic groups expressed in their humor as it indicates their status in and relations to dominant groups in the society at large (Rinder 1965; Rosenberg and Shapiro 1959). Jokes involving different ethnic groups have also been collected and analyzed in recent years to discern the underlying stereotypes.[4]

An awareness of ethnic plurality in America has also grown in the population at large. There has been a resurgence of the so-called ethnic joke anthologies (J. Adams 1975; Larkin 1975; Wilde 1973a, 1973b), many of which are old jokes transformed; similar anthologies have existed since the early twentieth century, and, in the case of some ethnic groups, such as the Irish, as far back as the eighteenth century (Barrick 1970). Many folklorists believe that ethnic riddles and jokes have been in oral circulation for a long time, though the group ridiculed may change, depending on contextual factors (Barrick 1970; Dundes 1971). Proverbs that make fun of ethnic groups and foreigners have been a part of traditional folklore in most societies since antiquity. According to A. Greenberg (1972), ethnic humor may have developed as an urban form because of the concentration of different ethnic groups in large cities. Despite the current popularity of the phase "ethnic humor," it was not used widely in the literature on humor until the 1970s. Instead, such expressions as "race-conscious humor," or merely "race" humor (Burma 1946); "racial humor," or "racial jokes" (R. Middleton 1959); "intergroup humor" (Barron 1950); and "inter-ethnic humor" (Zenner 1970) were used. In general, "ethnic humor" is the phrase commonly used in recent social science literature. It has also been well established in popular writings and humor anthologies. Note, for instance, that Joey Adams's *Ethnic Humor*, an anthology of the popular so-called ethnic jokes (1975), states on the cover: "I supply the humor ... you supply the ethnic."

This chapter will consider the nature of ethnic humor and its relationship to sociocultural systems. It will provide, first, a brief discussion of some relevant theoretical concepts; second, an examination of the forms and techniques of ethnic humor; third, an analytical discussion of the sociocultural bases of the text, context, and function of ethnic humor; and finally, some suggestions for anthropological research.

Conceptual Bases of Ethnic Humor

The closely related concepts of ethnic group, ethnic identity, and ethnicity, together with the notion of stereotype, are most crucial for any discussion of ethnic humor. They have been extensively discussed in the theoretical literature and in empirical studies investigating the nature of specific ethnic groups and their interactions.[5] While sociologists, political scientists, and psychologists have generally explored the subject of ethnicity and ethnic groups in the context of modern industrial societies and European nation-states, anthropologists traditionally accepted as self-evident the existence of small-scale, culturally homogeneous, discrete ethnic entities with bounded attributes. Malinowski (1941:535) viewed such ethnic entities, particularly tribes, as prototypes of European nationalities. The fundamental assumption on the part of anthropologists that there existed such discrete ethnic entities was necessary for ethnographic fieldwork. During the period after World War II, however, anthropologists began to question this assumption. On the basis of research during about the last twenty-five years, many writers have asked how culturally and linguistically homogeneous the societies traditionally studied by anthropologists really were and whether they were indeed self-contained, discrete ethnic entities, as had generally been assumed.[6]

Groups, Identity, and Ethnicity

No single definition of ethnic group, ethnic identity, or ethnicity is acceptable to all researchers because their disciplinary inputs and perspectives differ. No matter how concepts of ethnic groups and ethnicity are defined at the analytical level, they do not necessarily cover all empirical categories, if we assume that ethnic groups are indeed "real." Any definition is therefore bound to be somewhat arbitrary and hypothetical in nature. Human groups vary in size, composition, and nature. In some instances the concept of a group may be coterminous with that of a society or nation. On the other hand, complex societies consist of several groups, as do many newly independent multilingual nations that have been carved out of earlier European colonies. Such labels as "lineage," "clan," "tribe," "caste," "social class," "club," "neighborhood," "gang," and "association" have been used to identify different kinds of groups some of which have been either equated with or subsumed under ethnic groups.

Ethnic groups can be said to have several basic characteristics, such as ascribed status, shared cultural traits and values, some degree of internal cohesion and interaction, and self-awareness. Numerous attributes of ethnic groups mentioned in different definitions can be subsumed under these basic characteristics. In a survey of definitions used in sociological and anthropological studies that deal with aspects of ethnicity (Isajiw 1974), the most frequently mentioned attributes of ethnic groups were: common national or geographic origin or common ancestors; a common culture or customs; religion; race or physical characteristics; and language—in that order. Other attributes less frequently mentioned included consciousness of kind, common values or ethos, separate institutions, and minority or majority status. Anthropologist Geertz (1963:109–14) viewed the basic attributes that link members of an ethnic group—race, language, blood ties, custom, region, and religion—as "primordial" ties. Because of the development of new nations and an upsurge of nationalism, however, national identity has also become a major factor in group consciousness.

The attributes that I have listed can be broadly categorized as biological, sociocultural, and psychological dimensions of ethnic

111

groups. Members of an ethnic group may, for instance, share phenotypical traits due to group endogamy, descent, and common ancestry. Group status is then "ascribed," because it results from factors over which an individual has no control. Extreme phenotypical differences between ethnic groups have caused them to be considered as racial groups. Anthropologists in general, however, have denied the affinity of ethnic and racial groups and have rejected race as an important factor in defining ethnic groups (Fried 1965; Montagu 1964).

Common ancestry and geographical location generally but not necessarily lead, through the socialization process, to the acquisition of a common culture that, for the most part, includes language, religion, customs and behavioral patterns, social institutions, and ideologies and values, thus constituting the sociocultural dimension of ethnic groups. Individuals generally share with others of their ethnic group a conscious identity that is based on traits they perceive to be characteristic of the group. This is the psychological dimension of ethnic groups. Such ethnic identity is a subjective reality for individuals, whether or not it is supported by empirical facts.

Whether ethnic groups really exist, whether they are only analytical categories for explaining group dynamics, and whether they represent only a subjective psychological reality for individuals are issues that have been much debated by scholars. The controversy also involves the concept of ethnicity, which I have defined as referring to the existence of groups, real or imagined, characterized by some or all of the attributes discussed above. Therefore, both subjective and objective definitions of ethnic groups and ethnicity are to be found in the literature. The following definition is objective: "An ethnic group is a distinct category of the population in a larger society whose culture is usually different from its own. The members of such a group are, or feel themselves, or are thought to be, bound together by common ties of race or nationality or culture" (*International Encyclopedia of Social Sciences*, vol. 5, p. 167).

Ethnicity is closely tied to other social processes of group dynamics, such as conflict, cooperation, differentiation, and fusion and fission. These processes may wax and wane under differential political and economic conditions. Ethnicity also involves a double boundary, one drawn from within and the other drawn from without (Isajiw 1974:122). The former is maintained and perpetuated by the socialization process, while the latter is established through intergroup relations and interaction. Both subjective and objective approaches are relevant in analyzing ethnic humor, because individuals and groups have to believe in the existence of ethnic groups characterized by such attributes as language, religion, race, culture, and nationality before ethnic humor can occur. In addition, groups indeed emphasize their distinctiveness in their social dynamics, for whatever motives and whether or not the distinctiveness is supported by empirical facts. The primary objectives of groups in social dynamics may simply be the creation or maintenance of an ethnic boundary, real or imagined. Their focus may be on the "ethnic *boundary* that defines the group," because the "cultural features that signal the boundary may change, and the cultural characteristics of the members likewise be transformed" (Barth 1969:14–15).

Stereotypes

The concept of a stereotype was originally formulated by the journalist Walter Lippmann (1922). The importance of this concept in discussions of ethnicity and intergroup relations is clearly indicated by the numerous experimental studies in which social scientists have sought to refine the concept and to elaborate upon its relevance to intergroup dynamics and to cognitive development of individual thought processes (see the extensive bibliography in Brigham 1971). For many researchers the existence of stereotypes and their relevance to ethnic humor are self-evident.[7]

Lippmann defined stereotypes as mental pictures formulated by human beings to describe the world beyond their reach. He stated that stereotypes at least partially are culturally determined. He stressed, however, that their contents are factually incorrect, that they are the products of a faulty reasoning process, and that they tend to persist even in the face of knowledge and education. In general, most of the research has been devoted to the exploration of psychological processes involved in the formulation of stereotypes, their nature and types, their relationship to objective reality, attitudes, and behavior, and their perpetuation as well as the functions they serve. Stereotypes seem to be universally present in societies (Bogardus 1950:28; Harding 1968:261). Whether or not stereotypes exist without prejudice has been a controversial issue (Brigham 1971:28; Secord, Bevan, and Katz 1956; Vinacke 1949). Most scholars seem to link the two, however. Stereotypes can be positive or negative and other- or self-oriented and can involve a single trait or a configuration of many.

When a stereotype includes many traits, it is difficult to determine whether it is positive or negative, because some traits are favorably viewed, while others are stigmatized. Traits assigned to self-oriented stereotypes can be positive, favorable, and overvalued (Vinacke 1957:240) as well as negative (Abrahams 1970a; Rath and Sircar 1960; Rosenberg and Shapiro 1959). There are stereotypes of stereotypes—for example, "a Negro's conception of a white's conception of a Negro in contrast to a white" (Dundes 1971:188). While stereotypes may, and occasionally do, contain a "kernel of truth" (R. Brown 1965:172; Klineberg 1950), an often-quoted study (La Pierre 1936) showed that they have little or nothing to do with "objective reality" or "empirical truth," and they may persist despite strong evidence to the contrary. Therefore Dundes (1971:188) has emphasized the congruence between stereotypes and "social reality" rather than between stereotypes and "objective reality." The process of stereotyping has also been analyzed as an extension of ethnocentrism (R. Brown 1965; Campbell and LeVine 1961), and Abrahams (1972a:24) claims that when stereotypes include traits that negate the values held by a stereotyping group, the group will cite the stereotype as supplying evidence of lack of "culture." It has also been argued (R. Brown 1958) that stereotypes rationalize selfish behavior and hostility felt by individuals toward a group or that they verbally express prejudice or serve to rationalize or project it. This view, however, is not accepted by all scholars (Brigham 1971; Vinacke 1949).

Stereotypes are crucial to ethnic humor and its appreciation. Because they are widely accepted by members of individual cultures, they constitute a shared set of assumptions necessary for ethnic humor. Speed of development is crucial for the effectiveness of any humor, because appreciation slows down when humor depends on a concept that cannot be understood without an effort or when critical examination is invited. In order for ethnic humor to have the desired effect, it needs readymade and popular conceptualizations of the target group(s). Stereotypes fulfill this requirement admirably, and therein lies their significance in the development of ethnic humor.

THE ANALYSIS OF ETHNIC HUMOR

A basic assumption in ethnic humor is that it should be based on traits that are considered to be the consequence of ethnicity. Thus many popular jokes in the United States that are based on stereotypic images of professionals, such as lawyers, physicians, secretaries, construction workers, and waiters, cannot be considered ethnic humor. If an individual's social identity is based on ascribed status, however, and if occupational status results from it, then humor based on that identity constitutes ethnic humor. Many proverbs in various South Asian languages that make fun of goldsmiths, tailors, and barbers, for example, can be said to constitute ethnic humor because, in the context of Hindu society, these target groups are hereditary occupational caste groups, and the profession constitutes an integral part of members' ascribed status. A son of a barber is identified as a member of the barber caste, though he may pursue another profession, and certain stereotypic images are associated with him, irrespective of his occupation.

Forms and Types

Ethnic humor is mostly verbal, although it is frequently aided by gestures and other nonverbal modalities. Purely action-based ethnic humor without speech is rare. Even in cartoon humor that emphasizes visual stimuli, verbal messages are crucial. I use the phrase "verbal humor" in a broad sense to include written and printed representations of speech. Verbal ethnic humor, like most other humor, is developed through jokes, proverbs, riddles, riddle-jokes, rhymes, tales, anecdotes, and legends. By far the most popular form of ethnic humor in the Western world appears to be jokes, followed by riddles and rhymes. In many non-Western societies, proverbs and tales seem to constitute the major genres of ethnic humor (Champion 1938; Risley 1915)

Jokes. Of the many varieties of ethnic jokes, the most common is one that identifies an individual as a member of a specific ethnic group and portrays that individual in a disparaging light. Usually the portrayal involves developing an incongruity between verbal comments and actions or exaggerating a personality trait or behavior that is stereotypically associated with the group. Most often such jokes give the impression that a person of the target ethnic group is stupid, ignorant, or unclean. In the following representative joke, any ethnic group may be the target.

A ―――― husband was complaining to his wife that their neighbor kept sneaking up to him and slapping him on his chest, breaking all the cigars in his pocket. "But," said the husband, "I am going to teach him a lesson."

"What are you going to do?" asked his wife.

"I'm going to fix him," said the husband. "The next time he slaps me on the chest, he will be hitting three sticks of dynamite in my pocket instead of cigars!"

Another type of ethnic joke involves the "cross-cultural" listing of slurs, so that many ethnic groups are simultaneously targeted. Individuals from diferent groups face a common situation and respond to it in keeping with popular stereotypes involving their respective behavior, action, verbalization, or carrying out of a task. The following joke illustrates the type. "An American, an Englishman, a Frenchman, and a German managed to survive a shipwreck on an island. After a few months, the German had organized the natives into an army, the American had built a plant using native labor, the Frenchman had opened a brothel, and the Englishman was sitting on the beach waiting to be introduced."

Competition and one-upmanship are key elements in yet another type of ethnic joke in which two or three individuals of different ethnic groups compete with and try to outsmart each other. Winning often means coming up with the cleverest answer in verbal repartee, as the following joke shows.

An orthodox rabbi and a Catholic priest were playing golf together and were discussing religious differences when the priest turned to the rabbi and said, "Quite confidentially, Rabbi, have you ever eaten ham?"

The rabbi in a very soft voice answered, "Confidentially, yes."

As the two continued to play, the rabbi thoughtfully asked the priest, "Very confidentially, Father, have you ever gone to bed with a woman?"

The priest blushed, and, in a whisper, answered slowly, "Yes, I have."

"Better than ham, wasn't it?" The rabbi exclaimed.

Riddle-Jokes A popular type of ethnic humor is a combination of a joke and a riddle, which folklorists commonly call a riddle-joke (Brunvand 1970). The joke takes the form of a question and an answer, and the answer usually reveals some stereotypic attribute of an ethnic group mentioned in the question. Riddle-jokes are supposed to reflect common beliefs about the target groups. The most popular of these jokes in recent years involves the act of changing a lightbulb. The usual question is: "How many ——— does it take to change a lightbulb?" Various answers reveal presumed cultural traits of different ethnic groups. There are many types of riddle-jokes (A. Greenberg 1972). The following seem to be the most common.

1. A) What is ———?
Example: Q: What is a ——— car pool?
            A: Five ——— carrying a car to work.
   B) Who is/was ———?
Example: Q: Who was Alexander Graham Kowalski?
            A: The first telephone pole.
   C) What does ——— say or do?
Example: Q: What does a ——— cheerleader say at a football game?
            A: Get that quarter back.
   D) What has ———?
Example: Q: What has one brain, sixteen legs and lives in the forest?
            A: Snow White and the seven ———.
2. How do you ——— or How can you ———?
Example: Q: How do you get thirteen ——— in a Volkswagen?
            A: Throw a quarter (nickel) in.
3. What is the difference between ——— and ———?
Example: Q: What is the difference between a ——— and a bucket of garbage?
            A: The bucket.
4. What do you call a ———?
Example: Q: What do you call a ——— who doesn't lie, cheat, or steal?
            A: Deceased.
5. Why did ——— or Why does ———?
Example: Q: Why did the ——— couple get married in a bathtub?
            A: Because they wanted a double ring ceremony.

Jokes with Gestures and Actions. Gestures or actions constitute an essential part of some ethnic riddle-jokes. In one form, the narrator performs an action or makes a gesture and usually asks the question "What is this?" The answer generally mentions the action or gesture of an individual, revealing the underlying assumption of stupidity or of some other, similarly undesirable trait associated with the target. In another type, the narrator of a joke first asks a question pertaining to some trait of an ethnic individual and supplies the answer by way of a gesture or an action. Occasionally, the

117

narrator may need the cooperation of the listener for the successful development of an action-based joke. The following joke, for example, is first identified as a variation of the three-card trick played by two individuals of a particular ethnic group. The narrator asks the listener to put one fist on the table. The narrator then moves his or her two fists from the left of the listener's stationary fist to the right and back several times, as in the three-card trick, and asks the listener, "Which is your fist?"

Rhymes. Rhymes as a form of ethnic humor appear more widespread among children than among adults. Children have little inhibition and think nothing of singing slurs and deprecatory rhymes about ethnic group(s). Unfortunately, collections of such rhymes are available mostly for the Western languages, although we have an occasional example from other parts of the world (Jordan 1973). Mencken (1942) lists many nursery rhymes dating back to the mid-nineteenth century in which Jews and Negroes are the butt of slurs. Birnbaum (1971) quotes examples of Hungarian and German rhymes that ridicule different ethnic groups. Porter (1965) quotes examples of American children's rhymes that make fun of blacks. In his discussion of the "jokelore" about the Mormons in the United States, Brunvand (1970) lists many parody rhymes, one of which is the following. "Come, come, ye Saints; no toilet paper here /But with grass wipe your ass." It is a parody of a Mormon hymn played in every Tabernacle organ concert: "Come, come ye Saints; no toil nor labor fear / But with joy wend your way."

Proverbs. Proverbs constitute an important genre of oral literature in most societies, more so perhaps in those that do not have a written tradition. Proverbs often succinctly encode the dominant values of a culture and give expression to its collective, shared perception of the universe, including other human social groups. As part of their sociocultural reality, many cultures encapsulate their view of outsiders in proverbs that are then used as folk wisdom not only for passing judgments on outsiders but also for the perpetuation of the existing stereotypic images of other people and prejudicial attitudes toward them. Investigation of proverbs and their textual analysis may therefore provide useful insights into a culture's perception of other groups.

While several collections of ethnic and racial proverbs from many cultures exist (Champion 1938; Mencken 1942; Roback 1944; Taylor 1931/1962), few systematic attempts have been made to analyze proverbs with an eye to extrapolating ethnic stereotypes that may persist in a culture. Folklorists and other scholars, however, have been aware that, whenever intergroup hostilities occur, each group is likely to coin proverbs against the other. Hungarian, Slavic, French, and German proverbs, for example, reflect stereotypic images of and prejudicial attitudes toward each other (Birnbaum 1971). Jokes and proverbs are perhaps the single factor most responsible for attitudes that one group holds with respect to another.

In many Asian and African cultures, proverbs that stress the perceived drawbacks of neighboring groups are popular (Champion 1938; Feinberg 1971; Westermarck 1931). In India, proverbs with negative caste stereotypes are cited to justify intercaste hostilities. Risley (1915) lists many proverbs that project stereotypic images of brahmins, peasants, goldsmiths, barbers, and untouchables.

Techniques Used

The techniques of imitation and exaggeration are used extensively in ethnic humor to suggest the physical appearance, clothing, behavior, body movements and gestures, and language considered to be characteristic of the target groups. Actors who caricatured blacks in the nineteenth- and early twentieth-century minstrel, burlesque, variety, vaudeville, and musical comedies appeared on stage in tattered clothes and black faces. The "light circle around the mouth was an extravagant distortion of supposedly typical lips of the Negro" (H. E. Adams 1937:16). The actors imitated the singing, speech, shambling gait, and other supposed characteristics of blacks.

Caricatures of outgroups appear to be widespread across cultures. American Indians routinely made fun of other tribes and particularly of the white man by exaggerating outgroup behavior, mannerisms, and clothes in their ceremonial humor, much of which was performed by ritual clowns (Steward 1931:197). Kwakiutl Indians in their potlatch ceremonial skits made fun of the provider of the potlatch by identifying him as an European, thus indirectly lampooning the European personality and character (Codere 1956:340). The tradition of burlesquing the white man has obviously continued among the American Indians, as exemplified by impromptu humorous performances in which Western Apache men exaggeratedly imitate the white man's speaking style and other mannerisms (Basso 1979).

Foreign language imitations constitute major stimuli in ethnic humor. The popular "accent" humor discussed in Chapter 6 is ethnic in nature. Occasionally, parodying the language of an outgroup involves nonsense manifestations. Children in a Chinese community near Hongkong make mocking noises like "keiko-keiko" in quick chatter to imitate the Japanese language at a Japanese film. English is often parodied by children with phrases like "asikasekaso" suggesting that it is perceived as full of "s" sounds (Anderson 1967:95). Such parodying reflects the acoustic images formed by members of an ingroup when they listen to a foreign language. Once a few features and sounds are identified as characteristic of a particular language, they are sufficient to caricature the speech of that linguistic group. The fact that listeners laugh at the imitations suggests that such impressions may be widely accepted and considered amusing within a culture. On the other hand, the association of particular sounds with specific languages can spread easily from one person to another and can be acquired just as easily as stereotypes.

Ethnic groups are also nonverbally ridiculed by exaggerated imitations of dress, occupational behavior, and so forth, especially in the context of festivities. At village festivals in Okinawa, exaggerated imitation of the clothing and wood-cutting activities of the people in the Northern district portrays them as jolly country bumpkins (Glacken 1955:257). Many non-Western societies that were under European colonial rule during the eighteenth and nineteenth centuries caricatured the white man in their paintings and woodcarvings. The wooden masks and figures exaggerated the white man's clothes, hat, shoes, pipe, and other characteristics that the natives found ridiculous (Lips 1937/1966).

THEORETICAL PERSPECTIVES

A broad conceptual framework needs to be developed within which anthropological analyses of ethnic humor in individual cultures can be carried out and comparative studies can be undertaken. Such a framework and the subsequent analyses should permit us to formulate hypotheses regarding the general characteristics of ethnic humor and the nature of its integration into the sociocultural system. The following dimensions, crucial for developing a framework, are examined in the next several sections: ethnic humor as cultural text; contextual determinants of ethnic humor; functions of ethnic humor. The discussion of these dimensions raises questions that cannot be answered satisfactorily because of the paucity of data from many culture areas of the world. Still, I hope to pinpoint both methodological and analytical issues that need to be examined in future research.

Ethnic Humor as Cultural Text

Ethnic humor, like all other types of humor, is an integral part of expressive culture. It reflects a group's perception and evaluation of other groups' personality traits, customs, behavior patterns, and social institutions by the standards of ingroup culture, with its positive or negative attitudes toward others. Judgments proceed from intergroup interactions, but once established, they tend to become a part of cultural heritage and do not change substantively unless they are affected by significant historical events. Groups' perceptions of and attitudes toward each other can be discovered through textual analyses, which constitute a major part of the existing research on ethnic humor. The existing analyses show a wide range in their focus and objectives, the kind of data collected, and the methodology and techniques adopted. The subject matter of many such analyses is humor pertaining to a single ethnic group or to several.[8]

Ethnic groups in North America figure prominently in textual analyses, perhaps because considerable emphasis has been placed on research on ethnicity by scholars in the United States since World War II. At the same time, a dearth of textual analyses of humor pertaining to ethnic groups in the cultures of Asia and Africa hampers cross-cultural comparisons of ethnic humor. The data for textual analyses come from written and published materials, from records made of performances by comedians or from jokes recorded at specific joke-telling sessions, or from social events. In addition to jokes, folklorists, who do the lion's share of textual studies, also gather ethnic riddles, rhymes, and proverbs.

The primary objective of most textual analyses is apparently discerning from the contents the underlying stereotypes, and the covert attitudes, beliefs, and motives, regarding the targeted ethnic groups. The assumption is that ethnic humor directly or indirectly exhibits the stereotyper's mental images and deep-seated beliefs, attitudes, and primordial emotions toward people made the butt of such humor.

Many studies attempt to identify the esoteric-exoteric factor (Jansen 1959) in the jokelore. The esoteric factor "applies to what one

121

group thinks of itself and what it supposes others think of it" (p. 206), while the exoteric factor is "what one group thinks of another and what it thinks that other group thinks it thinks" (p. 207). Jansen's concept of "factor" includes beliefs and attitudes that, in his view, are reflected in folklore. Esoteric beliefs of a group may be unconscious, or a group may "know the exoteric concepts held about it" and either may reject them or may "recognize them tolerantly." Jansen's exoteric factor seems comparable to a group's stereotype as held by other groups, while his esoteric factor appears to be similar to a group's self-stereotype and its awareness of the stereotype regarding it that is held by others. It is also possible, as Jansen suggests, that exoteric and esoteric factors may overlap considerably.

The distinction between esoteric and exoteric factors has been equated with "ingroup" versus "outgroup" humor, especially slurs (Dundes 1971:100). It is generally assumed that ingroup humor by and large reflects a group's positive image of itself, while outgroup humor reflects a group's negative image. While it has been argued that such is not always the case, supporting evidence, such as actual observations of self-derogatory humor narrated by members of a group to each other, is rarely presented. It is merely asserted (Dundes 1971:189; A. Greenberg 1972:146; Klymasz 1970:169) that minority ethnic groups tell jokes that are self-deprecating and conform to the exoteric factor.

In one of the earliest textual analyses of ethnic humor (Barron 1950), 734 jokes pertaining to Jewish, Negro, and Irish ethnic groups in the United States were analyzed. The study raised some interesting questions about the textual and contextual nature of ethnic humor. Who invented and communicated ethnic jokes? What basis is there for the suspicion that minority groups themselves sometimes invent and communicate ethnic jokes, and to what extent is self-hatred involved? It was argued that, until some of these questions have been answered, the assumption underlying some theories of humor, namely that "the ingroup only supports the ingroup and attacks the outgroup whenever it engages in intergroup joke verbalization" (p. 94) must remain tenuous. I shall discuss textual analyses of humor pertaining to several ethnic groups with particular attention to Jews and Negroes, because many more studies involve them than involve other ethnic groups.

Jewish Humor. Many themes and traits considered to be Jewish have been extracted from the existing jokelore by scholars. Jokes are considered Jewish if one or more of their textual components—social situations, participants, topics, and targets—are identified as such. The primary thesis of one textual analysis (Rosenberg and Shapiro 1959) is that Jewish humor reflects the psychological ambiguity of Jewish life due to the marginal social position of Jews in American society. This ambiguity conditions many other aspects of Jewish personality and life, which include "self-criticism frequently amounting to deep revulsion that can only be called self-hatred" (p. 74), acceptance of "some of the stereotypes of Jews held by anti-Semites" (p. 75), anxiety stemming from ambiguous social status, exaggerated sensitivity to anti-Semitism and to the subsequent "anti-goyish anticipatory counter-aggression," and an exaggerated sense of tradition, wishful desire, and belief in the "myth of the ubiquitous Jew."

In another analysis of Jewish humor (Dundes 1971), the extrapolated stereotype of Jews includes such traits as "the concern with money, trade, status, professionalism, the large nose, the undesirability, and in fact, impossibility of renouncing one's ethnic identity as a Jew, a prideful consciousness of the Judaic elements in Christianity, and a fear for the loss of ethnic identity through conversion to Christianity or through marriage with gentiles" (p. 199). This stereotypic image of the Jew is said to be fairly consistent and composite and to have existed in the United States and in other parts of the world for some time. Yet another study (A. Greenberg 1972) sees conflict between "loyalty to the Jewish tradition and assimilation into the American way of life" as the most common theme of Jewish humor. The other themes are a denial of a Jewish heritage, a thirst for money, a perpetual search for anti-Semitism, Jews who are no longer truly Jewish, social pressure to convert and conform to the mainstream of American culture, and the superficiality of such conversion.

Ehrlich (1979) has provided a classificatory scheme for Jewish jokes, illustrating each category with examples. His themes do not, however, seem to vary in any significant way from those provided by other scholars except that he has added a few new ones. Interestingly, Ehrlich rejects Rosenberg's and Shapiro's main thesis that Jewish humor is a reaction to the marginal, ambiguous status of Jews in America. He claims that "not all Jewish humor, not even most, has this property." In his view, Jewish humor, like that of any ethnic group, reflects the group's dominant values and is "existential" in character. As these and other studies demonstrate, there seems to be a basic agreement, despite differences of inter-

123

pretation, about the image of the American Jew that emerges from Jewish humor. Interestingly, this profile of the Jew and the characteristics of Jewish humor do not seem to differ fundamentally from those presented by Freud in his classic study of jokes and their relation to the unconscious in 1905 (translation by Strachey 1960), although Freud's analysis did not focus on the American Jews.

It has been argued (A. Greenberg 1972) that the ambiguous role of the Jewish people has led them to tell two types of jokes about themselves. In the first type they see themselves "contemptuously, with exaggerated features either as an anachronism or as a deserving recipient of contempt from non-Jews" (p. 149). In the other type there is a "nostalgic praise of traditional culture, often in forms leading to group cohesion, such as the traditional symbol of the Jewish mother forcing food on anything with a mouth" (p. 149). Although jokes of the first type may seem derogatory when told by the Jews themselves, they appear to be fond remembrances of a past generation.

Negro Humor. There is a consensus among the researchers of Negro humor that, until the Civil Rights movement began to strongly influence and change the status of Negroes in the 1960s, they, like the Jews, accepted the whites' stereotype of them and told self-disparaging jokes. The white stereotype of the Negro that emerges from the textual analyses depicts him as lazy, stupid, dishonest, and sexually immoral, with a preference for chicken and watermelon and characterized by animal sensuality. He is depicted as holding mostly menial jobs, as being good in sports, as having a natural sense of rhythm, as being religious; other stereotypical traits include certain physical features, such as fat lips and large genitals, a shuffling gait, a substandard form of spoken language, and a childlike mentality.

A major aspect of Negro humor is its preoccupation with the Negro's relationship with whites. Negroes depicted in ethnic humor rarely interact with other Negroes; they mostly interact with whites. Although many jokes reflect the whites' stereotype of the Negro, in some—for example, the following joke—the Negro outsmarts the white by using the latter's stereotype of Negro as an advantage.

Three men, a Negro, a Mexican, and a white, were brought into a courtroom. The judge said that if they could show fifteen inches of

124

length between them, they would be set free. The Negro pulled out his penis, which measured seven and a half inches, the Mexican pulled out his, which was five and a half inches, and the white pulled out his, which was two inches. Since the total was fifteen inches, the judge set them free. Once outside, the Negro and the Mexican began to boast about the size of their penises when the white man said, "You two are lucky that I had a hard-on."

In another type of joke, a white individual is made to appear stupid for having assumed that all Negroes fit the stereotype; some such jokes show that the stereotype is simply not correct. "A Southern officer stationed in England was seated next to a Negro at an official dinner. He completely ignored the Negro until the end of the meal and then commented, 'Rastus, Ah reckon you-all miss yo' watermelon.' The Negro then was introduced as the guest of honor and a renowned Oxford scholar and gave a brilliant speech. When he returned to his seat he said sarcastically to the officer, 'Yes, Rastus sho' do miss his watermelon.' "

The distinctions emphasized in Negro jokes are said to be social rather than ethnic, and the Negro joke form of ethnic joke is considered to be devoid of any ethnic contrast, the reason being that, unlike other minority ethnic groups, the Negroes lack a "sense of cultural identity distinct from that of the dominant culture" (Abrahams 1970a:240). This lack of identity associated with a geographical place is reflected in the Negro jokes such as the following.

There was a Mexican, Frenchman, Chinaman and Negro sitting under a shade tree shooting the bull one afternoon. So they got to boasting about their countries and the Mexican said, "Hail to the green grass of Mexico that has never been surpassed by any country." The Frenchman said, "Hail to the great flag of France that is a symbol of power." The Chinaman said, "Hail to the Great Wall of China that has never been scaled."

Next it was the Negro's turn to boast but he hesitated because he couldn't think of anything to boast about. So just about the time he was fixing to give up he saw a black bird that was flying over at the time, so he said, "Hail to the black bird who flew over the Great Wall of China, shit on the green grass of Mexico and wiped his ass with the great flag of France." [Abrahams 1970a:240]

In Abrahams's opinion a major aspect of the recent Negro nationalistic movement has been the "fabrication of roots by learning African history and Swahili, by adopting West African modes of dress, and by forming a Black Nation" in the United States (p. 241).

Another characteristic of Negro humor is seen to be the denial of black racial identity by Negroes who have achieved middle-class status and have become socially acceptable in white society (A. Greenberg 1972). This view is supported by an earlier study (Middleton and Moland 1959) but is not acceptable to all scholars. It has been argued (Arnez and Anthony 1968) that, with increasing pride in Negro identity, its denial in earlier humor is giving way to an identity that leads to humor more caustic in nature toward whites and toward those Negroes who deny their identity and heritage.

The Humor of Other Ethnic Groups. Relatively few studies of jokes involving North American ethnic groups other than the Jews and Negroes have been carried out by researchers. Much of the humor involving the other ethnic groups appears to be of the type of riddle-jokes. Among the other ethnic groups subjected to humor are the Polish Americans, whose stereotypical image, as reflected in Polish humor, is that they are "poor, dirty, stupid, inept, vulgar, boorish and tasteless" (Dundes 1971:200–201). Dundes, however, and other researchers who have analyzed the so-called Polish jokes (Barrick 1970; Clements 1969; Welsch 1967) claim that the Polish stereotypic traits as extracted from such humor are really traits of the lower class and that they can be, and have been, transferred to other minority groups in the United States and Canada such as the Italian Americans, Irish Americans, Puerto Ricans, and Newfoundlanders, a claim supported by other investigators (Klymasz 1970; D. C. Simmons 1963).

While the studies of ethnic humor that I have discussed are primarily concerned with ethnic minority groups in the United States, Paredes (1966) has discussed the image of Anglo-Americans in Mexican folklore, including various humor genres. According to the emerging stereotypic image, Anglo-Americans are fond of eating ham and white bread; are fat and soft in contrast to the rugged Mexican and thus need cots, kitchen, and mosquito nets; have odd customs; have a tendency to be less than dominant over their women; and have an extremely white face, which in Mexican folklore symbolizes cowardice. In short, the Anglo-American is portrayed as stupid, insensitive, gullible, and incapable of speaking Spanish properly or of understanding Mexican customs. Anglo-Americans take polite conversations and clichès at their face value.

The Anglo-American woman is portrayed as insipid, thus incapable of properly satisfying a man sexually. Despite the negative image of the Anglo-American in Mexican folklore, the humor of Mexican Americans in the United States, like that of other ethnic minority groups, tends to be self-deprecating (Paredes 1966) and displays the same feeling of ambivalence toward the dominant whites that is found in other ethnic groups.

There is an awareness of pejorative stereotypes of foreigners in humor, anecdotes, and other folkloristic genres of societies in different parts of the world, especially in Asia and Africa (Beidelman 1964:33–34; Campbell and LeVine 1961; Steward 1931; Swartz 1961). In the past, however, very little research was carried out on ethnic humor in societies outside North America. Fortunately, the situation is changing, as evidenced by several new studies made since the start of the 1970s. Zenner (1970) has examined ethnic jokes among the Druze in Palestine. A new oral literary genre of humor called *Chizbat* developed in Israel has been analyzed by Oring (1973, 1981). In Oring's view Chizbat humor appears to explore the boundaries of Israeli Jews' self-identity by poking fun at the stereotypes of both the *Sabra*, the native-born Israeli, and the *Galut*, the immigrant Jew. The jokelore among the Andalusians in a Spanish town in which Gypsies are the targets has been studied by Brandes (1980). Kravits (1977) has analyzed the ethnic stereotypes of the West Indians, Pakistanis, Irish, Scots, and Jews in jokes told by white Londoners in pubs and parks and by four white comedians. Even the ethnic humor of American Indians has been examined anew, as demonstrated by Basso's (1979) analysis of the Western Apaches' caricature of the white man in their social interaction. These studies reflect diverse theoretical perspectives but are methodologically and analytically rigorous. They not only focus on textual analyses but also discuss the contextual factors and possible functions of ethnic humor in their explanations.

While many textual analyses of humor seek to identify the stereotypic traits that are assigned to various ethnic groups, some traits have been found to evoke universal negative reactions, and these tend to be assigned to any group that is to be ridiculed and mocked. Such traits as stupidity, dirtiness, brute force, and excessive sexuality are generally viewed negatively and can be linked to any target group. Thus there are "slot-filler" jokes that ridicule the traits just mentioned and in which any group—ethnic or nonethnic—will serve as the target. The imputation of universally disapproved traits to any group to be ridiculed amuses the people who narrate and enjoy such humor and expresses their feeling of superiority.

Textual analyses seem useful for discerning the existing stereotypes of specific ethnic groups. Few of them, however, discuss the extent to which such stereotypes accord with objective reality. The methodology for collecting jokes is not always stated. While folkloristic data, particularly jokes, are gathered from a few—often only one or two—informants, there is a tendency to assert that they are widespread and popular in a specific region and community or in the entire population. Such claims, which are rarely based on statistical validation, appear to reflect the subjective impressions of the researchers.

An ethnic joke can be analyzed and interpreted on the basis of its dominant theme. Occasionally, however, a single joke may reflect multiple themes, or it may lack a clear-cut theme. Determining what theme a joke reflects is also a matter of interpretation, and a researcher's theoretical orientation may influence his or her views, particularly when a joke reflects multiple themes. Determining how frequently a theme appears in ethnic humor is often difficult. It is important to rank order themes on the basis of the number of jokes that reflect them, although a researcher cannot always present all jokes from his or her data that reflect different themes. Few themes can be treated as dominant and as expressing the world view of a group unless they appear in many jokes. While a few studies (Barron 1950; Clements 1969; Kravitz 1977; Oring 1982) seek to show a theme's dominance, more commonly the researcher presents a theme and then simply gives one or two jokes that reflect it.

Some textual analyses tell when and where the data were collected. Such information usefully puts the analysis in a proper contextual perspective, making it possible to determine the effects of time and place on the creation and dissemination of jokes and other witticisms. A major drawback of textual analysis based on published collections of ethnic jokes is that the contextual information is often lacking, so that it is difficult to relate the analyses to external historical events and to sociocultural reality. It is also difficult to tell whether published jokes are in fact representative of those in circulation in a society at a particular time.

Occasionally, textual analyses and interpretations of jokes presented by some researchers seem rather far-fetched. Abrahams and Dundes (1969) analyzed a set of "elephant jokes," which became popular throughout the United States in the 1960s and "achieved notoriety that may have surpassed even that of the 'knock-knock,' 'little moron,' or 'sick joke' cycles" (Abrahams and Dundes 1969:225–26). An example of an elephant joke is the following. Q: "How do elephants make love in the water?" A: "They take their trunks down" (1969:231).

In support of their claim regarding the popularity of these jokes, Abrahams and Dundes (1969) cite several collections and papers on elephant jokes published in the 1960s (p. 239, n. 2). They call these jokes "patently childish and nonsensical" and argue that such childish jokes constitute a regressive means of achieving temporary sense of freedom from societal restraint. The principal thesis is that these elephant jokes, by their infantile and fantasized nature, provided relief by way of "harmless aggression" for whites, who felt threatened by blacks who had produced a new image that was "powerful, enigmatic, and occasionally vindictive (as in the Black Muslim movement)" (p. 237). The elephant jokes served a defensive function because, according to the authors, the elephant is a reflection "of the American Negro as the white sees him," and the "political and social assertion by the Negro has caused certain primal fears to be reactivated" (p. 236). Abrahams and Dundes suggest that the jokes began to occur and to be popular at the time of the increasing influence of the Civil Rights movement. They maintain that "there is obvious association in the minds of many Americans of both the elephant and the Negro with the African jungle" (p. 236). The authors further suggest that the sexual jokes involving elephants are very popular because both "the male Negro and the elephant are pictured as having unusually large genitals and commensurate sexual capacity"; "the public image of them relates to great size, strength and endurance" (p. 236). Abrahams and Dundes further contend that the "preoccupation with the elephant's color" in many jokes reflects "the public's concern with the Negro as either 'colored man' or 'man of color' " (p. 237).

As my discussion has indicated, textual analyses invite us to consider the validity of interpretations of humor. A common danger in any textual analysis is reading too much into the text. Perhaps some textual analyses are guilty of projecting the investigators' ideas onto the content of ethnic humor, especially when it is claimed that often even the people who tell ethnic jokes are not aware of the symbolic significance of their contents (Dundes 1977:142). Unless we can develop some ways of testing textual interpretations of the kind provided by Abrahams and Dundes, it is not possible to determine the validity of their analysis. One possibility would be to conduct an associational test among white subjects after telling them the elephant jokes. Any significant association between the elephant and the Negro would support at least to some extent the main thesis of Abrahams and Dundes.

In this connection Oring's (1975) criticism of the psychofunctional theoretical approach, by which all ethnic humor is seen as socially aggressive, deserves much attention. Oring argues that this theoretical approach is reductionist, so that "humorous communication is not significantly distinguishable from any other form of artistic expression." Because many researchers claim that different groups tell socially aggressive jokes about themselves, they all need to be viewed as having masochistic tendencies, and humor must be regarded as a "vehicle of self-aggression" that "weakens the explanatory power of aggression theory." But Oring's most important criticism is that so much emphasis on aggression theory "has led to a stultification of humor analysis." He presents an alternate analysis of the elephant jokes, claiming that they, like most humor genres, are "primarily structures of ideas to be perceived intellectually," which means that they should be based upon "the creation and perception of an appropriate incongruity."

The issue of determining how faithful to objective reality the group portrayals in ethnic humor are is complex and controversial, a matter closely related to the problem of the truthfulness or falsehood of stereotypes that I discussed earlier. In ethnic humor a single trait is frequently assigned to many groups. This recurrence suggests that a negative attitude is shared by people of different cultures toward that trait rather than that the trait is characteristic of a particular group. "Numskull" or "moron" jokes, for example, can apparently be attributed to any ethnic group; similar jokes and themes have demonstrably been used to ridicule and lampoon blacks, Polish Americans, and other minority groups in the United States, Ukrainians in Poland (Levy 1976); Newfoundlanders in Canada (Klymasz 1970); Gypsies in Spain (Brandes 1980); and Sikhs in India. In this connection, it is worthwhile to repeat the apt comment of Joey Adams (1975): "I supply the humor ... you supply the ethnic."

Ethnic humor frequently labels and portrays a member of a particular group as typical of the entire group. Such a practice reflects overgeneralization and a belief in uniformity. Intracultural variation and individuality are ignored in this practice as a matter of convenience. Stereotypes in general tend to be overgeneralized conceptualizations of ethnic groups. When ethnic humor is based on a stereotype that is developed without extensive contact and interaction, however, it is likely to be quite inaccurate: ethnic humor based on it may bear no resemblance to objective reality. An identical portrayal of a particular group in the humor of many cultures does not necessarily prove that the stereotype is faithful to objective reality. The humor and the stereotype may result from diffusion. The truthfulness of the underlying stereotype in such humor remains unconfirmed in such instances.

Many studies have claimed that members of ethnic groups tell jokes that are based on negative stereotypes of themselves.[9] A group's acceptance of its negative stereotype and of the humor based on it, however, does not prove that the portrayal is faithful to reality. Such acceptance merely suggests a lack of positive self-image and an inferiority complex on the part of the group, which may be due to its relatively low sociocultural status. Another possibility is that people who tell jokes derogatory of the ethnic group to which they belong are likely to disassociate themselves from the underlying stereotype, believing in intracultural diversity and in the existence of several subethnic groups differentiated on the basis of generation, occupation, degree of religious orthodoxy, immigrant status, education, and overall socioeconomic status. Such distinctions may or may not be verifiable. What matters, however, is the perception of the people who engage in the so-called self-deprecatory humor (Ben-Amos 1973).

It is sometimes suggested that, if ethnic humor is based on a specific trait uniquely attributed to a particular group, its faithfulness to objective reality may more easily be verified. Many jokes are based on the consumption of watermelon and chicken in large quantities by blacks, on the use of hand gestures by Italians while talking, or on "excessive" drinking by the Irish. Even with regard to these so-called verifiable traits, however, generalizations are not free from exceptions. The problem is that such behavior is assumed to be characteristic of the whole group but reflects the observation of only a few individuals. The truthfulness of ethnic humor can be assessed satisfactorily by emphasizing the inherent nature of all humor. Humor results from a creative process that uses exaggeration—distortion—as one of its major techniques. Therefore the portrayal of individuals, groups, actions, personality traits, and physical features is rarely, if ever, faithful to objective reality. In addition, prejudice and negative attitudes seem universally to play a major role in ethnic humor (Birnbaum 1971; Dundes 1975; Roback 1944), and therefore the degree of incongruity is often quite high. It is thus realistic to view much ethnic humor as based on prevalent associations of traits with diverse ethnic groups irrespective of whether or not such associations actually occur.

Another way of considering truthfulness with respect to objective reality is to argue that the issue is not relevant. Whether or not attributes associated with a particular group in ethnic humor are true, the fact remains that many individuals who narrate and enjoy such humor perceive the target group in the indicated fashion. In other words, the "knowledge" is accepted, maintained, and transmitted regardless of its ultimate validity or invalidity (Berger and Luckman 1966/1967:3). Ethnic humor and the stereotypes upon which it is based therfore represent "traditional images of reality rather than the reality itself" (Dundes 1975:24). In this regard, portrayals of groups in ethnic humor, then, should properly be regarded as "concept-systems with positive as well as negative functions, having the same general kinds of properties as other concepts, and serving to organize experience as do other concepts" (Vinacke 1957:229).

CONTEXTUAL DETERMINANTS

In exploring the influence of contextual factors on ethnic humor, it is useful for analytical purposes to recognize two interrelated basic types: Macro-level factors relevant to the societal, national, and international interaction; and micro-level factors relevant to small-group interaction within society. Macro-level contextual factors include the following: the nature of individual societies (whether they are simple or complex, small-scale or large-scale, homogeneous or heterogeneous); the nature of contact and interaction between societies; historical events of significant nature that affect societies (for instance, international conflicts, wars, large-scale migrations, social movements, and religious upheavals); major intrasocietal conflicts of a political and economic nature; and sociocultural change over a period of time that affects the social status of many ethnic groups within a society. Contextual factors at the micro level include, among others, the nature of settings in which ethnic humor occurs, such as informal social gatherings at home, among friends, in daily routine interaction at the place of work, and so on; the ethnic background of participants in such small-group interactions; the intentions and motives of individuals when they engage in ethnic humor; and the responses of participants to ethnic humor directed at others and at themselves.

Macro-Level Contextual Factors

The Nature of Society. The nature of ethnic humor, especially as regards its target(s), is closely associated with the nature of society as a whole. Ethnic humor is much less likely to occur in highly homogeneous small-scale societies simply because no ethnic groups are likely to be part of it. In contrast, ethnic humor disparaging various groups is much more likely to occur in many traditional and contemporary multiethnic societies. The existence of hundreds of caste groups in the traditional Hindu society of India is the primary reason for the widespread use of proverbs that poke fun at them (Risley 1915). The multiethnic nature of American society from its very inception can be cited as one of the major reasons for the popularity of ethnic humor in the United States. It has been pointed out (Barrick 1970:6; Dundes 1971:199; Welsch 1967:183) that any new immigrant group quickly becomes the target of ethnic humor by residents of longer standing in the United States.

Intersocietal Contact and Interaction. Ethnic humor in which "foreigners" are the target generally develops when societies come in contact with each other and have some degree of interaction. By the same token, one society is not likely to be the target of another's ethnic humor if the two have no extensive cultural contact. If a person does not know anything about another society, then there is nothing to share about it with members of the person's own culture: no image is developed of the other group. In the ethnic humor of European nations, the targets are often the neighboring European societies rather than some remote tribes of Asia and Africa. The targets in the folklore of Hungarians, Germans, and speakers of Slavic and other European languages, for instance, are their neighboring ethnic and linguistic groups (Birnbaum 1971). Much the same is true elsewhere. In Mexican folklore Anglo-Americans appear to be the main target (Paredes 1966).

Major Historical Events. Wars, large-scale migrations, major social movements, religious upheavals, and other similar national or international happenings can change ethnic groups' perception of each other and of themselves. As a result, ethnic humor and the stereotypes on which it is based may also change. During the occupation of Czechoslovakia by the Nazis during World War II, for example, the Czechs developed ethnic humor in which the Nazis were the target. The Nazis were ridiculed, belittled, and portrayed in a strongly disparaging light (Obrdlik 1942). Such humor kept up the morale of the Czechs as they tried to resist a strong adversary who could not be defeated. The most interesting aspect of this phenomenon was that the Germans could not stop the dissemination of such anti-Nazi humor. During the first Egyptian-Israeli war, in both Egypt and Israel many jokes made the Egyptian army the butt of ethnic humor. But after the second war, in which the Egyptians fared better, the Israelis created self-disparaging humor because of their failure to live up to their own expectations (Eliason 1974).

Sociocultural Change. Ethnic humor is influenced significantly by the sociocultural changes that may occur, especially if by such changes the social status of subordinate ethnic groups is altered. Sociocultural change may also be reflected, however, in the societal attitudes toward ethnic groups as a whole. There may develop sensitivity about the use and propagation of ethnic humor, or emphasis on acculturation and assimilation may give way to ethnic pride. The social conditions in America, for example, have changed during the last quarter century or so, so that now there is less emphasis on the "melting pot" and more on recognition of, and pride in, ethnic identity. This change has affected both the minority ethnic groups and the white majority. The nature of black humor, for example, has changed during this period. Instead of being self-deprecatory, black humorists have started poking fun at the whites' ethnocentricity and at whites' perceived racist attitudes. The humor of black comedians has become more caustic and includes satirical comments not only on the whites' stereotype of the black but also on the whites themselves, as demonstrated by Dick Gregory, Moms Mabley, Flip Wilson (Arnez and Anthony 1968), and, more recently, Richard Pryor.[10] In Great Britain, on the other hand, the Welsh-speaking people in recent years have begun to emphasize their Welsh identity. A recent study (Gadfield et al. 1979) found that, because the Welsh people are redefining their identity vis-à-vis the dominant group in Great Britain, they do not view aggressive self-directed humor favorably.

Sociocultural change due to migration may affect the nature of humor across generations, especially if it results in the improvement of overall socioeconomic status and a positive self-image. According to Ben-Amos, "Self-ridicule was the main trait of Jewish jokes in East and Central Europe and . . . it disappeared from their society as they crossed the Atlantic to the United States" (1973:130).

The younger generation rejected the self-deprecatory image, while the older generation may continue to view itself in a demeaning fashion. Sociocultural change may affect ethnic humor in yet another way. With the growing sensitivity of ethnic groups to their negative image in humor, prejudice and negative attitudes may be expressed metaphorically or covertly rather than directly and overtly. Such is the argument presented by Abrahams and Dundes (1969) to explain the popularity of elephant jokes in the 1960s, as I noted earlier. Dundes (1977) has also explained the later popularity of the "wide-mouth frog" joke using the same reasoning: again, its popularity reflected covert negative attitudes toward the black because of the intolerance of overt racist feelings due to sociocultural change. While the elephant jokes give expression to the perceived sexuality and image of the large genitals of the black male, the wide-mouth frog joke indirectly makes fun of black speech characteristics and dialects, with emphasis on how blacks need to learn to talk like whites.

There may be some reluctance to ridicule ethnic groups openly in ethnic humor by making them targets, but research and collections of ethnic humor published by folklorists in recent years suggest that humor that draws on the common transferable traits (such as those used in the numskull or moron jokes) seems ever more popular. The reason may be that such jokes may serve to portray any group. Some ethnic groups, however, seem strongly to oppose even this riddle-joke humor. Polish Americans, for example, have mounted concerted efforts to stop the perpetuation of numskull riddle-jokes that make Poles the target (Barrick 1970:13). Klymasz (1970:167) describes attempts made to enforce the Civil Rights Act when jokes about Polish-Americans began to circulate widely.

Micro-Level Contextual Factors

Little research evaluates the ways in which ethnic humor is affected by such micro-level contextual factors as social setting, participants and their ethnic background, their motives in narrating ethnic humor, and their response to it when they are or are not its target. In determining the connection between one of the contextual factors, namely, social setting, and ethnic humor, it is useful to see a dichotomy between the public and the private domain. The public domain includes large gatherings for cultural programs and entertainment, political rallies, public lectures, press conferences, and programs on television and radio. The private domain includes small gatherings in which family members, close friends, or members of the same ethnic groups interact. Ethnic humor in both types of social situations is viewed in ways that depend on the culture. In some, narration of ethnic humor in both the private and the public domain may be readily accepted. In others, ethnic humor may be considered inappropriate in the public domain, while it may be quite popular in the private. Changing societal attitudes also influence the use of ethnic humor in both domains.

Persons who are prominent in public life, such as politicians and actors, must be particularly discreet in using ethnic humor, especially if society's attitudes toward its use are negative. Although telling ethnic jokes in both the public and the private domain was considered quite acceptable in the United States twenty-five years ago, the situation has changed in recent years. An occasional indiscretion, or a press report of the joking disparagement of a particular ethnic group in private conversation, can ruin the careers of public figures. Well-known recent examples include Earl Butz, the secretary of agriculture during the Nixon administration who made fun of blacks and Italians and had to apologize publicly, and, more recently, Secretary of the Interior James Watt, in the Reagan administration, who resigned after having described the membership of a committee as consisting of one Jew, two blacks, one Hispanic, and one cripple. Nowadays, stand-up comedians in the United States generally do not poke fun at ethnic groups other than their own, with some notable exceptions. Lenny Bruce openly ridiculed many ethnic groups. Starting in the 1960s, some black comedians began to practice social satire at the expense of whites. In the last few years, Richard Pryor, the black comedian, has made whites the target of his ethnic humor in his public performances.

In social settings in the private domain, participants generally know each other's background and can predict the reactions to ethnic humor. On the other hand, it is difficult to know the background of participants in social situations in the public domain and to predict how they will react to ethnic humor. Comedians performing in clubs may use numerous techniques to identify the ethnic composition of their audience. They may ask how many people are from a particular ethnic group; they then generally avoid telling too many jokes that may offend the largest group in the audience. Sometimes, performing comedians start by identifying their own ethnic background and then telling self-deprecatory jokes; later the jokes are rotated, so that eventually several ethnic groups become the target of the humor. Self-degradation is particularly important if the comedian is a member of a minority group but wants to tell ethnic jokes, because it establishes his status as a member of a minority group. Even with such precautions, however, comedians occasionally face angry or hostile reactions from members of the audience, as Kravitz (1977) found during his research on ethnic jokes in London. (The comedians he interviewed described the techniques that I mentioned above).

In discussing how the background of participants affects the use of ethnic humor, researchers characterize social situations as being of either ingroup or intergroup type. A common assumption in ethnic humor research (Dundes 1971; A. Greenberg 1972) is that minority ethnic groups tell self-deriding jokes among themselves. Only a few studies (R. Middleton 1959; Paredes 1973; Prange and Vitols 1963), however, provide data-gathering techniques and other information to show that jokes were actually collected in social situations where all participants belonged to the same ethnic group and that a significant percentage of jokes told were self-disparaging. Participants of diverse backgrounds frequently react differently not only to ethnic humor but also to other types of humor. Research that systematically studies the nature of reactions to ethnic humor among participants of different ethnic backgrounds, including the people who become its target, is lacking, however. Only occasional comments emphasize that humor is an individual-oriented cognitive experience and does not reside in the situation itself (Burma 1946:712).

There may be many reasons why individuals either unconsciously fail to understand ethnic humor or purposely do not acknowledge it. If, for instance, a man had some previous experience during which his ethnic identity was ridiculed, so that he became defensive, angry, or resentful, he may unconsciously fail to understand and to appreciate humor directed at his ethnic identity, because its recognition and appreciation may lead to anxiety. Such a possibility has been suggested in clinical studies of individuals who failed to understand any humor at all (Levine and Redlich 1955). A person's strategy of deliberately refusing to understand, or of pretending not to understand, ethnic humor in which he or she is the target may succeed only if there are no other participants with an ethnic background different from that of the target group. Otherwise, participants who wish to see the ethnic identity of an individual ridiculed may go as far as "explaining" such humor to ascertain that it has been understood. Another possibility is that the listener, and in some instances even the narrator of a joke that deprecates the ethnic group he belongs to, may disassociate himself or herself from the target, viewing the stereotypic traits as characteristic of other social subgroups within the ethnic group. Such seems to be the case, according to Ben-Amos (1973), among people who tell Jewish dialect jokes. Ben-Amos states that such jokes are "part of the repertoire only of second generation immigrants whose own English is normative and who at the same time heard at home the accented speech of their parents" (p. 124). Ben-Amos further suggests the possibility that different occupational or otherwise distinct subgroups within an ethnic group may tell jokes disparaging each other that the outsiders may consider characteristic of the whole ethnic group. Among the Jews in the United States, for instance, rabbis and the laity tell jokes disparaging each other (pp. 125–29).

Ethnic humor deriding a dominant group may become a part of the folklore of minority ethnic groups. D. C. Simmons (1963, 1966), who has suggested such a possibility in his study of anti-Italian-American riddle-jokes in New England, uses the term "protest humor." He contends that, for protest humor to occur in a particular group, the tradition of maligning the group must have been long, as it has been for blacks and Jews in the United States. He explains the absence of protest humor among Italian-Americans as due to the fact that anti-Italian folklore in the United States, including humor, is of much more recent origin, starting only in 1961. Simmons's analysis indicates that, although every ethnic group may develop humor expressing its superiority to others, in reality sociocultural factors may delay or prevent such development. The interconnections between participants' ethnic background and their response to ethnic humor can lead to any of the following outcomes: (1) individuals may pretend not to understand a joke in which their ethnic group is the target if they have a strong loyalty to the ethnic group and/or are sensitive to its disparagement; (2) in ethnic humor development an individual of a maligned ethnic group may respond by engaging in humor ridiculing the ethnic group of the previous narrator, and the end result may be a competition for one-upmanship; (3) members of a subordinate ethnic group may tell jokes deriding the dominant group(s) in intragroup as well as intergroup social situations.

Researchers should specify contextual factors such as ethnic group membership, the identity of narrator(s) of ethnic humor, and the identity of listeners when they are linked with the text of such humor so that it can be analyzed into such meaningful categories

138

Table 1. Relationship of textual and contextual factors to categories of humor

Factors			
Textual:	Contextual		Categories of
target	Narrator	Listener	ethnic humor
Same	Same	Same	Intragroup and self-directed
Same	Same	Different	Intergroup and self-directed
Same	Different	Same	Intergroup and other directed
Different	Same	Same	Intragroup and other directed
Different	Different	Different	Intergroup and other directed

Note: The terms "same" and "different" denote ethnic group membership.

as intragroup versus intergroup humor and self-oriented versus other-oriented humor. An ethnic joke in which a Jew is the target, for example, belongs to the categories of intragroup and self-directed humor only if the narrator and the listener(s) are Jews. If a Jewish narrator tells the same joke to non-Jewish listeners, however, it falls into the category of intergroup humor, although it still belongs to the category of self-directed ethnic humor. If the same joke is told by a non-Jewish narrator to Jewish listeners, it falls into the category of other-directed intergroup humor. If the same joke is told by a non-Jewish narrator to listeners of his own ethnic group, it belongs to the intragroup and other-directed category of ethnic humor. Finally, if the same joke is told in a multiethnic social group that excludes Jews, it belongs to the intergroup and other-directed category of ethnic humor. These relationships between textual and contextual factors are illustrated in table 1.

While contextual factors are necessary for establishing categories within ethnic humor, they are not useful for defining it. Using them for this purpose narrows the nature and scope of ethnic humor considerably. Ehrlich (1979), however, has proposed a definition of ethnic humor that is based on contextual factors. In his view ethnic humor is ingroup humor: the narrator, the listener(s), and the subjects are all affiliated with the same ethnic group. He distinguishes ethnic humor from intergroup humor in which the speaker and the listener(s) hold different group memberships from the subjects of their humor. Ehrlich does not specify the theoretical advantage to be gained by his proposed distinction. I find Ehrlich's definition of ethnic humor too narrow. Ethnic humor mocks, caricatures, and generally makes fun of a specific group or its members by the virtue of their ethnic identity; or it portrays the superiority of one ethnic group over others. In addition, its thematic development must be based on factors that are the consequences of ethnicity, such as ethnocentrism, prejudice, stereotyping, and discrimination. Such a broad-based definition of ethnic humor subsumes many types within it, including Ehrlich's intergroup humor.

FUNCTIONS OF ETHNIC HUMOR

The perceived motives of individuals and groups in the use, propagation, and enjoyment of ethnic humor have been discussed extensively in the existing research literature. Many theories have been proposed to explain the widespread popularity and persistence of ethnic humor and its generally negative and disparaging nature. Among them, theories that assign psychological or sociological functions to ethnic humor seem to predominate. The former appear to emphasize the catharsis of some primordial emotions and the strengthening of others, while the latter seem to emphasize the relevance of ethnic humor to intergroup interaction and to the survival of individual groups. Two basic approaches can be discerned in the theoretical discussions. One is to explain the purpose(s) that ethnic humor of specific kind serves for a particular ethnic group, and the other is to explain the popularity of ethnic humor in general utilitarian terms. Sometimes these two approaches are combined, either inductively, moving from the specific to a general explanation, or deductively, from general premises to explanations of specific functions.

Investigators who propose psychological theories at the specific level do so with reference to a particular ethnic group and utilize specific themes extracted from textual analyses to support the theories. Jewish humor, for example, is seen to function as the relief-giving expression of the Jews' guilt and tensions, the feelings that attend their ambiguous position in American society (Rosenberg and Shapiro 1959). Many themes extracted from textual analysis have been presented to support this functional explanation. A major function of ethnic jokes that whites tell about blacks in the southern United States was seen to be the rationalization and justification of their discriminatory treatment, so that the jokes helped to reinforce the existing stereotype (Myrdal 1944). According to another theory, the harmless aggression by whites in the face of the increasing power of blacks in the 1960s, as previously noted, was reflected in the sudden popularity of elephant jokes (Abrahams and Dundes 1969). Another functional explanation sees anti-Italian-American riddle-jokes in New England as the expression of resentment felt by older groups due to competition from a new group (D. C. Simmons 1966). Ethnic jokes told against Pakistanis in London have been regarded as the expression of anger and xenophobia (Kravitz 1977). A careful analysis of Gypsy jokes told by Andalusians in a Spanish town (Brandes 1980) takes into acount both the text and the context and proposes differential functions for different kinds of jokes.

While some psychological theories explain the popularity of specific types of ethnic humor in particular contexts, as the above examples indicate, other functional explanations of ethnic humor are couched in general terms, distinguishing between majority and minority or dominant and subordinate ethnic groups. Protest ethnic humor developed by the minority groups, for example, is seen as functioning to relieve the "suppressed aggression" and "to preserve the ego identity of minority group members" who had to tolerate attacks on their group image that were expressed in unflattering stereotypes (D. C. Simmons 1963). A similar psychological function—the cathartic release of aggression—has been ascribed to the jokes told by American Jews as well (Cray 1964). Ethnic humor is also considered to reinforce a group's social position by relegating another's to an inferior level (A. Greenberg 1972).

The psychological functions of ethnic humor have been discussed in universalistic terms too. It is claimed that ethnic humor in general serves to satisfy the pan-human need to vent aggression (Dundes 1975; A. Greenberg 1972; Klymasz 1970). Such a view is clearly influenced by Freud's psychofunctional theory of jokes. On the other hand, this view has been criticized as unsatisfactory because it fails to take into account the diverse nature of ethnic humor (Oring 1975). Individuals and groups who narrate ethnic jokes do not necessarily accept the negative or pejorative stereotypes of the target groups. Rather, ethnic humor serves merely to amuse. R. Middleton, for example, is of the view that "even if a person does not accept the validity of a stereotype, he may be willing to suspend his disbelief temporarily in order to enjoy the humor of the joke" (1959:80).

A general psychological framework relevant in explaining the existence and worldwide popularity of ethnic humor can be found in the concept of ethnocentrism. A classic definition of this concept

(Sumner 1906:13) is the "view of things in which one's own group is the center of everything, and all others are scaled with reference to it. . . . Each group nourishes its own pride and vanity, boasts itself superior, exalts its own divinities and looks with contempt on outsiders." This definition has been further elaborated by Campbell and LeVine (1961) using theoretical propositions to be tested by extensive cross-cultural research. These authors have argued that "stereotyped imagery is an unconscious rationalization for the hostility" (p. 85) toward outgroups, such hostility being a concomitant of ethnocentrism.

In my view, attitudes of ingroup adulation and outgroup hate, stereotyping, and prejudice, must all be considered to be concomitants of ethnocentrism. Treating or thinking of other cultures and people as inferior, for example, is one way of strengthening self-image. Prejudice reinforces ethnocentrism, just as negation of the cultural values of other people nurtures self-esteem and feelings of superiority. Ethnographers are only too familiar with ethnocentrism and with the resultant ridicule of their own behavior—eating habits, clothing, and approach to everyday routine jobs—by the people they study. In the initial stages, ethnographers often find that they are laughed at because of their "strange" habits and their faltering and unsuccessful attempts to learn the "proper" cultural patterns and language of the people they study. Salinas (1975), a Mexican who worked with ethnographers, described in tongue-in-cheek style much of their "strange" behavior during his numerous encounters with them. Anthropologists tell other such stories about their early experiences in the field and about the ways in which they were often made the butt of native humor (Chagnon 1968; Lee 1969). In view of the widespread occurrence of ethnocentrism, prejudice, and stereotyping, it is not surprising that these tendencies constitute the main basis for the ethnic humor that reinforces them.

It has been claimed (Dundes 1971; Ehrlich 1979) that even seemingly self-disparaging humor strengthens ethnocentrism, primarily because traits seen as negative by outgroups are viewed as positive by ingroups. Although Jews may protest against ethnic humor derogatory of them, "they may secretly take pleasure in the fact that their group is vital enough to stimulate such [ethnic humor] traditions" (Dundes 1971:202). A similar view has been expressed by Morrison (1972), who studied the Bania caste in India. Members of this caste are primarily businessmen and are stereotypically viewed as shrewd, tight with their money, and materialistic. They are ridiculed for these traits, which are assumed to be negative. The caste members themselves, however, consider the traits positive and are proud to be the targets of the humor. Researchers who prefer particularistic explanations, then, appear to propose that contextual factors and psychological functions of ethnic humor are interdependent (Brandes 1980; Kravitz 1977). On the other hand, investigators who provide universalistic explanations seem to accept the view that certain emotions, feelings, and attitudes are primordial and find their outlet in ethnic humor. These perspectives combined may more realistically explain the occurrence of ethnic humor rather than the universalistic explanations do.

Intragroup control and intergroup conflict have been frquently mentioned as important sociological functions of ethnic humor (Barron 1950; Burma 1946; Obrdlik 1942; Stephenson 1950–51). Ethnic humor is presumed to have the function of intragroup social control when it directly or indirectly expresses approval of a group's sociocultural characteristics, encourages strong ethnic identity and positive self-image for group members, and disapproves by ridicule individuals who do not conform to existing cultural norms or who wish to hide or deny their ethnic identity for personal gains. Ethnic humor can be said to have this function also when it emphasizes that ethnic identity is permanent, is an integral part of an individual's personality, and cannot voluntarily be discarded. Many Jewish jokes display this viewpoint. The message is that, despite a change of name and concealment of background, a Jew is often identifiable because of certain behavior, a preference for certain foods, or speech habits.

In an ethnically pluralistic society, ethnic humor is more likely to be present among minority or subordinate groups, because of their need for social cohesion, than among majority or dominant groups who do not face the dilemma of choosing between acculturation and the maintenance of distinct ethnic identity. Not all ethnic humor, however, can be said to perform the function of social control. While many jokes display a positive attitude toward the retention of ethnic identity and cultural pride, others can also be found in which assimilation is emphasized or an ambivalent attitude is expressed toward the processes of assimilation and the maintenance of ethnic identity. Both textual and contextual factors must therefore be taken into account to determine whether or not specific examples of ethnic humor act to control society and whether or not such humor is used widely among the members of minority or subordinate groups. Social control is the function not only of

143

ethnic humor but also of other types of humor, as the discussions in many other chapters indicate. Humor in a religious context is used for the same purpose as children's humor, in which socialization is emphasized. Humor that makes fun of any socially inappropriate behavior can be said to promote social control because it emphasizes social conformity.

Ethnic humor is said to express intergroup conflict when it emphasizes disparagement of ethnic groups "to strengthen the morale of those who use it and to undermine the morale of those at whom it is aimed" (Stephenson 1950–51:569). Although this function of ethnic humor has been discussed in the literature primarily in the context of interracial relationships in the United States, especially between whites and blacks (Barron 1950; Burma 1946; Rinder 1965), it is not restricted to this situation alone. Ethnic or any other type of humor that emphasizes intergroup social and economic differences, the ensuing inequality, and the differential status of occupational and other social groups may be said to express conflict. In addition the conflict function can be related to the widespread existence of ethnocentrism. Any group may use ethnic humor as a device to malign, downgrade, and ridicule other group(s), thereby gaining ascendancy or advantage over them in its own eyes. Such perception of self-superiority on the part of a group need not even be supported by empirical evidence.

According to Stephenson (1950–51:569), irony, satire, sarcasm, caricature, parody, and burlesque serve to express the conflict. Humor is a most suitable medium because it "may conceal malice and allow expression of aggression without the consequence of other overt behavior" (p. 569). If undermining the morale of groups by means of humor is just as important an aspect as strengthening the morale of the people who use such humor, then direct contact and actual social interaction between ethnic or other types of groups are necessary prerequisites. This requirement has not, however, been mentioned in the discussions of the conflict function because of its conceptualization in the context of *actual* intergroup interaction in the United States (Barron 1950; Burma 1946; Rinder 1965). It has also been argued (Birnbaum 1971; Dundes 1975), however, that direct interaction between groups is not necessary if the principal motivation is merely self-superiority and the reinforcement of ethnocentrism and self-morale. The issue of the need for direct contact arises primarily because Stephenson (1950–51) and other researchers have emphasized both strengthening the self-image of ingroups and disparaging the morale of outgroups in their elaboration of the concept of conflict. In order for ethnic humor to express conflict, groups must compete with each other through humor, since one-upmanship can result only from such interaction.

Some general comments about functional theories of ethnic humor are in order at this stage. First, psychological functional theories rely on unconscious motivation. While they intuitively appear to be viable, they are speculative unless they are supported by empirical research. Little empirical work has been undertaken, however. Second, different psychological functions of ethnic humor are associated with different types of ethnic groups. Contextual factors therefore need to be taken into account to determine what psychological functions specific types of humor serve for particular kinds of ethnic groups. Third, a particular ethnic joke may serve several functions. It is therefore difficult to determine which function is primary. In other words, the relative importance of different psychological and sociological functions cannot be measured. Rather they seem to be presented as a group. Fourth, psychological and sociological functions of ethnic humor relevant to a particular ethnic group may change over a period of time if its social position vis-à-vis other groups changes. Fifth, both psychological and sociological functions are presented with the assumption that ethnic groups are homogeneous. Little attention is paid to intragroup differences, individuality, or subdivisions within them except in a couple of studies. It is important to emphasize that psychological functions are not equally operative for all individuals in a group. Sixth, in the discussion of functions of ethnic humor, groups are reified and treated as concrete wholes rather than as abstractions. While individuals tend to see groups in this way, researchers need to be aware of the various levels of abstraction and of the conceptualizations involved in any analytical discussions of the functions of ethnic humor. Finally, people who propose many theories of ethnic humor often ignore the fact that humor in general serves the purpose of entertainment and pleasure. Enjoyment of any humor, including ethnic humor, does not necessarily make individuals aggressive or hostile. Rather, a make-believe framework or state of mind is developed temporarily for sheer pleasure and is discarded when engagement in humorous exchange is over.

Occasionally, abstractions in analysis lead to the discussion of analytical units in isolation. If a functional approach is to be used in analyses of ethnic humor, the structural aspects of group dynamics need to be emphasized, especially the nature of relations among members within a group, relations among groups within a society, and relations of societies in the context of world population. Discussion of the functions of ethnic humor may take on different perspectives, depending on the level at which humor occurs.

ANTHROPOLOGICAL CONTRIBUTIONS TO RESEARCH

Occasional references to cultural stereotypes of foreigners are found in ethnographic and theoretical studies by anthropologists. As we have seen, anthropologists have described in humorous fashion having been the targets of practical jokes and ridicule by the people they have studied (Chagnon 1968; Fernea 1965/1969; Lee 1969). Such treatment of anthropologists can be attributed to ethnocentrism and to the universal inclination to make fun of foreigners, especially when they are ignorant of the culturally appropriate behavioral norms of a society in which they find themselves temporarily. Anthropologists have otherwise generally ignored the topic of ethnic humor unless they specialized in folklore. The absence of research on the topic was recognized only in an occasional comment (Beidelman 1964). Increasing attention is being given to this subject, however, as indicated by some recent studies that I discussed earlier. The absence of a systematic study of ethnic humor by anthropologists in the past can be traced to the early disciplinary orientation. Anthropologists concentrated on describing and analyzing preliterate, highly homogeneous, small-scale societies that lacked extensive contact with many outside groups. Studies of culture contact and acculturation received their impetus much later in anthropology (Beals 1953:621–25).

Descriptive-analytical studies of ethnic humor, both exclusively and as part of standard ethnographies of cultures in all areas of the world, represent a first step in any future anthropological research on ethnic humor. In addition anthropologists should search for the likely existence of ethnic humor in the emerging complex societies of new nation-states in Asia and Africa, because they have already started studying urban communities using ethnographic methods. The end of colonialism and the emergence of new nation-states accelerated the sociocultural change that had begun during the colonial era. Such change has particularly affected many preliterate small-scale societies as they have become parts of national polities and economies. Societies that were formerly hostile to one another are now pacified and encompassed by superordinate authorities. Anthropologists have already turned their attention to the process of incorporation, which is often accompanied by growing urbanization and industrialization and the emergence of multiethnic urban societies (Cohen and Middleton 1970; Fallers 1974; Geertz 1963). In this development of an urban milieu, ethnic groups often become specialized in particular institutionalized roles—as factory workers, merchants, bureaucrats, technicians, skilled laborers, or domestic servants—and develop specific modes of interaction (LeVine and Campbell 1972:157). Growing contact among ethnic groups and role specialization thus leads to the development of stereotypes that, as we have seen throughout this chapter, form the bases of ethnic humor. Some studies (Epstein 1959/1968; Handelman and Kapferer 1972) already indicate that ethnic humor may be developing in such emerging multiethnic urban communities in Asia and Africa.

The study of ethnic humor can be undertaken by anthropologists also as a part of the cooperative cross-cultural research on ethnocentrism proposed by LeVine and Campbell (1972), who suggested in their proposal the "topical areas and interview questions for ethnographic data collection on interethnic behavior, attitudes, and hypothetical correlates of such behavior and attitudes" (p. v). They also developed a systematic inventory of propositions about ethnocentrism. In their original list of attitudes and behaviors toward the outgroup that formed part of the ethnocentrism syndrome, LeVine and Campbell did not include ethnic humor. Their fieldwork procedure guide for the study of ethnocentrism (1972:251–96),however, includes extensive instructions for the interviewing of native informants. While collecting data concerning "imagery of the outgroup" anthropologists can easily gather samples of ethnic humor. Even if the investigator does not wish to be very specific, the field guide of LeVine and Campbell provides a general framework for the gathering of ethnic humor data in support of the many propositions that these authors have put forward concerning the nature of ethnocentrism.

THEORETICAL PROPOSITIONS

The following theoretical propositions follow from the discussion of ethnic humor in this chapter.

Certain pan-human primordial emotions and attitudes, such as ethnocentrism, ingroup adulation, outgroup resentment, prejudice, and intolerance of the life-styles of others, constitute a broad base for the development and popularity of ethnic humor.

Ethnic humor tends to reflect negative attitudes toward certain sociocultural traits, such as excessive sexuality, uncleanliness, and gluttony, which are projected onto other groups in order to make them the butt of such humor.

Stereotypes constitute a significant basis for ethnic humor because they provide ready-made and popular conceptualizations of groups intended to be targets.

Overgeneralization is a characteristic feature of ethnic humor whereby groups are seen as totally homogeneous and intracultural variation is ignored.

Textual factors are essential for defining the domain of ethnic humor, while contextual factors are necessary for establishing its specific categories, types, forms, and functions.

Ethnic humor is less likely to occur in highly homogeneous, small-scale societies than in heterogeneous, large-scale, and complex ones.

Major historical events such as war, migration, and social or religious movements can modify ethnic groups' perceptions of each other, thus changing the stereotypes and the ethnic humor based on these stereotypes.

Negative attitudes toward ethnic humor in a society may prevent its occurrence in the public domain, though it may occur in social interaction in the private domain.

In social interactions involving individuals of two or more ethnic groups, people with strong group loyalty usually respond to ethnic humor disparaging to their group by retaliating in similar fashion. Such a strategy may lead to competition and one-upmanship in the use of mutually disparaging ethnic humor.

PART II

CULTURAL EXPRESSIONS
OF HUMOR

5

Humor in Religion

Few aspects of human behavior have been studied as extensively as religion. Religion seems highly influential in shaping cultural values and in molding and maintaining social organization in human societies everywhere. It is a ubiquitous form of human behavior and is reflected in culturally complex elaborations. Religion resembles humor and language in being omnipresent, pervasive, and yet unobtrusive at the level of individual consciousness in the way in which it affects the rest of human behavior. Anthropological studies show that humor has been intimately connected with religion in many cultures. The concept of religion used in this chapter follows its broad-based interpretation in anthropological research (Malefijt 1968b; A. F. C. Wallace 1966), including the major components briefly described below.

Conceptualization. A primary concept of religion is that of the supernatural, which may include beings, objects, and spirits—in short, all metaphysical forces over which human beings exert little or no control. In addition, religion includes notions of the universe and incorporates ideas of morality and ethics that lead to distinctions between good and evil, benevolent and malevolent, and sacred and profane. These conceptualizations are closely interrelated and structurally interdependent.

Behavior. Any behavior that attempts to control or appease supernatural forces so as to affect human life positively from birth through death and beyond is considered religious. Such behavior is generally institutionalized and includes prayers, rituals, and rites. The primary purpose of such behavior is the well-being of a society and of individuals, from both the materialistic and the spiritualistic perspectives.

151

Actors and institutions. Certain individuals and institutions are primarily responsible for the propagation and sustenance of religious systems. Such individuals may claim to have special powers, enabling them to play a vital role in practicing and directing religious behavior of members of a culture and to act as links between them and the supernatural forces in the universe. Priests, shamans, saints, ritual clowns, and other religious leaders constitute a special group that develops religious instructions through customs, ceremonies, and rituals. I use the term "institution" to mean organized activity: it is patterned, recurrent, and involves aggregates of people.

Texts. Scriptures, mythologies, and other oral and/or written accumulated bodies of knowledge that explain the origin and the nature of the universe constitute religious texts. They also explain acts of creation and destruction of organisms, objects, and the life of human beings. Such a body of knowledge may also expound on the socially acquired moral and ethical codes and on their justification. All religions in the world have such accumulated knowledge.

After the joking relationship, humor in religion has received the most extensive attention from anthropologists. Clowning and other comical performances have been reported as part of religious ceremonies in ethnographic accounts of cultures from various parts of the world. Both ethnographic and ethnological studies of humor in religion exist, concentrating on the American Indians, and date from the last quarter of the nineteenth century to the present.[1] The primary reason for the existence of such extensive anthropological materials may be that humor has been a major feature of both rituals and mythologies of American Indian religions.

In their ethnographic and theoretical studies of African societies, British social anthropologists noted what they considered to be unusual acts that formed part of African religions. Rituals with clowning and other incongruous acts in North India and Sri Lanka have also been described. Rites involving comical and amusing acts as part of the popular Christian rituals in Europe during the medieval period have been analyzed, and accounts of such activities in some parts of Western Europe even in modern time are available. Humorous aspects of rituals have also been explored from a cross-cultural perspective.[2] The humorous and incongruous acts and the rites and rituals of which they are part have been labeled "Rites of Reversal" (Norbeck 1974), "Rituals of Conflict" (Norbeck 1963), "Rituals of Rebellion" (Gluckman 1963), "Institutionalized Licence" (Van den Berghe 1963), and "Licenced Rebellion" (D. B. Miller

1973). These labels suggest that one reason for the anthropological interest in the humorous aspects of religion in preliterate societies may have been the "exotic" nature of the rites, since they often involved scatological and sexual acts that appeared to be a strange combination of the "sacred" and the "profane" to the Western mind.

Interest in humor in religion from the perspective of play has also been growing. I discussed in an earlier chapter the complexity of the concept of play, the broad domain it covers, and the extensive research into its relevance for human existence. Because play has been viewed as the opposite of work, acts that seem antithetical to the seriousness and sacredness of religious rituals have been interpreted as playful acts contrasting with and reemphasizing symbolically the important ethical values of religion. The concept of play in this context includes sports and other games occurring at ceremonial occasions in many preliterate societies. Because play and humor have a close but complex interconnection, interest in "rites of reversal" within the framework of play has also been beneficial to studies of humor in religion. The notion that even the supernatural elements engage in play affecting the universe and human destiny has been significant in Hinduism and other religions.

In analyzing humor in religion, I shall focus on discerning its general attributes and the nature of its linkages to the institution of religion with respect to social-structural factors, behavioral patterns, and ideologies and values in a cross-cultural perspective. My objective is to formulate some hypotheses based on analyses of the interconnections between humor and religion. I shall also briefly evaluate theories of humor in religion. The dichotomy between religious behavior and the religious conceptual system is crucial to my overall discussion; religious behavior includes rituals and their characteristics, while the conceptual system subsumes mythologies and other religious texts. In this chapter I shall discuss only ritual humor. Humor in mythology and folklore, espectially the widespread trickster theme, will be analyzed in a later chapter.

Ceremonial Bases of Humor

Rituals, rites, and ceremonials are conventional activities involving interaction with supernatural forces. Ceremonies constitute ways of appeasing nature and of coming to terms with it for the continued well-being of individuals and social groups. Anthropologists generally classify such activities into two broad categories: calendrical rituals and life cycle rituals.

Calendrical rituals are associated with seasonal changes, especially the transition from a winter to a summer solstice or the start and completion of agricultural cycles. Depending on geographical location and climate, a particular season can be a time for much religious activity. Calendrical rituals also include other important events, such as birth and death anniversaries of mythical heroes, saints, and saviors. Such ceremonial occasions seem to occur more frequently in societies that have well-established scriptures, which usually indicate important events in the life of prophets and other mythical and epic heroes.

Life cycle rituals, commonly known as "rites of passage" (Van Gennep 1909/1960), are religious activities associated with important events in the human life cycle—birth, puberty, entry into adulthood, marriage, pregnancy, childbirth, old age, and finally death. Such rituals signify the transition from one life stage to another and the accompanying change in social status. They are important because of the widespread belief that individuals who are in a transitional or liminal stage, that is, in between clearly identified life stages, are likely to be more affected by supernatural spirits and thus need to be protected. Rites of passage acquire significance also because certain rights and privileges publicly accrue to individuals in specific life states. Initiation rites in many societies, for example, mark the transition to manhood, and the new status permits young men to participate in activities from which they were formerly excluded.

Although calendrical rituals are generally more group oriented than rites of passage, both can and do involve group participation. Initiation and puberty rites in many African societies, for instance, involve large-scale group activities when they are performed for several individuals simultaneously. Religious ceremonies serve as occasions for changes of pace and for change of routine. They provide diversions from work, opportunities for entertainment and fun, a change in diet, and a relaxation of social norms. Rituals, then, signify the importance of religion to members of a culture, mark important social and calendrical occasions, and note the ensuing special status accorded to some individuals. Dramatization is the most effective and significant technique used within the framework of rituals. It takes many forms. Its most essential ingredients are action, play, cultural symbols, masks, costumes, tools

154

and other paraphernalia, and special means of communication. Drama is both entertaining and educational. Humor plays a significant role in dramatization and is often the primary mode of entertainment, especially in preliterate societies.

RITUAL HUMOR: GENERAL ATTRIBUTES
AND TECHNIQUES USED

Numerous ethnographic accounts of rituals in different cultures suggest that the following properties are typical of ritual humor: an absence of social control; behavior contrary to established cultural norms; extensive sexual and scatological elements; a burlesque of rituals, people in authority, and foreigners; and an appearance of disorder and chaos.

The Suspension of Social Control

Much ritual humor appears to be rooted in the suspension of social control over verbal and nonverbal behavior and appearance. Individuals who engage in ritual humor have considerable freedom to depart from conventional behavior and to parody activities that are strongly disapproved in normal everyday social interaction or are even taboo. The removal of social control during rituals results in both unstructured and structured humor stimuli. The unstructured nature of humor is evident in the spontaneous and often unpredictable behavior of entertainers, who may engage in whatever suits their fancy, impulsively switching from one activity to another. They chase spectators, play practical jokes on members of the audience and on each other, engage in banter and horseplay, simulate sexual behavior, drink and eat all kinds of nonedible objects, wear absurd-looking costumes or no clothes at all, jump, dance, exaggeratedly imitate others, perform numerous types of antics, and generally frolic.

On the other hand, behavior as a part of ritual humor can be considered structured in the sense that it may be the exact reverse of behavior commensurate with social roles and customs. Alternatively, humor creation may be highly routinized in that the same stimuli may be used regularly year after year, and actions and their sequences, costumes, and props may become standardized. The same skits and short dramas may be presented routinely, with the same individuals playing the same roles. Although the dichotomy between the structured and the unstructured development of ritual humor is theoretically relevant, the two aspects are not totally separate in reality. Even when behavior is highly conventionalized, individual innovation often occurs. There is much improvisation and variation among individual entertainers, who display fervor and originality in humor.

Contrary Behavior

The reversal of established or common behavioral patterns associated with sex, social roles, and social status in characteristic of ritual humor. In every society people essentially follow the established cultural ways of eating, dressing, sleeping, playing, talking, and carrying out other routine tasks. Interpersonal interaction in social situations is also governed by cultural norms, as is behavior appropriate to specific roles. During rituals humorists often do the opposite. Anthropological literature commonly refers to such conduct as contrary behavior, inverse behavior, or reversal. Reversal occurs not only in behavior but also in physical appearances and in other aspects. Contrary behavior can occur collectively or individually. Ethnographic data indicate that such behavior is manifested primarily in three ways: by sexual inversion, by status inversion, and by routine behavioral inversion.

Transvestism is one of the most common modes of sexual inversion within ceremonial contexts. One sex simulates not only the appearance but also the overall behavioral patterns of members of the other sex and is achieved by the use of clothing, ornaments, body decoration, and even artificial sexual organs. Body motions as well as stylistic acts characteristic of the sexes are imitated. Much humor associated with ritual transvestism is generated by the incongruity between physical features and costumes characteristic of one sex and exaggeration of behavior associated with the other. Such transvestism is widespread in African societies during initiation ceremonies for boys and girls. Among the Masai of Central Africa, for example, young men wear the dress of married women during periods of recovery from circumcision (Huntingford 1953:116). Among the Nupe of Nigeria, transvestite boys comically imitate the walk, gestures, and manners of dancing women (Nadel 1954:82, 218).[3] The inversion of sex roles also occurs in the context of other rituals and ceremonials. In the Zinacantecan communities of Highland Chiapas in Mexico, men masquerade as grandmothers

156

during the Christmas and New Year festivals, wearing outfits normally worn by women, but behave like men and "express most dramatically how incongruous and inappropriate masculine behavior is for those who wear women's clothing" (Bricker 1973:15). Feminine conduct seems to be a common theme of clowns in spiritual and seasonal rituals among many American Indian tribes (Parsons and Beals 1934; Steward 1931).

The inversion of social status in manifested by the ridicule of people in authority. In everyday social interaction, persons of high status have power and authority. This pattern is reversed during ceremonies. Individuals with status often become the butt of caricature, pantomine, parody, and burlesque and are ridiculed especially if they have overused their authority and power. Such spoofs are often carried out by people with low social status and without authority and power. At the other extreme are people of high social status who behave in a manner totally incongruent with their position by acting like common people. Both, then, manifest status inversion. During the potlatch ceremonies among the Kwakiutl Indians, skits are presented in which the host and his family are made to look foolish for the amusement of participants, and this is done with the host family's full participation (Codere 1956:339); the family just demonstrated high status by giving the potlatch. During the spring festival of *Holi* in North India, women of low castes chase and pretend to beat up elderly Brahmin men, especially those who are otherwise considered to be village leaders. Young men shout obscenities at old men and on occasion may make them the victims of practical jokes. The elders are not supposed to retaliate but are merely expected to protect themselves by running away or by taking shelter (Marriott 1966/1968; D. B. Miller 1973).

Contrary behavior not related to social status and sex roles also occurs as part of rituals. Such behavior is merely the reverse of everyday routine acts of speaking, walking, sitting, and so forth. Among the American Indians of the plains and southwestern United States, for instance, clowns speak in terms that are contrary to their actual meaning. The Arapaho clowns pretend not to notice carrying a heavy load but groan under the weight of a light object (Kroeber 1902–1907:192, as quoted in Makarius 1970:63).[4]

Sexual and Scatological Elements

Ritual humor is characterized by verbal and nonverbal activities of a sexual and scatological nature, perhaps because of the absence of social control. Obscene singing by participants and verbal re-partee among clowns or between clowns and the audience with references to sexual organs and activities often form part of the ceremonials. Ba-Thonga men, for example, sing obscene songs and insult women, who retaliate by uttering obscenities at the men's expense during the selection of a new site for a village (Evans-Pritchard 1929). During the Christmas Day celebration among the Abron of Ivory Coast, male performers insult the crowd by uttering obscenities, which are greeted with much laughter (Alland 1975:138). Obscene banter and joke telling occur during the carnival in the regions of Rhineland and Bavaria in Germany (Van den Berghe 1963).[5]

Nonverbal obscene and scatological behavior as part of ritual humor is also widespread. Ritual clowns among the Hopi, Zuni, Arapaho, and Mayo Indians wear large artificial penes made of wooden sticks or knives (Crumrine 1969:7; Steward 1931:193). A lump of wood is bound to a boy's penis during the initiation ceremony among the A-Kamba in Africa and "in this condition he marches amid roars of laughter" (Evans-Pritchard 1929:318).[6] Obscene horseplay, the touching and grabbing of sexual organs, the chasing of women and young girls, and pretended phallic advances toward them are common practices on the part of clowns at rituals among the Yakut, Yuki, Ponca, and other American Indian tribes. Simulated sexual intercourse with each other or suggestive play with an artificial phallus and simulated masturbation are also part of ritual obscenity among these clowns.[7]

The scatological aspects of ritual humor are just as varied. Ritual clowns of the Pueblo Indians "simulated eating and drinking the excreta they would pretend to catch in their wooden machete from the body of passing burro or horse or man or woman, even of one kneeling in prayer" (Parsons and Beals 1934:491). The drenching of other clowns or even spectators with urine or with urine mixed with feces or mud is widespread in ritual humor recorded among American Indians and villagers in North India. Simulated defecation is a common scatological act of clowns and occurs in various contexts.[8]

Burlesque

Humor development within the context of rituals also draws on caricature, burlesque, and the parody of social institutions, of the ritual themselves, and of foreigners and authority figures. This

158

practice seems quite widespread, as the following examples illustrate. There is much cross-cultural variation, however. Humor development of this kind may be carried out individually by a person of either sex, regardless of age or social status, or collectively by a whole group. The social status of people who burlesque the various targets may have significance in some societies and not in others. On the other hand, among many American Indian tribes, such acts may be carried out only by ritual clowns. The question of the performer's identity will be discussed later in this chapter.

Occasionally it is difficult to identify the target of burlesque during the rituals. The reason is that the object of ridicule depends on the focus within the context of rituals, which may shift periodically. Furthermore, the burlesque of the ritual itself cannot be considered apart from the identity of the performers; because the performers of rituals may themselves be persons of authority, humor of this kind caricatures not only the rituals per se but also the authority figures. Sometimes nonperformers of social prominence are ridiculed, and at other times outsiders become the target. The main point, however, is that rituals provide immunity to individuals who want to ridicule persons in authority within their own society.

Among the Yaqui Indians in Arizona, the traditional clowns known as *pascolas* and *fariseos* burlesque serious things in public ceremonies. While a marriage ceremony is being solemnly affirmed, the pascolas just a few feet away carry out an absurd burlesque of it that is charged with obscenity. During the Easter ritual, the masked pascolas leap and shiver and scrape imaginary filth from their legs whenever the name of Mary or God is mentioned. The clowns interfere with the members of the ceremonial societies, dangling toy monkeys before their faces in the middle of their prayers and sacred chants (Spicer 1940). Zinacantecan ritual clowns mock ceremonies, ritual curing prayers, and dances by introducing sexual and obscene connotations (Bricker 1973:31, 37). They also mock prayers of religious officials by exaggerated actions, crossing themselves with their rattles and praying loudly and ludicrously. The ritual clowns disguised as grandfathers exchange stick horses, mimicking the exchange of ceremonial flags between religious officials.

Among the Kiwai Papuans, characters called Imigi perform clowning acts during the great secret ceremony associated with the cult of the dead. The Imigi make obscene gestures at women, run helter-skelter, and also pretend to attack the spirits. All of this activity is considered very amusing by the audience (Landtman

1927:394, as quoted in Charles 1945:28). Women conduct play pot-latching among the Kwakiutl Indians of the northwest coast, during which ridiculously small and valueless objects are distributed and participants are given funny names. Objects that are given away are often not owned by the donors. The customary giving of speeches is lampooned by the making of ridiculous claims. In general, then, play potlatches mock the whole potlatch ritual (Codere 1956).[9]

Such mockery of the sacred elements and rituals is not of recent origin. During the holiday known as the "Feast of Fools," which flourished in parts of Europe during the medieval period, serious-minded commoners and priests who were ordinarily pious painted their faces, "strutted about in the robes of their superiors," and in general "mocked the stately rituals of the church and court" (Cox 1969/1972:1). Sometimes an ass was introduced into church during this festival while the Prose of the Ass was chanted. On such occasions a solemn mass was punctuated with brays and howls. In general, the composition of satirical verse, the performance of topical plays, and the preaching of burlesque sermons formed an important part of the Feast of Fools activities (Welsford 1935:200–203). The ceremony was condemned and criticized by the higher officials of the church. Nonetheless, it survived until the sixteenth century and gradually died out during the Reformation and Counter Reformation.

The burlesquing of foreigners appears to be a major stimulus of ritual humor, especially among American Indians. Steward (1931:197) described it as one of the major themes of humor and provided many examples from previous ethnographic accounts of rituals among the Hopi and other tribes of the southwestern United States and among the Kwakiutl, Winnebago, and Iroquois. During the rituals, the appearance, costumes, and customs of the white man were spoofed. Occasionally, individual tribes caricatured other neighboring Indian tribes in similar fashion; the Yoruk and Maidu Indians seem to do so. Such humor probably helped develop community solidarity, because the whole community could empathize with the performer. No community member was the butt, and the caricaturing helped express collective fear, envy, contempt, or feeling of superiority with respect to the outsiders.

Disorder and Chaos

Although the burlesque of rituals, authority figures, and foreigners is a major aspect of ritual humor, other ceremonial activities, such as dancing, food preparation, sports and games, and processions are also imitated. Such imitations, however, must be out of tune with the activities being burlesqued before humor can develop. When clowns in American Indian rituals imitate dancers, for example, they are always one step behind and pretend to miss the rhythm. In sports and games, the clowns fumble and break the rules. While the ritual ceremonies are going on, they dart in and out of processions, interrupt verbal incantations with their loud remarks and comments, perform all sorts of disruptive antics, and generally try to undermine any organized activity. In other words, the creation of disorder in the middle of order to give the appearance of incongruity is a chief goal of people who develop ritual humor.

Verbal obscenities, insults, ridicule, practical jokes, the exaggerated imitation of events, actions, and persons, and uninhibited behavior culminating in simulation of sexual and scatological acts appear to be the primary techniques used in ritual humor. Audio and visual aids and modalities are equally important in humor development because of the emphasis on imitating appearance and nonverbal behavior in addition to verbal communication. Costumes, masks, and other paraphernalia are generally used. The ethnographic accounts suggest that, on the whole, visual and action-oriented stimuli are just as important as verbal in ritual humor.

RITUAL HUMORISTS: IDENTITY AND SOCIAL STATUS

There is much cross-cultural variation regarding the choice of ritual humorists on the basis of such factors as their position within the context of ceremonials and their overall social status in the society at large. Cultures range from those in which any person of whatever social background and status can participate in humor-generating activities to those in which only a specially designated and socially high-ranking group of individuals can do so. Similarly, a single individual, or one or more groups of persons each identified on the basis of some specific sociocultural attributes, may be humorists. In some cultures, such groups may consists of specialists whose primary role is humor development, and they may act in an organized manner. In other cultures, engaging in humor may be a mass activity, so that a "free-for-all" situation exists. A major reason for the cross-cultural differences in the choice of ritual humorists is that such selection is structurally interconnected with the rest of the cultural system. It depends on and is affected by such sociocultural factors as the type of ritual involved and its significance for participants and for the community at large, the fundamental religious ideology underlying the ritual(s), the nature of social organization, ecological factors, and attitudes toward ritual humor in terms of the techniques used and the humor's effects.

The dichotomy between calendrical rituals and rites of passage is significant in determining who will engage in humor. It appears that, in rituals of the latter type, humor-generating activities are generally undertaken by relatives or friends of the individuals going through the ritual or by people who are connected with the ceremony itself in some way. Some examples follow. During funeral rites in such East African tribes as the Plateau Tonga, Kaguru, Luguru and others, only the funeral partner who is also the joking partner of the deceased in the utani relationship described in Chapter 1 is supposed to joke and ridicule the deceased. Such a funeral relationship may exist either with one or more members of a clan that has the utani relationship with the deceased's clan (Beidelman 1966; Christensen 1963; Colson 1953:53–54). During the final phase of Tiwi funeral rites in Australia attended by the relatives of the deceased and members of other clans, mock fighting between all actual and potential spouses takes place. There is a great deal of shouting, with squeals of laughter, because tickling is also part of the fighting activity (Goodale 1971:287–88).[10]

During wedding ceremonies in some cultures, women of either the bride's or the groom's side have the prerogative to engage in humor, and they do so mostly by burlesquing sexual activity, by singing obscene songs that may make fun of the bridegroom, or by parodying local social events. Such is the case in North India (E. O. Henry 1975; Jacobson 1977) and among the Magars in Nepal (Hitchcock 1966) and the Gimi of New Guinea (Gillison 1977). In many African tribes mock battles take place between members of the bride's kinsmen and those of the bridegroom (Norbeck 1963:1264). Puberty rites of boys and girls are also occasions for specific groups or individuals to engage in humor. Among the Gusii of East Africa, only mothers and other female relatives perform obscene and lewd acting and dancing, using artificial phalli during the girls' puberty rites (B. B. Whiting 1963:189). On the other hand, boys put on women's clothes and burlesque women's behavior during their initiation ceremonies in some African tribes (Norbeck 1963:1257–58).

Sometimes beliefs concerning life seem to influence the choice of the person who will engage in humor. In some African societies, calendrical rites at the start of the agricultural cycle involve licentious behavior, obscene joking, and nude dancing by women. The same thing occurs when a new site for a village is to be chosen. Perhaps women perform these activities because of their association with fertility, because the goal is a bountiful harvest or rapid growth of a new village. Among the American Indian tribes of the Southwest, however, only male sacred clowns are associated with fertility rites (Steward 1931:199).

Social status and specific roles appear to determine which individuals will develop humor and which will be the target in the context of some ritual. It appears that in certain rituals the normally subordinate segments of society ignore behavioral constraints and take the lead in humor development. Generally, women constitute such a group in patrilineal societies; young men and women in societies with a gerontocracy; and several groups with menial occupations and low socioeconomic status in highly stratified societies. These groups ignore societal norms and poke fun at their superiors during some rituals, and hence these are rites of reversal.[11] Membership in secret societies, fraternities, or similar organizations often brings with it the privilege of humor development at specific rituals, as has been recorded for many American Indian tribes. Among the Plains Indians, only members of secret societies participate in contrary behavior at rituals that provide many humor stimuli. Among the Yaqui, Hopi, and other Indians of the southwestern United States, there are clown societies, and only members seem to develop humor during rituals.

Perhaps no category of individuals occupies so distinct a position in developing humor among the American Indian tribes of North and Central America as the ceremonial buffoons (Steward 1931), sacred fools (Beck and Walters 1977), sacred clowns (Parsons and Beals 1934), and ritual clowns (Crumrine 1969; Honigmann 1942; Makarius 1970). Although clowning has been noted to occur in many societies (Charles 1945), American Indian ritual clowns and their activities constitute perhaps the most institutionalized development of ritual humor in any culture area of the world. The ritual clowning complex was a highly developed phenomenon among the Indians in much of North and Central America except the east coast (Steward 1931). Much cross-cultural variation concerning the form and substantive aspects of ritual clowning existed in areas where it was well developed, but some generalizations can be made.

Ritual clowns among the American Indians seem to have two major attributes: they belong to specific types of associations, fraternities, secret societies, and cults; and they are associated with various supernatural spirits and special powers. These attributes are reflected in the kind of humor in which ritual clowns engage and in the objects and techniques they use. Among the Yaqui, Hopi, and other southwestern Indians there are phallic clown societies. Ritual clowns belong to medicine societies in some Indian tribes, while in others they are members of military and secret societies or are associated with fertility cults. Clowns among the Zuni, Acoma, Hopi, Navaho, Apache, Iroquois, Cheyenne, Papago, and other Indian tribes are believed to have powers to ensure success in war and hunting. They are also believed able to cure sickness through magical healing (Makarius 1970:47ff.). Among some Indian groups it is believed that ritual clowns practice black magic (Makarius 1970:55).

It should be obvious, then, that ritual clowns occupy a unique position in many American Indian cultures. They are laughed at, but they are also respected. They are loved for the humor they provide but are also feared. People regard them with awe and associate them with supernatural origins and power. They are allowed considerable liberty in their interactions with religious authorities and with other participants in rituals. While the nature and degree of the clowns' distinctness varies across cultures, they generally seem to have a unique identity both in the context of rituals and in society at large. In addition to providing entertainment and humor, they serve other functions that I shall discuss shortly.

THE RELEVANCE OF HUMOR TO RITUALS

Determining the relevance of humor to rituals is a complex task, since relevance may be manifested by the linkages between the two through form, techniques, content, performers, underlying myths, and so on. The type and nature of these linkages as well as the degree of relevance vary cross-culturally. Theoretically, the range of variation may include cultures in which humor is extraneous to rituals and those in which humor cannot be separated at all from rituals formally, conceptually, or in any other way. In reality, ritual humor in most cultures seems to fall somewhere in the middle in the sense that some of it is well integrated into the rituals, while some is marginally linked. For the purposes of my discussion, two types of linkages are considered significant in judging the relevance of humor to rituals: conceptual integration and functional integration.

Conceptual Integration

Humor can be relevant to rituals because of its integration into myths and into the religious ideologies that constitute the bases of rituals. Individuals who engage in humor within the context of rituals often assume an identity with supernatural spirits or mythological characters. In the myths of some American Indian tribes, the spirits and other mythological figures are not only supernatural but antinatural in the sense that their appearance and behavior are contrary to nature and customs (Ray 1945:87). The assumed identity of both supernatural and antinatural spirits allows the humorists to simulate anatomical deformations and extraordinary verbal and nonverbal behaviors, including contrary behavior. Such appearances and behavior appear to be the major humor stimuli during rituals. During the winter, guardian spirit dances among many southeastern Plateau Indians such as the Flathead, Spokane, and Kalispel, for example, the ritual involves assumed identification with the bluejay character of mythological times. This identification permits the individuals to appear in unusual costumes and to behave in a contrary fashion. The audience is specifically directed *not* to laugh at the antics (Ray 1945:80), which suggests that they are indeed comic.[12] Among the Plains Cree and Northern Paiute Indians, buffoons imitating antinatural spirits wear costumes that produce the effect of a great hump on the back. Other distorted anatomical features include elongated noses, faces made grotesque with paint, and lumps on the legs and belly (Ray 1945:85, 103, 107). An association of anatomical deformation and antinatural spirits such as monsters also occurs in Balinese puppet theater, where clowns appear with pot bellies, enormous mouths, and very short legs as they amuse the spectators (Charles 1945:27).

The association between supernatural or antinatural elements and mythological characters on the one hand and ritual clowns or buffoons on the other is further reflected in the identification of the American Indian clowns with mythological figures including tricksters, who are discussed in Chapter 7. The ceremonial clowns among the Acoma Indians represent Koshari, the original clown (Stirling 1942:65, as quoted in Makarius 1970:45), or trickster. The clowns among the Iroquois are traditionally related to a legendary hero called False Face. They wear masks with twisted noses symbolic of the contest between False Face and the Great Spirit, during which False Face's nose struck the mountain he was supposed to push (Speck 1949:69–70, as quoted in Makarius 1970:45–46). In several other Indian tribes, either similar associations between clowns and mythological trickster figures occur or the clowns are supposed to have originated from tricksters (Makarius 1970:45–46). The trickster's antics are a part of the mythological oral tradition in many American Indian groups. The buffoons are treated as the trickster's descendants and are obligated to imitate him in their antics.

Although the nature and degree of the clowns' power vary cross-culturally, power in most cases in perceived to derive from the violation of rules and prohibitions. The clowns' magical and healing powers are often attributed to their breach of taboo, and a parallel is found in the case of the mythological trickster figure. Sexual and scatological humor based on sexual, oral, and anal behavior and humor based on ridiculing sacred decrees, mocking religious rituals, and symbolically defiling sacred objects result from the breaking of taboos. The numerous breaches of taboo committed by ritual clowns have been noted in anthropological literature, and Makarius (1970:53) even suggests that violation of taboo is the clowns' raison d'être.

In many instances of the representation of supernatural spirits, the role playing must be comical and witty because the character from mythology is so perceived (Ray 1945:89–90). Among the Dakota Indians the clowns, who are members of the Heyoka society, are assumed to be threatened by thunder and lightning if they do not perform the contrary ceremony. Thus they are clowns "by the direct necessity, by the imperative demands of a vision" (Steward 1931:202). Among some Indian tribes individuals cannot be clowns unless they have had a vision or a dream. Among the Dakota Indians a person can become a ritual clown by having in a dream a vision of the god Iktomi or of one of the beasts associated with him. Iktomi can be considered an ideal representative of the pure trickster (Makarius 1970:45). The clowns among the Arapaho Indians belong to a "Fools' Lodge," the founder of which is Nihaca, the trickster (Makarius 1970:46, n. 2). The clowns among the Plains Indians perform contrary speech and action only as a result of a vision, usually of thunder or lightening. Thus religious sanction is the basis of ritual humor in many American Indian groups.

Humor itself is often ritualized and is thus integrated into the religious system. Among the Dakota Indians, the Heyoka ritual is antinatural, as it is among the Ponca Indians. In other words, antinaturalness is an essential aspect of religious conceptualization as well as of ritual humor. In some American Indian tribes, the ritualization of antinaturalness is highly institutionalized by the establishment of "contrary" societies, whose members regularly engage in antinatural rituals. Such societies exist among the Mandan, Hidatsa, Arapaho, Atsina, and Blackfoot Indians and have been adopted as part of the contrary ceremonies by other Indian tribes such as the Cheyenne (Ray 1945:104). The Cheyenne even developed a cult called the Contraries, while among the Arikari Indians the cult of Foolish People existed. The Mandan and Hidatsa Indians had such names as Crazy Dog or Real Dog for these societies.

The primary activities of the members of such societies are dancing and contrary behavior within the context of rituals. The dancers have considerable freedom and are permitted to engage in all manner of mischief; they act in foolish and extravagant ways that are reflected in contrary actions and speech and in animal imitations, for example, the howling of dogs. Among the Hidatsa, one form of unnatural behavior is the ceremonial practice of randomly embracing women regardless of closeness of kinship. Sacred objects are shown no respect, and proprieties are disregarded. Contrary behavior includes such activities as shooting arrows backward over the shoulder, interpreting instructions in reverse, and use of reverse speech, all of which are humor-generating stimuli. The most antinatural behavior among several tribes includes the trick of withdrawing meat from boiling water as part of the ceremony (Ray 1945:91ff.).

The Functional Relevance of Ritual Humorists

Humor is integrated into the overall structure of rituals in still other ways. Clowns are connected with ceremonies in numerous capacities and assist the organizers in successfully performing them. The degree of the clowns' involvement in rituals and ceremonies in capacities other than as humorists, however, varies across cultures.

As members of various societies, clowns among different American Indian tribes undertake curing, fertility, or military functions (Steward 1931:198). In general, clowns may act as messengers, wood cutters, and water carriers; may urge people to attend church during Lent and Easter ceremonies; may maintain law and order; and may punish antisocial behavior (Bricker 1973; Crumrine 1969; Parsons and Beals 1934:507). Ritual clowns are disciplinarians of children among some tribes and are also used as bogeymen. As if their masks, appearance, and impersonations of supernatural beings were not sufficiently scary, the clowns often threaten to whip the children and frighten them in other ways (Norbeck 1961:309). Ritual clowns also have alternating duties as priests (Crumrine 1969; Makarius 1970), fulfilling many sacred duties and on occasion acting as priests. Among the Zuni Indians, for instance, the Koyemshi, that is, the ritual clowns, perform several rites, especially the rain and fertility ceremonies.

Ritual clowns among some American Indian groups function as medicine men. Since they are presumed to have supernatural powers, they are often credited with healing. Body wastes such as urine and excrement of both humans and animals, or dirty water that the clowns pretend is urine and use in their scatological antics, are presumed to have magical power. These substances are sprinkled on the spectators or are drunk and spat upon individuals (Makarius 1970:47–51; Ray 1945:85). Among some American Indian groups, the ritual clowns rarely do anything except engage in humor and thus are not fully integrated into rituals either conceptually or functionally. Such seems to be the case among the Hopi Indians (Parsons and Beals 1934:494).

RITUAL HUMOR AS PERCEIVED BY THE INDIGENOUS POPULATION

Two issues have not been discussed by anthropologists analyzing ritual humor: first, how to determine whether or not the indigenous participants in and spectators at ceremonials consider the clowns' behavior humorous, and second, what kinds of evidence should be adequate for such a determination. Without some explicit statements regarding these matters, the ethnographers' views regarding the occurrence of ritual humor remain etic, that is, observer oriented and formed from outside the cultural system. In regard to the second issue, another problem arises, namely, the extent of indigenous opinions. When it comes to determining what is humorous, there is much intracultural variation. All generalizations therefore need to be viewed as tendencies rather than as absolute statements. If we keep this caveat in mind, various observations

168

can be considered to provide evidence of the humorousness of clowns' acts; observed evidence would include spectators' frequent laughter at the clowns' behavior, ceremony officials' specific prohibition of laughter (Ray 1945:80; Seligman and Seligman 1950:356; Steward 1931:200), and so on. Occasionally, ethnographers have commented on the negative responses of spectators and participants to clowns' acts (Crumrine 1969:4, 12), in which case the acts constitute ritual humor only from the anthropologists' perspective. Similarly, broad generalizations without adequate evidence need to be treated as anthropologists' own views rather than as factual statements. Norbeck's (1961:207) generalization that ritual reversals among the American Indians are perceived by the people to be funny but that similar behavior in African cultures is not necessarily so, for example, should be considered as his own opinion rather than as a factual generalization.

THEORETICAL CONSIDERATIONS

The widespread occurrence and diversity of ritual humor has led to a plethora of interpretations, theories, and explanations that are psychological, sociological, cyclical, historical, or symbolic in orientation.[13] Among them, psychological and sociological theories seem prominent and have a functional focus. Some explanations are multifarious because the researchers who propose them feel that all aspects of ritual humor cannot be satisfactorily explained within a single theoretical framework. Some of the theories are particularistic, addressing ritual humor within the context of rituals, while others are universal, viewing ritual humor within the framework of presumed universal psychological attributes of humans.

A common thread that runs through psychological theories is the emphasis on conflict resolution and on release from tension. Theories differ, however, regarding the nature of the tension, its causes, and its release. Some theories draw on the Freudian theoretical framework, while others refer to the context of the rituals themselves. Jacob Levine (1961), for instance, claims that tension exists due to intrapsychic struggle between impulse and defense: on the one hand, there are infantile, instinctual impulses of aggression and sexuality in an individual, and on the other, these are inhibited because of the censuring function of the superego, which causes guilt and anxiety leading to tension. Ritual humor makes possible the dissipation or release of such tension. Unfortunately, this explanation can be applied equally well to sexual and aggressive humor in secular social situations, and thus it fails to explain the significance of humor in the context of rituals satisfactorily. The same is true of other theoretical explanations.

Honigmann (1942) and Spicer (1954) also explain the role of ritual humor as the reduction of tension, but they see the occurrence of tension within the context of rituals. Honigmann claims that tension arises from feelings of frustration, powerlessness, and insecurity, which develop because opportunities for understanding the mystical experience of the ritual are lacking. Spicer argues that tension occurs primarily because of the extremely intense and complex interaction during rituals. Both writers see ritual humor as functioning to reduce tension: it produces social release, according to Honigmann, and comic relief, according to Spicer.

Particularistic psychological theories such as Spicer's appear plausible, because the occurrence of ritual humor is explained by the very nature of the rituals themselves. Spicer claims that increasing tension results from the intense and extended ceremonialism and also from the complex and highly charged social interaction. The tension needs to be dissipated for the continuation of the rituals. Spicer's theory seems possible in view of the fact that human beings are rarely, if ever, able to sustain any emotional state, or intense concentration, whether grief, anger, sorrow, mirth, or hilarity, for extended periods of time except when pathological conditions exist. In this context we should recall Darwin's comment (1872/1965:197) that only imbeciles have a perpetual smile on their faces or laugh frequently; most normal individuals smile and laugh only when appropriate stimuli are present. Ritual humor is necessary to allow participants to relieve their intense concentration and seriousness. Accounts of some ceremonies (Gossen 1976; Howard 1962) indicate precisely this transition from seriousness to light moods in ceremonies.

The nature of tension may vary, depending on the rituals involved. Gluckman (1963), for instance, states that, during the boys' circumcision ceremony among the Wiko people in Africa, tension occurs party because aggression and sexual pleasure are banned in the village during the rites and also perhaps because circumcision symbolically signifies the separation of boys from their mothers as they enter the men's world. The tension is released by obscene humor, horseplay, mock fighting, and other similar activities in which adult men and women participate and symbolically display the sexual organs of the opposite sex.

Psychological theories that attempt to explain ritual humor in universalistic terms by alluding to human psychic tendencies emphasize neurosis, repression, and other psychopathological conditions. This is a rather negativistic perspecitve on human societies. In reality a culture is rarely a perfect functioning whole, just as it is rarely, if ever, in total anomie. Furthermore, the "innocent release of aggression" by way of catharsis becomes a catch-all concept for explaining ritual humor, if universalistic psychological theories of aggression dissipation are to be accepted. But such explanations are provided for other types of humor as well, including ethnic humor.

While Honigmann and Levine see the psychological function of ritual clowning as operating at both in individual and the societal levels, other researchers emphasize that it is primarily a "safety valve" mechanism for the whole community, reinforcing the existing social order (Gluckman 1954, 1959; D. B. Miller 1973; Parsons and Beals 1934). The sexual and scatological nature of ritual humor and its emphasis on reversal of everyday social relations and social status are seen as catharses of repressed biological and psychological tendencies in all human beings. Norbeck's (1974:50–54) premise that inverse rituals serve as "a channeling device that both permits and controls" appears similar to the views of other writers though not couched in a psychological framework.

According to one theory (Crumrine 1969), both the conflict and its resolution are executed by ritual clowns. They blur the existing structural distinctions in society and culture, which creates perceptual conflict, leading to heightened participant arousal and focus on resolving the conflict. When the Mayo ritual clowns are baptized and become men, they shed their clowning role. Participants and spectators going through this experience perceive traditional social relations and cultural values in greater depth. Thus clowns ritually mediate between numerous oppositions within the structure of Mayo culture and society. Crumrine calls his theory cultural-cognitive and uses a dialectical approach.

The sociological theories by and large emphasize social criticism and social control as the primary function of ritual humor. They differ, however, regarding the nature of social criticism. Codere (1956), for instance, claims that ritual humor in the play potlatch among the Kwakiutl Indians criticizes the "stuffed rigidities of potlatch" and also the emphasis on rank order and competition that permeates society. Bricker (1973), on the other hand, states that the social criticism of ritual humor is directed toward people who deviate from established sexual and social norms. In her opinion, ritual humor also emphasizes morality and thus also ridicules excessive sexuality. Some theories (Spicer 1954; Steward 1931) see the social function of ritual humor as primarily highlighting key values and conflicts in the sociocultural system and in group activities. Why humor should do so in the ritual context, however, and not in any other social situations remains unexplained. Universal psychological and sociological theories emphasize a functional linkage between ritual humor on the one hand and tension reduction and maintenance of social order on the other. Because statistical relationships for such theories cannot be easily established, they can be evaluated only on the basis on their internal logic and feasibility. One problem is their failure to explain why rituals are selected as the mechanism for catharsis to relieve tension and antisocial feelings. Unless cultures in which ritual humor is said to serve these functions share certain distinguishing traits, such theories are post facto explanations.

According to the cyclical theory proposed by Van den Berghe (1963), societies can be "viewed as going through a normative cycle consisting of a long 'normal' phase and a short 'licentious' phase" (p. 415). The two phases stand "reciprocally in the same antithetical relationship as the norms stressed in each phase" (p. 415).

Some schools of anthropological theory emphasize cultural contact and the subsequent diffusion of cultural traits as the primary reason for cultural and linguistic similarities among different societies (Harris 1968:376ff.). Diffusion is regarded as the principal reason for the existence of ritual humor among many American Indian tribes by writers who propose historical explanations (Bricker 1973:167ff.; Parsons and Beals 1934; Ray 1945). The question of historical origins and diffusion with respect to ritual humor among American Indians is interesting in part because of its occurrence during the Easter ceremonies, which postdate the Spanish influence. Bricker (1973:216–18) believes that the syncretism between the American Indian and Spanish traditions occurred after the Spanish conquest. The Spaniards noted the similarities between their own tradition of humor and that of ritual humor in many areas of Middle America, which was primarily due to the Aztec influence. They therefore encouraged the Indians to incorporate Spanish customs in their social satire. Bricker sees the unity of the tradition of ritual humor as resulting not only from cultural diffusion during the pre-Columbian period but also from contact with Spanish culture.

Researchers who propose historical explanations emphasize that intercultural variation in the ritual clowning complex among the American Indians, and even the Spanish influence, is unevenly reflected in its many aspects. These historical explanations lack answers to such questions as why and how the institution of ritual humor, especially clowning, originated in the first place. It appears from the sources listed in Bricker (1973:191–94) that the Aztec nobles maintained jesters to amuse them and that ritual humor took place during the fiesta in honor of Quetzalcóatl.

Makarius (1970) suggested that mythological tricksters and ritual clowns both essentially express "a general, basic, contradictory human experience that gives rise to dramatic situations" (p. 53). On the one hand, the clowns are humorists and breakers of social and ritual taboos and on the other hand serve as healers and guardians of traditions and ritual sanctity. The contradictory aspect is reflected even in the ambivalent behavior of the spectators, who respond with laughter but at the same time fear the clowns' magical power. Theories of ritual humor that concentrate on clowns and their activities seem to emphasize two sets of factors: the freedom accorded to ritual clowns and the emphasis on taboo breaking, and the so-called anomalous position of ritual clowns due to their roles, which straddle the Durkheimian dichotomy of the Sacred and the Profane. Makarius emphasizes the breaking of taboo as a major factor in her symbolic theory, expressed in terms of "collective social psyche." In explaining the actions of the Koyemshi sacred clowns among the Zuni Indians, she states that "the violation of taboo which they symbolize, namely incest, is that which persistently haunts the mind of the tribal people, giving rise to frantic imaginary elaborations" (1970:58).

Makarius sees the basic contradictory characteristic of ritual clowns as a conflict between the individual and society, because only individuals break taboos, and while such violation is good for the group, the violator is not rewarded but ridiculed. In order for Makarius's theory to apply, clowns have to act individually. She claims (p. 54) that they do indeed do so in many American Indian groups; the clowns give individualistic performances even when they are in group. Many of the ethnographic data, however, indicate that ritual humor is collective activity, a characteristic that separates it from forms occurring on other social occasions. Humorous episodes and acts developed by ritual clowns generally need team effort. Even when ritual clowns are engaged in their own idiosyncratic form of humor, each is performing simultaneously with others who are similarly engaged. Such group participation has several consequences: first, it helps eliminate self-consciousness, which on such occasions is already reduced because of the masks or other costumes; second, it provides mutual reinforcement; and third, it encourages healthy competition that makes the clown innovative and creative in impromptu ways, an aspect that to some extent explains the daredevil activities in which ritual clowns engage in many American Indian groups.

Zucker (1967) combines the symbolic and psychological perspectives in his theory of ritual clowns, calling his approach theological. According to his theory, self-contradiction is the most significant feature of the ritual clown, who expresses the absurdity and paradox of human existence. The clown produces a peculiar mixture of laughter and indignation in the audience. He accepts the "twofold role of breaking all taboos and receiving all the punishment for it" (p. 312). The audience has the opportunity "to experience vicariously the assault on order and to witness simultaneously the reduction to nothingness of the transgressor!"(p. 312).

In general, the following caveats need to be noted with regard to theoretical explanations of ritual humor. First, ritual humor appears by nature diverse, as are the ceremonies in which it occurs. Therefore, unitary theories explaining it beyond the constraints of individual cultures are likely to be low-level abstractions and as a result somewhat trivial. Such theories cannot be viable unless they demonstrate that such humor universally shows features associated with the universally shared features of rituals. In other words, intercultural and intracultural variations need to be taken into account.

Second, theories that explain humor in functional terms need to show its relevance to an integration into rituals. If humor is extraneous to rituals, then little significance can be attached to its occurrence in that context except with respect to its entertainment value. On the other hand, if humor appears to be highly integrated into rituals, then we need to explain why and how it is so integrated. Comparative studies therefore need to be undertaken, first, to determine the degree to which humor is integrated into rituals, using criteria similar to those that I discussed in a previous section, and second, to learn what cultural factors are responsible for it.

174

Third, indigenous explanations for the occurrence of humor should be sought. Although many theories of ritual humor have been proposed by scholars and have been discussed above, none has presented any indigenous views. Such explanations would provide insight into what people think about humor occurring within the context of their religious ceremonies and would suggest how they perceive its relevance to and significance for various other aspects of culture.

Fourth, general theories proposing functional explanations should take into account that humor either may serve several functions or may simply be an epiphenomenon with purely entertainment value.

The existing theories of ritual humor appear to be based on the questionable assumption that ritual humor is qualitatively different from humor in other forms of social interaction. Much ritual humor, however, like other types of humor, appears to be based on incongruity and exaggeration. Thus such humor highlights the existing nature of sociocultural systems because of "association by opposition." It emphasizes reversal of existing social reality or simply its absence. It stresses either reversal or existing structure or total freedom from it. This aspect cannot be cognitively perceived, however, without drawing attention to the existence of both social reality and social structure. In other words, humor is experienced because of an association by opposition with the existing social order, cultural norms, statuses, roles, and so forth. It is also noteworthy that ceremonies, especially in preliterate societies, merely provide a context for the engagement in humor, because on these occasions most members of the community come together. Ceremonies therefore provide a suitable setting for public entertainment by way of humor. Humor may not be an essential ingredient of rituals; they do exist without it in many societies, and even in those societies in which ritual humor occurs, it is not always present.

I would like to suggest that ritual humor per se is not fundamentally different from humor in other social interactions. Rather the rituals provide a special framework intensifying the degree, mode of exaggeration, and incongruity of humor. Rituals enable humorists to behave outrageously and to have immunity from public ridicule and punishment for such behavior. Individuals who engage in humor temporarily transcend their usual social roles and take on another role for which they are not held responsible. Rituals thus permit transformation of personalities, either individually or collectively and in direct or indirect ways. The direct ways result in extreme behavior and breach of etiquette, while the indirect ways result in freedom to express mirthful laughter at acts ordinarily considered so outrageous as to arouse shame and anxiety.

The discussion so far permits us to formulate the following theoretical propositions concerning ritual humor.

The degree to which humor is integrated in rituals seems to vary not only across cultures but from ritual to ritual within individual cultures.

Social relationships and membership in specific groups are important criteria in the selection of ritual humorists. Thus at rites of passage, relatives and close friends of individuals going through the rituals engage in humor. At other types of ceremonies, members of secret societies, cults, or other similar organizations predominate as ritual clowns.

Ritual clowns play an important role in ceremonials because they not only act as humorists but also carry out other important tasks.

The security of the group and of the ritual context enables ritual clowns to engage in all kinds of outrageous and ludicrous acts.

The chief purpose of ritual humor appears to be community entertainment; religious ceremonies are the main events for large group interaction, especially in preliterate societies.

Ritual humor is not qualitatively different from humor in other social interaction. Rather, the rituals provide a special context whereby humorists and participants are both temporarily freed from social sanction for whatever acts they wish to simulate.

6

Humor and Language

In this chapter I shall delineate some similarities in the nature and position of both humor and language within the sociocultural system; describe and analyze humor that uses the structure of language as its basis; and discuss sociolinguistic aspects of humor.

HUMOR AND LANGUAGE COMPARED

It is inconceivable that the human race could exist without either language or humor. Anthropologists and other scholars have defined *Homo sapiens* as a creature with language. "Certainly it is language as much or more than any other human trait that sets us off as unique within the animal kingdom" (Burling 1970:1). The same can be said of humor. Human beings seem to have a mental framework suitable for perceiving experiences both in natural surroundings and in culturally symbolic surroundings for purposes of amusement and fun. "True laughter, like true language, exists only among human beings" (Hertzler 1970:27). Although we may not share Hertzler's rather strong view, given recent work on animal communication (Linden 1981), the fact remains that the faculties of language and humor have advanced in human beings to a degree considerably greater than that found in any other animals.

Both language and humor have universal and culture-specific attributes. The universal attributes are mainly formal in nature, while the culture-specific ones are substantive. It is an accepted premise in modern linguistics that all languages share certain properties, such as productivity, interchangeability, displacement, and arbitrariness in the relation of form and meaning (Hockett 1960;

177

Thorpe 1972). In addition languages display common structural features. All languages, for instance, use vocalic and consonantal sounds that have phonemic status. They use morphemes, which are classified into certain basic classes, such as nouns and verbs. Finally, languages use certain morphological and syntactic processes to juxtapose the various types of units. In short, human languages exhibit a certain degree of structural similarity in having phonological and grammatical units of similar types and in using similar techniques to put them together (Falk 1973:196ff.; J. H. Greenberg 1968; Langacker 1973:239ff.). The number of such units and their substantive nature, however, vary from language to language.

Humor too has both universal and culture-specific attributes. The techniques used in humor are universal, although they may not be as extensively defined as the numerous structural processes in language. Mimicry, exaggeration, reversal, mockery, punning, and nicknaming, however, are probably used in all cultures. This assumption must remain hypothetical at present, in contrast to the established universality of linguistic structures and processes, because systematic and extensive cross-cultural studies of humor are lacking. The substantive nature of humor, like that of language, varies across cultures: what is mocked may vary from one culture to another, like the degree and direction of exaggeration. Similarly, what is considered obscene may be culturally determined, but obscene humor as a category is probably universal. Other universal types of humor probably include proverbs, riddles, verbal games, and so on.

The proposition just articulated is based on the common biological traits of *Homo sapiens*, which needs to satisfy hunger, to eliminate body waste, to satisfy sexual desire, and to protect itself from the environment. Humans all share certain mental faculties, chief among which are the abilities to learn language, to make tools, and to adapt to whatever environment they find themselves in. It can be argued that humans also have the ability to engage in humor or to respond to humor stimuli by smiling and laughing. Language is used to nurture and socialize the young, to transmit sociocultural and behavioral patterns, to preserve cultural values, and to conduct a multitude of transactions among the members of a culture. Humor, it can be argued, plays a somewhat similar role, being quite widespread and serving many functions.

Humor and language show not only similarities but also interdependence, which is manifested in two important ways. First, the very nature of language becomes the subject matter of humor. Its phonological, morphological, syntactic, and semantic elements and their interrelationships are exploited in creating humor. This "linguistic humor" I shall discuss in the next section. Second, the development, comprehension, and appreciation of humor are determined to a considerable degree by the use and function of language in society and by the cultural attitudes and values associated with it. An explanation of the rather complex nature of this influence on humor constitutes a sociolinguistic perspective and is undertaken in the final section.

LINGUISTIC HUMOR

At the basis of much linguistic humor are the various types of linguistic units and their interrelationship. The notion of incongruity is crucial to such humor. It involves the disarray of phonological and grammatical elements, the twisting of the relationship between form and meaning, the reinterpretation of familiar words and phrases, and the overall misuse of language. Like most other types of humor, linguistic humor can occur accidentally or can be created deliberately. It depends, however, on the speakers' awareness of linguistic structure and of vocabulary. The degree of comprehension and appreciation of such humor closely parallels the extent of linguistic proficiency. As Rosten has remarked, "You must have a word and know it and have it understood by your peers before its misuse will trigger a giggle" (1972:13). I examine different types of linguistic humor below. My examples are mostly English, and my discussion is by no means exhaustive. Other investigators have provided extensive listing of many types of linguistic humor (Esar 1952; Hertzler 1970:175–88; Hockett 1967, 1972).

The Pun

The most common linguistic humor is the pun, which is usually defined as a play on words and involves the use of homonyms in a single context in which only one meaning is appropriate, while the other meaning may appear so only by extension or by association and in some instances may seem incongruent. An example would be: "The first thing that strikes a stranger in New York is a big car." Attitudes toward puns vary across cultures and over time. Reactions may vary even within a society, depending on how fre-

quently puns occur and in what social contexts. Punning in conversation and in literature was frequent during the Elizabethan
period in England (Greenough and Kittredge 1900–1901/1961:119),
while English-speaking communities nowadays regard the pun as
a very low form of humor (Farb 1975:99). According to Edwin
Newman, "There are millions of people who groan when they hear
a pun" (1974:185). He feels, however, that this response is standard, and people who groan do so because they either are envious
or like to deny themselves the pleasures offered by their language.

Punning has become an integral part of advertising in the modern
mass media, especially in the V/estern world. The advertisers of
many products often try to coin clever one-liners with puns so that
listeners or readers not only may enjoy and remember them but
also may be unconsciously persuaded to buy the products so advertised. This use of puns is illustrated by Quirk (1951), who analyzed those found in advertisements designed to attract London
railway passengers. Player brand cigarettes were advertised by two
slogans: "Say PLAYERS PLEASE—they always do" and "People
are saying PLAYERS PLEASE more than ever." Makers of a cham-
pagne cleverly used the brand name in the slogan "Hip Hip IR-
ROY!" The capital letters combined three functions, symbolizing
the familiar cheer, pointing to the pun, and giving prominence to
the brand name. Similar examples are quite common in the United
States. Success brand rice is advertised with such phrases as "Din-
nertime Success Stories" and "Success and the single girl." A per-
fume called "Embracing" is advertised with a picture of a young,
handsome man hugging a beautiful woman, with the caption "Embracing makes things happen!"

Although single-word puns are more common, punning techniques can be used morphologically and syntactically as well. The
following examples are from Milner (1972:17). "Love is a conflict
between reflexes and reflexions." A: "Won't you give up smoking
for me?" B: "Why do you think I am smoking for you?" The text
on a printed card titled "Bridge Party" from a restaurant-cum-gift
shop in Virginia was full of sentence puns. It supposedly reproduced the dialect monologue of a maid who quit her job after
overhearing conversation at a bridge game in the house where she
worked. The text included the following sentences, given here in
standard English but appearing in a southern dialect on the card.
They can readily be recognized as expressions common at any
bridge game but can be also interpreted obscenely. All of them are

double entendres. "Take your hands off my trick. Lay down and let me see what you have got. You forced me and I had to take you out when I had already been down twice. You jumped me twice when you didn't have stuff enough for one good raise. Well, I guess we should stop now as this is my last rubber."

Puns involving the literal and the metaphorical or extended meanings of words and phrases are popular in children's riddles. The right answer to the riddle depends on a literal interpretation of the question, as the following examples illustrate.

Q: Who crosses the river twice and is still not clean?
A: A dirty double-crosser.
Q: Why is tennis such a noisy game?
A: Because each player raises a racket.
Q: What goes through a door, but never goes in or comes out?
A: A keyhole.

A caption to a "Dennis the Menace" cartoon depicts Dennis's father leaving for the office as Dennis says to him: "I hope your rat wins the race, dad."

Linguists have analyzed puns in many different languages[1] and believe that punning and plays on words are a universal phenomenon. There also have been attempts to classify puns into many types on the basis of their degree of perfectness, the kind of linguistic units involved (that is, single words, phrases, and whole sentences), and their subject matter.[2]

The Interlingual Pun. Generally, interlingual puns are phonetically imperfect. They occur when individuals use a lexical item from a language that is phonetically similar to a lexical item from another but has a different meaning. Such puns are especially noted when one of the meanings is obscene. They may occur unintentionally, because of a person's insufficient knowledge of a foreign language, or may be used deliberately by bilingual speakers during word play. Once bilinguals become aware of phonetic similarities and semantic differences between words in the different languages they speak, such words are generally avoided, especially if the pun has an obscene connotation. Alternatively, knowledge of such phonetic similarity between words of different languages may be used in linguistic games with the goal of enhancing a person's linguistic skills in a foreign language. Thai students living in the United States, for example, avoided using such Thai words as *phrig* (chili pepper), *fag* (sheath, [bean-] pod), and *khan* (to crush), regarding them as phonetically similar to obscene English words. On the other hand imperfect interlingual puns are an important part of a Thai game called "Rhyming Translation," which is played by children and by adolescents who are learning English (Haas 1957a, 1957b). One unintentional interlingual pun occurred when an instructor of the Hindi language was conducting a class in a woman's dormitory with both male and female students present. When a new Hindi word *kaṇṭh* (neck) was introduced and students were asked to repeat it, there was no response. Being unaware that the word was phonetically similar to a four-letter English word, the instructor repeated it aloud several times, encouraging the students to do the same. The male students burst into laughter, and the female students seemed very embarrassed until someone explained the situation to the teacher.[3]

The occurrences of interlingual puns need to be investigated in greater depth because they indicate the differential attitudes of various language speakers as to which semantic domains are considered vulgar, obscene, derogatory, and taboo. The avoidance of certain words or, conversely, their deliberate use by speakers of one language or another in bilingual situations indicates not only dominant cultural values concerning linguistic etiquette but also the positive or negative attitudes toward certain topics. In the Thai case mentioned above, Thai students avoided taboo words in the presence of speakers of English because of acute anxiety about the proprieties and niceties of speech. Such anxiety has its basis in the Thai language itself, because it is characterized by the existence of numerous synonymous sets of words that are differentiated only by the varying degrees of vulgarity and politeness associated with their use (Haas 1957b:340–41). In this context the following hypothesis seems relevant: a person can become a "true" bilingual in the sense of internalizing a foreign language only after becoming able to use without embarrassment words in it that are phonetically similar to obscene words from his or her native language.

Malapropism

Malapropism is defined as a "ridiculous misuse of a word, in place of one it resembles in sound, especially when the speaker is seeking a more elevated or technical style than is his wont and the blunder destroys the intended effect" (Hockett 1967:927). The term is derived from the name of a character, Mrs. Malaprop, in the comedy *The Rivals*, by Sheridan. Mrs. Malaprop used wrong words in social situations because of their phonetic similarity to words appropriate in such contexts (Esar 1952:114). Malapropisms are generally the result of inadequate knowledge of vocabulary and a desire to use sophisticated words to impress others.

Examples of malapropism can be found in many introductory textbooks on linguistics and English grammar. The following are from Bolinger (1968): "harassing the atom" and "rising to higher platitudes of achievements" (Mayor Richard Daley of Chicago); "five below zero, nominally a safe temperature for driving" (spoken by a weather forecaster). In recent years, Archie Bunker, the main character in the popular television comedy "All in the Family," was shown to be very prone to malapropisms: "There you stand in your ivory shower"; "I say, 'Survival of the Fattest'"; "Capital punishment is a detergent to crime"; and "UFO CIA" (for "AFL CIO"). Malapropisms may occur also in the speech of nonnative speakers of a language, who are likely to confuse two similar sounding words as having the same meaning.

Spoonerism

A spoonerism involves the transposition of linguistic units such as phonemes, morphemes, words, or phrases in an utterance, thereby creating another. The term derives from William A. Spooner, dean and warden of New College in Oxford, who was famous for his presumed "slips of tongue." Although he is credited with many such slips, it is not certain that he said them all. Spooner's colleagues and friends stressed the fact that slips of the tongue were absent in his conversation (Robbins 1967:459). Yet many popular spoonerisms are attributed to him (Fromkin 1973:110): "Noble tons of soil"; "You have hissed all my mystery lectures"; "I saw you fight a liar in the back quad"; "You have tasted the whole worm"; and "The queer old dean." These examples illustrate the transposition of single sounds, but transposition of consonant clusters, syllables, or words is not uncommon (Hockett 1972:924).

It is not always easy to separate spoonerism from any simple transposition, which is commonly called metathesis in linguistics. To be a true spoonerism, not only should individual letters be transposed between words or complete syllables or words be transposed, the change must create equally intelligible utterances that generally do not fit the context and thus create an unexpected incongruity (Robbins 1967:460). Not all spoonerisms are humorous. Spoonerisms can be either intentional or accidental and, when they are the former, may be a part of children's games. Although the term "spoonerism" is new, such transpositions of sounds and words have long been noted (Esar 1952:58–60; Fromkin 1973:110). Spoonerisms probably occur in all languages. They have been reported in Southeast Asian languages (Milner 1971:256).

The Tongue Twister

Somewhat similar to spoonerisms are tongue twisters. They are sequences of words, phrases, sentences, or verses that include a series of phonetically similar sounds, so that, if the text is uttered at a fast tempo, the sequence is mixed up. Only by reciting a tongue twister carefully and slowly can a person produce the correct version. Tongue twisters are part of children's games and occur in many cultures. New ones are often created by children, and old ones become a part of folklore. In English, for example, such utterances as "Peter Piper picked a peck of pickled peppers," and the stanza that appears below, have been popular for many years.

> She sells seashells on the seashore
> The shells she sells are seashells, I am sure.
> For if she sells seashells on the seashore.
> Then I am sure she sells seashore seashells.

Anyone who has tried to recite this stanza can easily appreciate the problem of keeping the two sibilants [s] and [š] apart.

An interesting aspect of tongue twisters is the creation of obscene or scatological words when consonants are interchanged. An unwary subject is asked to recite a verse or to utter a sentence rapidly, only to realize that he or she is uttering a series of obscene words when the order of consonants changes. One such example in English is "She sits and shells, she shells and sits." Tongue twisters are used by children to test each other's linguistic abilities. True skill is demonstrated by reciting a tongue twister very fast and still retaining the correct sequence of proper words. Tongue twisters are therefore used by children in competition and for one-upmanship. There have been several descriptive studies of tongue twisters in non-Western languages (Arnott 1957; Lowie 1914).

Printing Errors

Humor due to typographical or printing errors is quite common because of the enormous volume of publications produced by the modern mass media. Despite careful proofreading, errors creep up. Those that occur in headlines receive the most attention. *Reader's Digest* magazine regularly publishes factual humorous printing errors as one of its features. Such humor is common in all societies that have well-developed mass media and extensive publications. Esar (1952:135–38) provides some classification of such humor. Most of it occurs when spelling errors result in puns or when words with quite unintended meaning are created as a result of inadvertent omissions or additions. The change of "importance" into "impotence," and the change of "laughter" into "slaughter," are examples.

Speech Impediments

Speech impediments such as stuttering or stammering and the inability to make certain phonetic distinctions cause blunders in speech. Laughing at such blunders, however, is not approved in all societies. Disapproval stems primarily from the cultural belief that laughing at speech impediments, especially those over which individuals have no control, is cruel. Children find speech blunders funny, however, and may laugh openly when they have not yet internalized the cultural norms of adults. In some cultures, there is no social sanction against laughing at blunders due to speech impediments, and an individual having a speech problem may even be given a nickname derived from it.

A child's inability to articulate certain speech sounds or to make phonemic contrasts can occasionally become a topic of humor for adults, especially during the early stages of childhood when speech is still being acquired. Baby talk is amusing to adults, who may occasionally use it themselves while communicating with infants and very young children. This phenomenon appears to be widespread across cultures (Ferguson 1964). Even in societies with social norms against laughing at blunders caused by speech impediments, jokes and other forms of humor on the topic do exist. In

Anglo-American culture, laughing at stutterers in real life situations is generally disapproved, yet there are many stutterer's jokes.

Analogy and Patterning

Humor based on analogy and patterning occurs most commonly in children's speech because children are unable to recognize word boundaries and attempt to create new utterances on the basis of patterns already acquired. If children do not understand the meaning of part of an utterance, they tend to break it into different words by analogy, using the patterns they already know. As a result they may ask questions or make comments that amuse adults but not children. A few examples follow. An older sister, commenting on a male acquaintance, said, "He's got poise." Her little brother asked, "What's a poy?" At breakfast, a woman said, "Please pass the cheese," and her young daughter said, "Mummy, I want a chee too" (Hockett 1958:288, 425).[4] These and other similar examples suggest linguistic experimentation on children's part. Although occasionally incongruent or unacceptable, the errors reflect children's creativity and their ability to use analogy and patterning. Adults are amused by the mistakes but may correct them. Such cases are regularly reported in *Family Weekly, Parade, Reader's Digest*, and other magazines.

Hypercorrections

Social climbers who are insecure about their speech try to adopt dialect or speech style that seems to them more prestigious than their own. The linguistic patterns of such speech varieties, however, are not totally uniform. Eager to acquire the new variety, such individuals learn a few grammatical, phonological, and stylistic rules and apply them uniformly, ignoring exceptions. As a result, people change pronunciations of even words that do not fit specific patterns or add prefixes or suffixes to words that occur without them in the prestige variety. Such verbal faux pas make the speakers the object of ridicule and humor for individuals who regularly speak the prestige style. Among the Javanese, people who speak the Prijaji dialect consider it to be the most prestigious and "correct" among the many that exist and make fun of "ignorant" villagers who use the wrong forms in attempting to speak it. The villagers add the Prijaji ending -*en* to the word *tjina* (Chinese), for example, in attempting to speak Prijaji, although, according to

186

Prijaji speakers, proper names should never be altered (Geertz 1960:259).

Slangs

Slangs are specialized languages developed by certain groups and used for both ingroup communication and to establish identity. To outsiders who do not understand them because of strange coinages, arbitrarily changed meanings of common words, and the extravagant use of numerous figures of speech and rhyming, slangs may sound funny. Sometimes slangs are developed and displayed in front of the outsiders precisely for the purpose of baffling them. An individual may also want to distinguish himself by oddity or grotesque humor (Greenough and Kittredge 1900–1901/1961:55). Slangs are frequently used by underprivileged groups and adolescents in many societies and may be considered foolish speech behavior that is indulged in by only young people (Kirshenblatt-Gimblett 1976:6).

Slangs have been a special topic of linguistic studies (see bibliography in Hymes 1964:403). The one that has received the most attention is the "Rhyming Slang" of the Cockney speakers in London (Franklyn 1960; Matthews 1938; Partridge 1937/1970). Cockney speech has certain well-publicized features, namely the dropping of h's from standard English words and excessive diphthongization. Cockney rhyming slang appeared in the early nineteenth century when London was undergoing a period of considerable activity, particularly construction work, and it was created partly to relieve the strain of hard work and to make fun of the Irishmen (Franklyn 1960:8).

Rhyming is occasionally used by Cockney speakers even today to show off their superior linguistic skills. The following, quoted from Franklyn, appears under the heading "Show Off." The words underlined are slang expressions that rhyme with the regular words they replace.

In a public-house, under normal conditions, a request for a pint of "brown" or of "wallop" will be made; but in the presence of an observer, when the Cockney uses his rhyming slang excessively and ostentatiously, partly to mystify and partly to establish his superiority, the request will be for a *Walter Scott* (pot) of *pig's ear* (beer). He may

187

add that he will not get *elephant's trunk*—or he may abbreviate to elephant's—(drunk) on it because it is half *fisherman's daughter* (water); but if he does he can be sure his *trouble and strife* (wife) will soon pick him up off the *Rory O'More* (floor) and get him into *Uncle Ned* (bed). [Franklyn 1960:71]

My discussion thus far has highlighted some major types of linguistic humor widespread among the languages of the world. Linguistic humor offers considerable scope for creativity and pleasure. Virtuosity also brings recognition among a person's peers. For children linguistic humor and speech play in general are most enjoyable, encouraging the children to feel that they have mastered their language. But linguistic humor is not the exclusive prerogative of children. Adults too seem to take great pleasure in it. Although linguistic humor draws attention to the structural and semantic peculiarities of a language, it reflects little of the rest of the culture.

SOCIOLINGUISTIC ASPECTS

Language is such an essential part of human social interaction that it is taken for granted and is used unconsciously in most social situations. Yet if we are in the middle of some social activity, a silence suddenly develops, and individuals rush to fill it by saying something, no matter how irrelevant—then we realize that language is indispensable.

Exploration of the sociolinguistic aspects of humor, much of which is verbal, is a complex task. In a broad sense it is necessary to evaluate the multitudinous ways in which language shapes humor and the ways in which this shaping process is affected by the relationship between language and the sociocultural system. This relationship in turn is influenced by the beliefs and attitudes of people toward the structure, function, and status of their own language vis-à-vis the rest of the culture. Such beliefs and attitudes vary not only cross-culturally but also intraculturally over a period of time. A broad goal in exploring the sociolinguistic aspects of humor is to investigate the cross-culturally differential ways in which language shapes humor and the kinds of generalizations that can be developed on the basis of comparative studies.

Linguists and anthropologists have only recently recognized that the status and use of language vary cross-culturally. People in different societies think differently about their language, value it differently, acquire it through diverse social mechanisms, and use it in all sorts of dissimilar ways. Some cultures place considerable emphasis on verbal virtuosity, and much attention is given to developing linguistic skills, which enable individuals to achieve prestige and high status. The Anang in Nigeria, whose very name was given to them by the neighboring Ibos and means "ability to speak wittily yet meaningfully upon any occasion," take great pride in their eloquence. Their youths are trained from early childhood to develop verbal skills (Messenger 1960:229). The Burundi (Albert 1972) and the Bella Coola Indians (McIlwraith 1948) are similar in this respect. On the other hand, in some cultures excessive verbalization is actively discouraged, and silence is considered more meaningful and appropriate to many social occasions. Such seems to be the case among the Western Apache (Basso 1970) and the Warm Springs Indians (Philips 1976). Some cultures may exhibit total unconcern with speech in general, as do the Gbeya (Samarin 1969), so that little attention is paid to how well children acquire the language of the community. There simply may not be any incentive for individuals in some cultures to derive pleasure from speech. The Paliyans of South India, for example, "communicate very little at all times and become almost silent by the age of 40" (Gardner 1966:398).

The diversity with respect to the status and use of language vis-à-vis the rest of the cultural system suggests that detailed ethnographic accounts of the functions of language in social interaction as well as of language attitudes in individual cultures are a prerequisite to fully understanding how humor is influenced by language cross-culturally. My discussion above, suggests the following hypothesis: the degree of language-related humor is more extensive in those cultures where the nature and use of language receive more conscious attention than in those cultures where attitudes toward language are either indifferent or negative. Thus, not much verbal humor, either language-related or otherwise, is likely to be found among the Paliyans of South India, whereas much the opposite is true of the Anangs of Nigeria and the Burundis of Western Africa.

The theoretical model called "Ethnography of Speaking" developed by Hymes (1962, 1968, 1972, 1974) is useful in exploring the sociolinguistic aspects of humor in a cross-cultural perspective. It aims to describe culture-specific patterns of language use on the basis of such concepts as "speech event," "components of speech event," and "functions of speech event." The components of speech event, as outlined by Hymes, are: setting (in terms of time and place), participants and their sociocultural backgrounds, the linguistic code used, channels of communication, the message form, topics, and cultural norms of interaction and interpretations. An exploration of all the interconnections of these components in individual cultures produces what Hymes calls "rules of speaking." Hymes's model and the many concepts elaborated by him constitute the basis of much of the discussion in the remainder of this chapter. The topics that I shall examine manifest the interdependence of language and the rest of the sociocultural system and show the effects of language on humor at the culture-specific and intercultural levels.

Linguistic Instrumentalities

Following Hymes (1972:63) I use the term "instrumentalities" here to refer to both mediums of transmission and various forms of speech used in humor. My concern is with the cultural preferences shown in choosing a particular speech form as an appropriate medium for humor, whether it is language, dialect, speech variety, style, register, or what have you, the possible reasons behind such a choice, and the ways in which it affects humor.

Available ethnographic data suggest that only some varieties of speech are considered appropriate for humor. If we use Joos's (1961/1967:11) classification and terminology, it can be argued that the casual rather than formal style for humor appears widespread, although speakers may not always be consciously aware of the existence of such styles or of their distinctive nature. In societies with diglossia (Ferguson 1959), speakers are not only aware of the "high" and "low" varieties of language but are also likely to use only the low variety for humor. In illustrating the functions of the high and low varieties in different social situations, Ferguson states that the low variety may be used in a caption for a political cartoon, in a radio soap opera, and in conversation with friends, family, and colleagues and is suitable for the development of humor. In the diglossia situation of the South Indian language Tamil, the spoken variety is used for jokes. In Tamil movies, buffoons always use the spoken variety, while the heroine, who is "purer" than other characters and embodies "certain virtues as chastity and honor," speaks the literary variety (Schiffman 1978:98, 107).

Various degrees of linguistic formality are recognized in many societies with emphasis on linguistic niceties, although a formal diglossia situation may not exist. In such societies the least formal talk, sometimes labeled "idle talk" or "frivolous speech," is used for joking and humor primarily because it is flexible and is least burdened with rigid conventions, rules of formality, and other similar restrictions. Among the Burundi of Africa, joking activity between joking kinsmen has the least degree of linguistic formality (Albert 1972:80). Most Zinacantecan Indian verbal joking occurs in the informal style (Bricker 1974:376). Among the Chamula Indians of Mexico, "truly frivolous talk" constitutes a "verbal game that is performed anywhere that conversation occurs provided the participants are in correct joking relationship" (Gossen 1976:127). Chamula Indians, however, consider truly frivolous talk inappropriate to a ritual setting, which probably involves much formality. The Chamula Indian folk taxonomy of verbal behavior indicates that the more elevated the verbal behavior, the greater the restriction of form and content and the greater the specification of setting (Gossen 1974:395). These observations explain why verbal humor among the Chamula Indians occurs in the least formal conversational style.

In societies with diglossia, but occasionally in those without, pairs of words often have the same meaning. One word is used for formal occasions and the other for informal chatting, gossiping, and joking. The former belongs to the high variety and the latter to the low variety. In the languages spoken by the native tribes of Cape York Peninsula in Australia, for instance, "there are at least two, often a number, of words for each object, or for parts of the body.... One of these words is generally considered to be the proper term to be used in ordinary polite conversation, the other is, in the words of my informant, 'half swear'" (Thomson 1935:466). Honigmann (1944) noted that in the discussion of sexual activities and reproductive organs, English does not have neutral terms. One set of terms is considered obscene, while the other is unnecessarily formal and scientific.

Not only certain speech styles but occasionally even specific dialects or languages are perceived as more suitable media for humor than others, although it is almost impossible to validate such perceptions empirically. In Lebanon a clown on various popular television shows was usually a man who spoke a dialect common to one middle-class section of the city of Zahle. The same dialect would have been imitated if someone had been telling a joke (Nader 1962:29). In a small town in northern Norway where people are bidialectal, the standard variety is used in speaking with outside researchers and for any serious talk; the local dialect is used to provide local color and to indicate humor (Blom and Gumperz 1972:421).

Whenever two or more languages are used in a society or nation, one of them is likely to be perceived as being more suitable for humor. Bilingualism is widespread in Paraguay, where Spanish and the American Indian language Guarani exist with well established diglossic patterns. Paraguayans consider Guarani as more suitable for humor than Spanish in all social situations. "In general, jokes are in Guarani in all spheres. . . . Many informants said that jokes were more humorous in Guarani or that Guarani lent itself to the expression of humor" (Rubin 1968:107).

Occasionally, pidgin languages in culture contact situations offer better opportunities for linguistic innovation and creativity, which plays a major role in development of humorous and catchy expressions by way of new words, phrases, and proverbs. Because the linguistic structure is still fluid and few restraints based on the notions of correctness are imposed, people can instantly react linguistically to new sociocultural experiences by creating appropriate and humorous labels. For this reason pidgins, or pidginized versions of colonial languages, seem more conducive to the development of linguistic humor. The linguistic scene in the urban copperbelt centers of Northern Rhodesia as described by Epstein (1968:320–39) is a case in point. Epstein cites many examples of humorous and extemporaneous coinages in English by the urban Africans. They reflect "a striking freshness and vividness of imagery which escapes the more orthodox idiom." In labeling different types of houses in the urban housing sections, for instance, urban Africans emphasize the special character of each section in humorous ways. One section consisted of semidetached one-room houses of very poor quality. They were commonly known as *way-alezi* (wireless) or *telefon* (telephone), because everything that went on in the house was immediately broadcast to the neighbors. Residents of a new suburb with large houses designated themselves *fwe bamafour-roomed* ("we people who have four-room houses"), in contrast with residents of the old location, who were labeled *aba mu mabottle* ("those who live in bottles"). The interesting aspect of these humorous expressions is that they are combinations of English and native African languages, and people who create them do not have a high degree of proficiency in spoken English.

Code Switching and Code Mixing in Social Interaction

Although language at an abstract level is seen as a structurally uniform system, its realization as speech in social context is diverse and fluid. Individuals do not always speak the same way but vary their speech in social encounters. The notions of code switching and code mixing have been developed in sociolinguistics to explain this phenomenon and refer to the alternate use of two or more speech styles, registers, varieties of language, or languages in social context and to their respective mixtures.

Social interactions are frequently evaluated by people in terms of their formality along a scale ranging from the most serious, formal, stylized or ceremonial to the most casual, loose, or unstructured. Many factors, such as setting, backgrounds of participants, the roles they play, their moods, motives, and expectations, and nonverbal activities, are crucial for such evaluation. Some of these factors, however, are more influential than others. In a social situation, for instance, the type of speech used is often more significant than, say, nonverbal activities, in judging the degree of formality because of its association with particular social categories of participants or with certain social settings and therefore with certain cultural values. My discussion in the previous section clearly suggests that awareness of the culturally perceived appropriateness of certain speech varieties for humor generally leads to their proper use on the part of the speakers in suitable social situations. Hence code switching becomes important because it reflects the norms of speech as they relate to humor.

Code switching is both a consequence of and dependent upon various other factors that I have mentioned that indicate the formality of social situations. Occasionally, for instance, code switching may be deliberately used as a device to change the nature of the social interaction. A speaker may communicate the intention of reducing the rigidity and formality of the situation by switching from a formal to a casual style. Because of the association of humor with casual style, humor itself may create an informal atmosphere, although the other components of a social situation may not necessarily change. Such is frequently the case in American culture, where humor is ubiquitous; it is enjoyed by most people and is regarded positively even in most formal social situations. Speakers often start even a formal address with a joke or some witty comments in a colloquial style, although the speech itself may be delivered in a formal style. Similar code switching takes place frequently in classroom lectures in colleges and universities, at political meetings, in courtrooms, and in sermons.

Code switching for the development of humor seems more prevalent among blacks in the United States, who emphasize verbal skills and performance more than other groups in American culture. Blacks readily alternate between the different kinds of speech styles in natural conversation, depending on their motives. Such speech varieties are identified with distinctive folk labels. Signifying, rapping, and marking are some of the types of talks recognized by blacks themselves and have been analyzed by sociolinguists (Abrahams 1963/1970b; Kochman 1972). Rapping and marking are often used for humor as well as for other purposes, such as the establishment of a person's reputation as a good talker among his or her peers. Mitchell-Kernan (1972:170–72) provides an example. She was discussing her research on black speech with three young men. One of them engaged her in an extended conversation as he switched back and forth from serious talk to rapping, especially when he found out that she was able to participate in such a game. People who are not accustomed to such frequent code switching, however, can become bewildered and are likely to be off balance—which on occasion may be the intention of the speaker.

Similar code switching takes place among the Chamula Indians. It was mentioned earlier that "truly frivolous talk" is inappropriate in ritual settings among the Chamulas. Such talk, however, "often occurs as 'filler' in idle moments of ritual sequences between players who would not have a joking relationship" (Gossen 1976:128). Gossen saw a ritual official completing a prayer and beginning to drink *pos*, a powerful liquor "to the happy accompaniment of 'truly frivolous talk' " (p. 127). In the Norwegian situation that I mentioned above, people switch from the standard to the local dialect in the same social situation if nonserious topics are introduced. Among the peyote-using tribes of American Indians, there are formal ritualistic ceremonies, including prayers and music when peyote is consumed. These all-night ceremonies last for ten or eleven hours, ending with a breakfast provided by the individuals who sponsor them. At breakfast time participants may stand to stretch their cramped limbs, may smoke, and may chat freely, thus changing the nature of social interaction from the serious and formal to the casual. This is also the appropriate time for telling jokes and other humorous exchanges relating to the ceremony that directly contrast with the seriousness of the ritual (Howard 1962:10).

What are the reasons for the notion, which seems widely shared across cultures, that informal speech styles are more suitable for humor? One explanation lies in the association of informal speech styles with a relaxed and unrestrained atmosphere. In any formal social situation, speakers must be careful about the manner of their speech; they must pay meticulous attention to their pronunciation, must carefully follow grammatical rules, and must be precise in their choice of vocabulary. Spoken words must be organized and explicit, often at the expense of pedantry. If any set phrases or stereotyped linguistic formulas are to be used on ceremonial occasions, they must be accurately produced; any mistakes can lower the esteem of the speaker in the eyes of the audience. Thus both the speech styles and the overall atmosphere are formal and rigid.

The reverse is true in social encounters conducive to humor. The atmosphere is relaxed, and participants are not burdened by the formality of the occasion. Various activities are engaged in purely for their own sake. Colloquial speech styles, which take liberties with structural norms, are therefore more appropriate to such occasions. As Joos comments, casual style is "for friends, acquaintances, insiders; addressed to a stranger, it serves to make him an insider simply by treating him as an insider" (1961/1967:23). In informal verbal interaction, there is elision of sounds, various words are used in their weak or shortened forms, gramatical rules are not always strictly followed, and speech shows an overall fluidity rather than a highly grammatical and carefully enunciated nature.

It is not surprising that informal speech forms and casual speech styles are suitable for humor. Humor and joking exchanges need a familiar setting in which such barriers to communication as age, rank, and social status are considerably reduced, if not totally removed, and togetherness is emphasized (Gossen 1976:138). The overall atmosphere is relaxed, and the personal barriers are let down. There is less attention to strict observation of grammatical niceties, because personal linguistic abilities are not under scrutiny. In other words, speakers are freed from the somewhat tyrannical linguistic constraints characteristic of formal speech and can converse creatively, extemporaneously, and without inhibitions. Formal speech, which suggests distance and politeness, is much less appropriate for such occasions.

Formal social situations are often marked by the use of appropriate stylized linguistic expressions in a proper manner. Ritualistic exchanges of such set expressions are an essential aspect of polite behavior in social interaction. Occasionally, the very act of code mixing involves the deliberate twisting of such set linguistic expressions for the development of humor. An unexpected word or phrase is substituted in place of the usual ones. Such manipulation may result in recognition of the speaker's motives by the listener(s), leading to amusement and laughter. In Syrian Arabic, a person responding to a greeting can choose from only the four set phrases, translated as "hello," "hellos," "two hellos," or "hundred hellos." When a linguist purposely changed the response to "two hundred hellos" or "one thousand hellos," the shift brought amused smiles (Ferguson 1976:144).

Just as substituting a word or two in stereotypic linguistic formulas leads to humor, so does code mixing of styles, which creates a mismatching of the mode of communication and the topic. In every culture different speech styles are firmly associated with different social situations and topics. Halliday remarks that "linguistic humor often depends on the inappropriate choice and the mixing of registers" and quotes a version other than the one commonly used to end the well-known children's story of the "house that Jack built": "that disturbed the equanimity of the domesticated feline mammal that exterminated the noxious rodent that masticated the farinaceous produce deposited in the domiciliary edifice erected by Master John" (Halliday 1968:150).

Although fluid and loosely structured speech styles seem more conducive to humor, once linguistic humor of a particular variety becomes well established, it develops its own structure. It tends to become stylized, leading to the creation of specific genres of verbal art. After such genres have been established, humor must occur within the bounds of their formal, substantive, and symbolic structures. Some well-known examples of humor genres are jokes, riddles, proverbs, and ritual insults or verbal duels, discussed in previous chapters.

Language and Speech as Topics of Humor

Just as the objects, behavior, persons, institutions, and customs of a culture are admired, disliked, or ridiculed, so is language. Negative or positive attitudes toward other cultures are based on stereotypes prevalent in a person's own culture, and the same is true of language. In this sense language itself becomes the topic of humor. Generally, fun is made of languages that are considered "inferior," "primitive," or "crude." A negative view of language is often just one aspect of the overall deprecatory way in which a society and culture are evaluated. Such views are part of ethnocentrism, which exists in all cultures. Its "normal" component is the common language myth that a person's own language is superior to other languages (Ferguson 1968:376).

Negative stereotypic attitudes about a specific language often result in its becoming the butt of humor. The Kaguru and Ngulu tribes of east-central Tanzania in Africa, for example, make fun of their neighbors' languages. The Kaguru and Ngulu are proud of the purity of their dialect and are inclined to refer to the persons in neighboring areas as *Wandubu*, meaning "those who garble their words." The term refers to the confusion and mixture not only of speech but also of other customs (Beidelman 1964:43). A well-known Marathi humorist made fun of South Indian languages by suggesting that, while conversing with speakers of these languages, a Marathi speaker should carry an earthen pot with a few pebbles in it. In response to anything said, the Marathi speaker would need only to shake the pot so that the pebbles would rattle inside; the South Indian language speaker would feel satisfied that the reply had been appropriate. This humorous advice probably reflected the fact that South Indian languages have considerable retroflexion and sounded "very harsh" to the humorist's ears. The advice is all the more interesting because Marathi also has considerable retroflexion.[5] The stereotypic assumption that a particular language is "funny" may be so firmly entrenched in the mind of members of a particular culture that mere mention of it or allusion to its structural characteristics may evoke laughter. Such seems to be the case with regard to Yiddish in the modern American mass media (Altman 1971:84–86).

What is true of languages in this respect is also true of dialects or of any other speech varieties distinctly identifiable and associated with a specific group, whether ethnic, religious, political, or social. Making fun of the speech habits of a target group is a major component of ethnic humor. Such humor is popularly known as "dialect," or "accent," humor. The practice of making fun of some language(s), dialect(s), or speech style(s) other than a person's own is widespread. In the United States the speech variety that is often treated in this fashion is the so-called southern dialect. Several popular humor books claim to instruct a person in speaking it (Dwyer 1971; S. Mitchell 1976; Wilder 1977). Wilder's book is *You All Spoken Here: A Handy Illustrated Guide to Carryin' on in the South*. The popular television comedy "Gomer Pyle" was based on the stereotypic image of a southern rural person in the army whose southern speech was much emphasized. The so-called Boston, or New England, and Brooklyn dialects are sometimes treated in similar fashion.[6]

Once a language, dialect, or speech style is stereotyped as "funny" primarily because it is stigmatized, any of its structural features—a single sound, word, phrase, or sentence—is sufficient to evoke laughter. Often certain structural features become the stereotyped stock stimuli for amusement and laughter, first by repeated mocking and later by established convention. Examples include the use of "y'all" and of centralized diphthongs in such words as "eye," "I," "my," and so forth to imitate southern speech in American English; use of the diphthong [oy] in place of the consonant [r] in such words as "bird" and "third," so that they are pronounced "boyd" and "toyd," in imitation of the Brooklyn variety of American English; and the dropping of the consonant [r] in postvocalic positions—"Pahk youh car in the Hahvahd squah"—to imitate Boston English. Similarly, nasalization or drawl is a sufficient cue to create the illusion of American English when the Dutch speakers make fun of it (P. Suzuki 1977).

Sometimes a mere word or phrase, though not necessarily stereotyped by convention, is a sufficient humor stimulus. Among the Mehinaku Indians of Brazil, creating linguistic humor involves imitating a word or a phrase from any of the languages of the neighboring tribes or from Portuguese. Mehinaku Indians believe that many of these tribes have ugly speech. During his fieldwork, anthropologist Gregor noticed that some villagers were calling each other by the Auiti tribe's term for brother-in-law, a word that sounded funny to the Mehinaku ear. After some time this fad died out, and everyone was using the Txicao tribe's interrogative *wa*? as a new source for humor (Gregor 1977:188). Interestingly enough, speakers who make fun of linguistic features in other languages are often unaware that phonetically identical sounds occur in their own native language. Dutch speakers, for instance, exaggerate the German velar voiceless fricative consonant [X] in caricaturing German speech, without realizing that an identical sound occurs in Dutch (P. Suzuki 1977:425).

Although a specific language may become the butt of humor in several cultures, different structural features may be chosen to caricature it. The choice is likely to be determined individually in each culture, and the reasons for it lie in each society's ideas about what is funny and why. Exaggeration may be a universal technique used in the development of humor everywhere, but its direction and manner are uniquely determined by each society.

Verbal Performance as the Basis for Humor

The term "performance" is used here both in its popular sense of dramatization and also in the linguistically technical sense to refer to "the actual use of language in concrete situations" (Chomsky 1965:4). Although the linguistic performance of most native speakers of a language is suitable for everyday social interaction, few individuals excel in using speech for the purpose of dramatization.

Artistic verbal performance is achieved by applying many linguistic techniques judiciously. Words, phrases, intonation patterns, tempo, voice quality, volume, and other rhetorical devices such as repetition, ellipsis, metaphor, and alliteration are employed in ways suitable to a specific setting and topic of conversation. Much imagination and verbal dexterity are required for verbal dramatization. Because much humor is verbal, the ways in which it is verbalized become crucial, and its effectiveness is closely tied to overall quality of verbal performance.

Ethnographers, sociolinguists, and folklorists have been paying increasing attention to artistic verbal performance as a major part of speech activities in different societies in recent years (Bauman and Sherzer 1974, sec. v; Hymes 1964, pt. vi). Some researchers have analyzed specific speech genres related to humor. Others have analyzed joke telling, the most popular humor-generating verbal activity in American and other Western cultures (Hockett 1972; C. A. Mitchell 1977; Sacks 1974). Even without such analyses, the ubiquitous joke-telling activity in American culture makes it obvious that verbal performance is crucial for humor. A joke told by a skilled narrator is enjoyed most, while the same joke told clumsily may fall flat.

Joke-telling performance involves memorization, editing, and improvisation. Because most jokes are not created anew but are repeated, the narrator generally memorizes the exact wording of key parts such as the pivot and the punch. The sequence of events covered in the joke is also memorized but only in a skeleton, nonverbal form. When a person is about to tell a joke, "he takes off from the part memorized verbally and the skeleton memorized nonverbally, and fleshes out the rest to fit" (Hockett 1972:177–78).

199

Individual variations in these abilities lead to different kinds of performers. The following shortcomings are common: joke tellers who spend too much time in the preliminary details, so that the joke goes on and on; performers who botch the punch line, the most crucial part of a joke, so that it goes down the drain (some individuals in this category do not even realize that they spoiled the punch line and are amazed when nobody laughs); people who take over someone else's narration in the middle because they think they can do better; joke tellers who omit some crucial detail in the preliminaries on which the effectiveness of the punch line is based, so that no one can understand the joke. Performance is even more crucial when the joke's punch line turns on some structural peculiarity of language.

Individuals whose linguistic performance, for whatever reasons, is consistently and noticeably defective in some way often become the butt of humor. Linguistic humor, such as the malapropisms and spoonerisms, discussed earlier, is based on defective performance. The most prevalent and popular type that uses defective performance as its basis, however, is the so-called accent humor. Accent humor is basically a caricature in that it exaggerates, or "accentuates," mispronunciation and incorrect use of grammar and vocabulary. These defects are most common in the speech of non-native speakers of a language but also occur when speakers of one dialect attempt to speak the standard variety or another dialect within a speech community. Anthropologists and linguists unwittingly become the butt of humor during their fieldwork when they try to speak the local language and not only commit many errors but also "sound funny," or "strange," to the people of the community (Bowen 1964:19–20; Chagnon 1968:11).

Even when the grammatical structure and vocabulary of a foreign language have been mastered, it is almost impossible to achieve total phonological control, especially over the proper articulation of allophonic variations of phonemes. Thus most of the time persons who speak a foreign language or unfamiliar dialect do so with varying degrees of "accent," that is, with phonetic peculiarities that may sound "funny" to native speakers. In real life, norms of politeness and social grace in some cultures do not always permit laughing at funny accents. Peculiar speech constitutes the basis of accent humor, however, especially when the technique of exaggeration is used—for example, by comedians—to highlight its oddness. Such humor is based on just the right mixture of verisimilitude and distortion.

Spoofs of inadequate linguistic performance are quite wide-spread. In the United States, accent humor was common in the minstrel and comedy shows, farces, and other plays of the late nineteenth and early twentieth century. The minstrel shows primarily made fun of blacks by exaggerating their appearance, mannerisms, and speech. As increasing numbers of immigrants of various nationalities began to come to the United States, however, they too became the butt of humor on the stage. The exaggerated imitation of the Irish, the Germans, and Jews in their efforts to speak English was by far the most common theme for humor development in the minstrel and comedy shows (H. E. Adams 1937). Even today American television comedies continue to exploit accent humor. Increasingly, however, such shows seem to use regional varieties of American English rather than foreign accents of English for humor development, as "All in the Family" and "Alice" recently demonstrated. Perhaps the reason for the change is the increasing sensitivity of various ethnic groups in the United States to such ridicule.

Not only has accent humor been popular on stage and in movies and television shows in the United States, but techniques for such humor have been developed in print media, especially in cartoon series. Conventions have been established to represent dialects or accents in speech for different characters. One is the use of "eye dialect" (Falk 1973:295), in which spelling differences represent substandard speech or accent. The inability of speakers to articulate the fricative consonant [ð] of standard American English, for example, is indicated by spelling words "this" and "that" as "dis" and "dat." Other examples of such conventionalized spellings of eye dialect are: "says" spelled as "sez"; words that end in "ing" spelled with "in" substituted, as in "goin" or "interestin"; "can" rendered as "kin," "get" as "git," "going to" as "gonna," and so on.

The linguistic exploits of Hyman Kaplan, a fictional character, and those of his classmates of different ethnic and linguistic backgrounds, represent one of the most successful examples of eye dialect used for accent humor (Rosten 1937, 1959). Kaplan, an immigrant in New York City, is enrolled in the beginner's grade of the American Night Preparatory School for Adults. He is a very enthusiastic speaker not in the least inhibited by his inability to pronounce American English correctly. Kaplan's speech illustrates the nature of Rosten's accent humor. 'I'm hearink it in de stritt. Sometimes I'm stendink in de stritt, talkink to a frand, or mine vife, mine brodder—or may be only stendink. An' somvun is pessnink arond me. An' by hexident he's givink me a bump, you know, a *poosh*! Vell, he says, 'Axcuse me!' no? But somtimes, an' *dis* is vat I minn, he's sayink, 'I *big de pottment*!' '' (Rosten 1937:11–12).

Accent humor is attempted in many social interactions. When scholars who have worked in South Asia assemble for meetings or conferences, they enjoy imitating Indian English with considerable exaggeration during informal drinking sessions. These attempts at accent humor generally include a few obvious features of Indian English, such as excessive overall retroflexion, use of the retroflex voiceless and voiced stops for the English alveolar stop consonants [t d], and use of certain grammatical peculiarities, such as the phrase "isn't it," as a tag question after every declarative sentence, as in "you are going to a movie, isn't it?" People who can further discriminate among the regional varieties within Indian English try to imitate the Bengali, Hindi, or Dravidian accents. Native speakers of languages other than English also use foreigners trying to speak their language as a humor stimulus. In Marathi literature, the speech of Christian missionaries attempting to speak Marathi is frequently used to create accent humor (Dandekar 1973:13).[7]

Linguistic performance does not necessarily have to be defective, by whatever standards, in order to become the butt of humor. In reality, any linguistic performance can be used in this fashion as long as it is perceived by listeners to be unusual or just plain "funny." This type of humor is effective primarily because of its association with an individual, a group, a profession, a role, or a prescribed status that is evaluated deprecatingly by participants in social interaction. In a culture-contact situation, a whole culture and its members may be so viewed and may be spoofed by outsiders. Basso's (1979) description of the joking imitations of the "Whiteman" by the Western Apache Indians is illustrative.

According to Basso (pp. 48–64) almost everything that the white man does in interacting with the Western Apaches is contrary to their cultural values, social relations, modes of conduct, and norms of social interaction, including verbal and nonverbal behavior. To show their disdain for their perceived image of the white man as "a loud-talking, overbearing, self-righteous, unswervingly presumptuous bumbler" (p. 61), Western Apache Indians exaggeratedly imitate the white man's way of talking, which the Apache audience finds very amusing.

The Linguistic Aspects of Social Roles

In many societies the speech styles associated with different sexes, ages, and occupational role, show clear distinctions of which people are generally aware. The imitation of a speech style characteristic of a specific role by people who are not identified with it is used as a stimulus for humor in social interaction, particularly when ascribed roles based on sex and age are involved. In cultures where there is a marked difference between men's and women's speech, for example, among the Carib Indians, a man either unintentionally or intentionally using speech style associated with women may generate humor (Trudgill 1974:94). For the same reasons, adults think it funny when children unintentionally imitate adult speech.

The caricature of speech styles characteristic of occupational roles—those of lawyers, physicians, businessmen, politicians, professors, and television newscasters—is a favorite technique of comedians in Western societies. The haranguing sermons of the Baptist ministers, especially blacks in the southern United States, have also been a frequent target of caricature in comedy shows.

The Key of Verbal Humor

The term "key" was introduced by Hymes (1972:62) to indicate the tone, manner, intent, or spirit of speech acts. Speech acts that may have the same components—setting, participants, and topic—may differ in key, being mock or serious, perfunctory or painstaking.

It is important to investigate the techniques that are used to convey different motives, manners, or spirit behind a communicative act. Most individuals are generally able to distinguish between a serious conversation and a humorous one. What cultural, linguistic, paralinguistic, and gestural cues are available to them? Although the semantic content can aid in making such a distinction, other cues are crucial, because often the same utterance can be communicated with a different intent. Thus listeners usually know when to take an utterance seriously and when to interpret it metaphorically or in a playful, humorous manner. No doubt there are occasions when the appropriate cues are either missing or the listener fails to interpret them properly, thus misunderstanding a remark. At such times, the speaker must make his intentions explicit. Witness, for instance, the often-heard remark, "I was just joking" or "I was kidding" by speakers in social interactions in American society when it is obvious that the intent was misinterpreted by the listener. Most of the time, however, the cues are sufficient for the appropriate decoding of the message.

By and large, the humorous intent is conveyed by the use of appropriate speech variety as well as of other techniques, including many paralinguistic and nonverbal features. A slightly pejorative remark accompanied by a wink or a smile, for instance, is obviously intended as teasing and joking, and the speaker expects it to be so interpreted. Once a particular speech style or technique is recognized as having a specific social meaning, it becomes stylized and is routinely used to convey such meaning. Equally important is the fact that such a style generally contrasts with others that convey a different attitude and spirit altogether. The greater the contrast between such varieties of speech, especially in their paralinguistic and nonverbal cues, the easier it is for participants to identify the intentions of the speaker. In some societies the use of established cues may further lead to the establishment of specific genres of verbal art with the primary function of humor creation.

"Marking" is one of the genres of black American verbal art and is essentially a mode of characterization. Such characterization is highlighted and is simultaneously separated from the rest of the conversation by specific techniques. According to Mitchell-Kernan (1972), one common social type that is marked by blacks in their interaction includes individuals "who are characterized as 'trying to talk proper.' " When their speech is imitated, it is "marked in a tone of voice which is rather falsetto" (p. 177). Mitchell-Kernan describes one of her informants who caricatured a woman. Not only were her exact words repeated, but the "quote was delivered at a pitch considerably higher than was usual for the informant and the words were enunciated carefully so as to avoid loss of sounds and elision characteristic of fluid speech" (p. 177). The performance was accompanied by a parody of appropriate gestures. Mitchell-Kernan comments that these features suggested the speaker was engaged in creating an impression that was contextually inappropriate. In another instance reported by her, a speaker used an exaggerated stereotyped southern speech with appropriate compromising and denigrating content to characterize an individual as an "Uncle Tom."

Basso (1979) similarly describes how the Western Apache mark the context of joking imitations of the white man. When Apaches normally converse with Anglo-Americans, "English is spoken in a careful and deliberate manner, softly and slowly, with minimal variation in pitch and tone" (p. 106). There is an overall effect of flatness and a lack of animation. In contrast, the style in joking imitations is "loud, freewheeling, and exuberant." There is an increased speech volume and tempo, with exaggerated elevation in pitch. Vowels are heavily nasalized. Whole phrases are repeated. Jerky and exaggeratedly abrupt movements accompany the imitation. Visual and body contact is lengthened (Basso 1979:45). Even the nonverbal cues in these joking imitations contrast sharply with those ordinarily used by Apaches when they converse among themselves.

The Role of Gestures in Verbal Humor

As the examples that I have discussed demonstrate, nonverbal expressive movements, especially gestures, constitute an important element of the key of verbal humor. Although nonverbal communication has been studied extensively (Morris et al. 1979; Weitz 1979), little systematic research has explored the role of gestures in verbal humor. Existing studies usually distinguish (Morris et al. 1979:xx) between illustrators, actions that accompany verbal utterances and serve to illustrate them, and emblems, actions that can replace speech and can act as substitutes for verbal utterances. Both types are relevant to humor.

Much verbal interaction is accompanied by gestures. In many instances gestures are essential to convey the nonserious intent of the verbal message. They can also be exaggerated more readily for visual impact. Gestures are important in humor that depends heavily on performance and acting. As illustrated in Chapter 4, many ethnic jokes need gestures to be effective because they need to be both heard and seen. In discussing the recent popularity of the "wide-mouth frog" joke in the United States, in which a loud-mouthed inquisitive frog changes his speaking habit when threatened, Dundes observed that "most of the power of the joke lies in the performance and specifically the shifts of 'dialect' from wide mouth speech, to normal speech, and finally to 'narrow-mouth' speech" (1977:14).

In some social interactions the humorous intent becomes clear only when gestures accompany the verbal interaction with which they are incongruent. In a parody of a Mayan bone setter's prayer, carried out by a mock curing ceremony among the Zinacantecans in Mexico, both gestures and proper context are necessary for humor (Bricker 1974:378). The curer impersonator pretends to cure a female impersonator and her "husband" of imaginary wounds that are supposedly inflicted on them by a bull impersonator. The curer strikes his patients' genitals whenever he speaks of healing their broken bones and torn muscles. The nonlinguistic behavior provides a context in which "bone" and "muscle" together connote "penis," and "cave" and "place" together connote "vagina."

Ordinary gestures are used for diverse messages, including humorous ones. A commonly occurring pointed lip gesture among the San Blas Cuna Indians of Panama is used in humorous social contexts both to initiate messages and to respond to them. One use of this gesture is to suggest that whatever exchange is taking place should be treated as humorous, so that when a pointed lip gesture follows an insulting or derogatory statement, it indicates that the preceding remarks are not to be taken seriously. It is also used as a mock greeting between two individuals who have a social relationship in which joking is permitted. The gesture is then exaggerated and is often accompanied by smiling, laughter, or arm pointing (Sherzer 1973). Gestures are used in similar fashion in many cultures. In the United States and other Western cultures, for instance, a wink directed at an audience and accompanying verbal praise or similar comments intended for a specific listener suggest that the listener is about to become a target of some fun or that the remarks are facetious.

Gestures can and do constitute humor stimuli by themselves. Various European gestures that are emblems and have derogatory implications are often used for ridicule and insult and can make someone the butt of humor without any verbal communication. When used unobtrusively or behind someone's back, they generate laughter. The palm-back V-sign is so well known as a gesture of insult in England that it became the subject of a cartoon in *Punch*. Two aristocratic gentlemen were shown standing just outside a gate on one side of which an enormous palm-back V-sign had been trimmed out of the hedge. The caption read: "I understand you've sacked your gardener" (Morris et al. 1979:230).

Gestures are relevant to humor because the incongruence between verbal communication and accompanying gestures can be humorous. By deliberate or accidental use of inappropriate gestures, comedians in particular often create an incongruence that leads to humor. Emphasis on gestures and their use in verbal communication including humor varies cross-culturally. As a result, different cultures are viewed stereotypically in this respect. Thus the French, the Italians, and other South Europeans are popularly considered to speak more "with their hands" than the British and the Scandinavians. Such shared stereotypic views help generate humor in caricaturing members of these ethnic groups, whom the audience can readily identify.

Ethnosemantic Considerations

The culture-specific interdependence of humor and language can be explored in yet another way by systematically studying the meanings of words in individual languages and their semantic relationships in the cognitive domain of humor. The primary goal is to discover and describe the principles of organization of the domain by extrapolating the existing arrangements of oppositions, inclusion and contrast, or intersection among the many lexical items of the relevant linguistic set. There is an extensive methodological and analytical literature on ethnosemantics. Ethnosemantic techniques have been applied to terminological sets of color, kinship, plants, and disease in different cultures despite the difficulty of determining the boundaries of semantic domains in individual languages.[8] No attempts have been made to analyze the semantic structure of the culturally defined domain of humor, however. It is necessary to discover how the realm of humor is bounded in individual cultures and what the indigenous categories subsumed under it are. In collaboration with my student Richard Franklin I carried out the first such ethnosemantic study of humor in American English. Six white male college students who were native speakers of American English were used as informants. Instead of using the standard ethnosemantic technique of elicitation, we presented the informants with a comprehensive set of forty-six terms that we had prepared with the help of a dictionary and a thesaurus after surveying the literature on humor. These terms are:

Absurdity	Humor	Repartee
		Ribaldry
Banter	Irony	Ridicule
Buffoonery		Ridiculousness
Burlesque	Jest	
	Joke	Sarcasm
Caricature	Jocularity	Satire
Clowning		Scurrility
Comedy	Lampooning	Slapstick
	Lark	Spoofery
Derision	Ludicrousness	
Drollery		Taunting
	Mockery	Teasing
Facetiousness		Tomfoolery
Farce	Pantomime	Travesty
	Parody	
Gallows humor	Pleasantry	Waggishness
	Practical joking	Whimsy
Hoax	Prank	Wit
Horseplay	Pun	Workplay

Each informant was given the following specific instructions, in accordance with which he was asked to select his own terminological set: he was to select only terms of which he definitely knew the meanings and which he considered to be relevant to the domain of humor; if any two terms appeared synonymous to him, he was to choose only one of them; he was to add any new terms not included in the set if he felt that they were pertinent to the domain of humor. None of the informants added any new terms to the original set. All included the term "humor" in their individual sets. The largest set consisted of thirty-one terms, apart from the term "humor," while the smallest set consisted of fourteen terms, apart from "humor." The sets chosen by all six informants appear in table 2. The columns represent the informants' sets and are arranged in descending order, starting from the set of maximum terms. An x in a row indicates the occurrence of a given term in an individual set. As table 2 shows, only four terms (apart from "humor") were shared by all six informants. Three other terms were shared by five informants; nine by four informants; six by three informants; and eight by two informants. Seven terms occurred in the set of only one informant, and eight terms were excluded from all sets.

After all informants individually selected their own sets of terms, a folk key division method was used to elicit placement of the terms in categories. The informants were asked to divide the terms of their individual sets into two or more groups, placing terms sharing some meaning in the same group and the contrasting terms in separate groups. This process was to be repeated until the informants could make no further divisions. The informants were asked what they considered to be the shared and contrasting meanings at each stage of the division. Such questions as "What features distinguish this group from the other(s)?" or, in reference to the terms within a particular group, "What do these terms have in common that influenced you to place them in the same group?" usually resulted in the discovery of the dimensions of contrast.

The term "humor" was chosen as the root of the domain by all informants. Five sets had a tree structure, while one set showed both a tree structure and a partial paradigmatic relationship. None had taxonomic structure because of the absence of humor taxa at the intermediate levels of contrast. In other words, the terms in each informant's set were distinguished at each level of division by the presence or absence of some defining feature. Only two or three levels of contrast appeared to be significant in the six semantic

Table 2. Informants' sets as compared with the comprehensive set, in descending order

Comprehensive set	Informant's set						Comprehensive set	Informant's set					
	6	3	1	2	4	5		6	3	1	2	4	5
Caricature	X	X	X	X	X	X	Gallows humor	X	X				
Pun	X	X	X	X	X	X	Hoax	X	X				
Satire	X	X	X	X	X	X	Lark	X	X				
Teasing	X	X	X	X	X	X	Ludicrousness	X	X				
Farce	X	X	X		X	X	Ridicule	X	X				
Mockery	X	X	X		X	X	Spoofery	X	X				
Pantomime	X		X	X	X	X	Tomfoolery	X	X				
Burlesque	X			X	X	X	Facetiousness	X					
Clowning	X	X		X		X	Ribaldry					X	
Comedy		X		X	X	X	Repartee				X		
Jest	X	X	X	X			Ridiculousness	X					
Joke	X	X			X	X	Taunting						X
Practical joke	X	X	X	X			Travesty		X				
Prank	X	X			X	X	Whimsy		X				
Slapstick	X	X			X	X	Wordplay	X					
Wit	X	X	X	X			Banter						
Absurdity	X		X	X			Drollery						
Derision	X	X		X			Jocularity						
Horseplay	X	X	X				Lampooning						
Irony	X	X			X		Pleasantry						
Parody	X			X	X		Scurrility						
Sarcasm	X		X	X			Waggishness						
Buffoonery	X	X											

Note: The term "humor" has been excluded from the table, although it occurred in all sets.

structures. The subsequent divisions appeared arbitrary. This characteristic precluded the possibility of extending the folk key division until each term contrasted with every other term on at least one dimension.

In order to remove any possibility that the nature of the methods was responsible for the fact that all of the semantic structures basically developed as trees, attempts were made to reapply each informant's dimensions of contrast at other places in the structure so as to develop a paradigm. In each instance, however, the informant considered this procedure inappropriate and made some comment such as "That's not the way I see it." The results demonstrated that the informants shared the same dimensions of contrast, although they were not necessarily ranked in the same way. The final structural sets therefore did not necessarily coincide. The five dimensions of contrast shared among the informants are listed in table 3 in descending order of sharedness. Dimensions not shared

Table 3. Dimensions of contrast in the semantic domain of humor

Number of informants sharing the dimension	Rank of dimension	Nature of contrast	
5	I	A. Humor based on performance	B. Absence of performance
4	II	A. Other-directed humor	B. Non-other-directed humor
3	III	A. Verbal humor	B. Nonverbal, physical humor
3	IV	A. Malicious or harmful humor	B. Benign or harmless humor
3	V	A. Intelligent/skillful humor	B. Humor without intelligence or skill

by at least three informants are not included. The maximum number of informants having the same dimension of contrast at some level in their structural sets was five. In dimension IB, absence of performance was explained as humor occurring in everyday interaction. Similarly, in dimension IIB, the informants explained that non-other-directed humor could be either neutral or self-directed. A term such as "caricature," for instance, had the following criterial attributes for most informants: IA, IIA, IIIA, and IVA. On the other hand, a term such as "pun" had any of the following configurations of attributes: IB, IVB; IB, IIIA; IIB, IIIA; IB, IIB, VA.

The results in general suggest that dimensions of contrast listed in table 3 are to a considerable degree culturally determined, although some individual differences exist, as should be expected in view of the complex nature of the domain of humor. The results do reveal the cultural notions associated with humor in American culture. The fact that the criterion of performance was used by the largest number of informants, for instance, indicates that, in American culture, humor is a major means of entertainment and is much emphasized in the mass media, especially in movies and on television. Similarly, the fact that humor is regarded as directed toward other people suggests that it is a major aspect of social interaction. The fact that maliciousness is a criterion for classification indicates that humor is also a way of expressing aggression toward others. The verbal-nonverbal dichotomy indicates that humor is a means of communication. The results of the study clearly show that one way of understanding the culture-specific cognitive nature of humor as reflected in individual languages is to carry out ethnosemantic studies of its domain as reflected in a structured set of relevant linguistic terms.

THEORETICAL PROPOSITIONS

The discussion in this chapter of the relationship between humor and language permits us to formulate the following cross-culturally significant theoretical propositions.

The similarities between language and humor are significant for understanding their nature and interdependence. Both have evolved in humans to a much higher degree of complexity than in other animals. Both have general and culture-specific attributes, and both pervade social interaction.

Language and humor are interdependent in two important ways: language itself becomes the subject matter of humor; and the use and function of language and the cultural attitudes and values associated with it considerably influence the occurrence, comprehension, and appreciation of humor.

The degree of an individual's linguistic proficiency directly affects his or her comprehension and appreciation of linguistic humor.

Interlingual puns indicate the different attitudes of speakers with respect to semantic domains that may be labeled vulgar, obscene, derogatory, or taboo.

Language-related humor is more extensive in those cultures in which the nature and use of language receives more conscious attention than in cultures where attitudes toward language and speech are indifferent or negative.

The use of a casual rather than formal style of speech is more widespread for humor because of its association with greater freedom of speech and less emphasis on linguistic structure; formal speech is associated with serious and important activities.

Negative attitudes and prejudice toward specific languages are often expressed in linguistic stereotypes that become the basis of humor in which language itself is the topic.

Gestures are essential to humor, since its effectiveness depends on performance and acting.

7

The Trickster in Folklore

Humor in folklore[1] takes many forms, some of which—such as riddles, jokes, and tall tales—become genres in their own right. This chapter analyzes the humor in folklore that is associated with certain types of characters commonly labeled tricksters, buffoons, and fools. The tales of their adventures and mishaps constitute a significant part of folklore in many cultures and have been categorized as myths, episodes, folktales, and so on.[2] I will consider all trickster tales as prose narratives,[3] distinct from other categories of folklore, such as proverbs, riddles, and ballads. The labels "trickster," "buffoon," and "fool," which overlap in semantic range, are problematic. Because the whole issue of how to define the concept of trickster and of how to separate it from other related concepts is the main concern of this chapter, I shall not define the term "trickster."

Anthropological and folkloristic studies focusing on the trickster, especially in the prose narratives of North American Indians that go back to the last century, have a long tradition. The initial efforts were primarily data oriented and concentrated on gathering the so-called trickster tales from many tribes. Such collections were part of the large-scale, systematic efforts undertaken by anthropologists and folklorists to record as much of the American Indian oral literature as possible before it was lost.[4] Such efforts have continued throughout the twentieth century (Ahenakew 1929; Bernard and Pedraza 1976). In the theoretical studies of the trickster throughout this long period, the emphasis has been on discussing the nature of trickster figure as revealed by the comparison of data from numerous American Indian tribes. Theories have been proposed for explaining the origins and persistence of the trickster in the prose narratives of American Indians and his relevance to religious ideology and to sociocultural reality.[5]

Relatively few studies of tricksters in other culture areas of the world are to be found, in contrast to the extensive collection and analyses of the American Indian material.[6] Similarly, only a couple of studies (Kerényi 1956/1969; Street 1972) specifically emphasize a cross-cultural comparative perspective in discussing the trickster theme, using data from culture areas outside North America. Studies of the related topic of clowns and fools are many and can be classified into: specific and general anthologies of prose narratives (Feinberg 1971; S. Thompson 1946:190ff.); analytical studies of specific clowns ancient and modern appearing in the literature of individual writers such as Shakespeare and occurring in the folklore and arts of specific cultures;[7] and general works that discuss the historical origins of such figures and evaluate their physical, psychological, symbolic, and sociocultural aspects while proposing different theories to explain their overall nature and function.[8]

Only a couple of anthropologists (Jacobs 1959, 1960; Skeels 1954) have undertaken analyses of humor in general in prose narratives of specific preliterate societies. Similarly, only a few scholars outside the disciplines of anthropology and folklore (Hyers 1973; Trueblood 1964; Webster 1960) have analyzed humor in the scriptures and mythologies of some major religions of the world.

TRICKSTERS IN DIFFERENT PARTS OF THE WORLD

Brief descriptive accounts of tricksters in the prose narratives of cultures in North America, Oceania, South Asia, and Africa are presented in this section as background material for examination of the trickster concept in a cross-cultural perspective.

The Indians of North America

The label "trickster" was probably used initially in the last decade of the nineteenth century in describing certain figures in the prose narratives of the American Indians (Boas 1898; Brinton 1896). Because of their unusual nature, tricksters became the focus of much anthropological discussion. Their amorphous nature and incongruous characteristics intrigued anthropologists and folklorists, because no comparable figures could be readily found in the oral literature of the West. The enormous textual material on North

213

American trickster tales gathered in the early years attests to their popularity and widespread occurrence. Despite the textual diversity in these tales, common traits can be found. I shall delineate the major attributes of the trickster among the American Indians on the basis of a few major sources.[9]

The trickster figures among various Indian tribes have different forms and are identified with different animals. The trickster is Coyote over much of the Great Plains, the Great Basin, the Plateau, the Southwest, and California; Raven or Mink on the northwest coast; Bluejay among some Indian groups in the state of Washington; and Hare among the Algonquin Indians and in the Southeast (Ricketts 1966:328). Individual trickster figures are assumed to possess the physical characteristics of the specific animals associated with them. Among some tribes the trickster is generally an anthropomorphic being and has such names as Gluskabe, Iktomi, Wakdajunkaga, Nihasan, Manabozho, and Wisaka. In both the theriomorphic and anthropomorphic forms, the tricksters are basically considered to be males.

The origin of the trickster is not always clear in the tales of various tribes. He is often depicted as simply being present at the time of the creation of the earth or during the transformation of the world. He is sometimes portrayed as simply a wanderer and is found drifting on earth or on a large mass of water. His birth is frequently of an unusual nature. The trickster in the Winnebago Hare tales, for instance, is described as having been born to a virginal young girl (Radin 1956/1969:63). He is generally portrayed as having a family. He is also depicted as an immortal character having some divine or mythical qualities (Radin 1956/1969:155). Even when trickster tales constitute a series of episodes (labeled a "cycle") associated with a specific trickster, his death in one episode does not preclude his having another adventure in the next tale. In other words, each tale starts with the premise that the trickster is alive. He is capable of transforming himself into any object, animal, or human being of any age and sex.

Although the physical and psychological nature of the trickster varies across the American Indian tribes, some traits and incidents appear to be widespread (Boas 1940/1966:473). The trickster is both a buffoon and a culture hero. His acquisition of such elements as fire, water, rock, and sun for the benefit of the human race makes him a culture hero. Yet he often embodies all basal, infantile instincts and animal qualities. Thus two or more seemingly contradictory roles are combined in a single personality. The trickster personality reflects mutually reinforcing biological and psychological incongruities. The biological incongruities involve such traits as grotesque form, intestines placed outside his body, a long penis wrapped around his body, with the scrotum on the top, eyes that are uneven and both inside and outside the sockets, or a sharpened leg (Radin 1956/1969:x; S. Thompson 1929/1966:63–64).

The trickster often lacks a sense of unity and cannot coordinate his body parts. He treats his organs as if they were independent of him. He talks to his organs (S. Thompson 1929/1966:56) and attempts to punish or to eat them. In one episode a quarrel takes place between his right and left hand in which the latter is cut up badly (Radin 1956/1969:5). In another story he instructs his anus to keep watch over the roasted ducks while he sleeps, and when he finds out that they have been eaten by foxes, he tries to punish the offender by sitting on the fire but cannot endure the pain. In the same episode, he discovers that he has been devouring his own intestines while commenting on how delicious they are (Radin 1956/1969:17–18). In another episode he sends his penis across water in order to have intercourse with the chief's daughter (Radin 1956/1969:18–19; S. Thompson 1929/1966:305 for variations of this theme). He can coil up his penis and put it in a box, or he can use it to attack other animals.

The trickster's basic biological urges know no bounds. He is always hungry and constantly looks for opportunities to obtain food. Many episodes revolve around his attempts to steal or acquire food by tricking other animals and humans. He is willing to change into any shape, form, or object to get food. In one incident he changes his sex and marries the chief's son, primarily to obtain food, but later his identity is revealed when his mother-in-law chases him around the fire and his vulva drops (Radin 1956/1969:20–22; S. Thompson 1929/1966:304 for variations of this theme). The trickster also has an insatiable desire for sexual gratification. He is willing to break taboos in order to have sexual intercourse. In the most widespread trickster tale among the American Indians, he seduces his daughter by employing tricks, including the feigning of his death. Variations of this theme and other similar episodes portray him as a lecherous brother or son-in-law (Schmerler 1931; S. Thompson 1929/1966:305). He has no control over the bodily processes of waste elimination, especially when he does not heed warnings about not eating certain things. Once he eats a bulb despite a warning that it will lead to defecation and almost drowns in the mountain of his own excrement (Radin 1956/1969:25–27).

215

The other personality traits of the trickster, such as cruelty, stupidity, lack of control to resist temptation, and inability either to identify objects or animals or to differentiate among them, match his biologically incongruous nature. In many episodes he is cruel to animals, inflicts injuries on them, ridicules and mocks them, tries to trick them, and laughs at their expense. He gets into trouble in turn, however, because of his ignorance. He too is mocked, ridiculed, and laughed at by others. His inability to recognize things as they are or to identify his surroundings frequently leads him into trouble, as do other actions (S. Thompson 1929/1966:54, 295). He likes to imitate others as they perform tricks but often fails and pays a penalty for not heeding a warning or because he uses excessive magical power. The eye-juggling episode (S. Thompson 1929/1966:63, 299) and other similar incidents reflect this characteristic. The overall personality that emerges from the trickster tales incorporates opposites of all kinds. The trickster is both foolish and clever. He tricks others but is himself often tricked. He is infantile and readily yields to his desires. His physical and psychological traits lead him to acts that are ludicrous and of a contrary nature. Furthermore, the trickster ridicules sacred customs, breaks taboos, and is the world's greatest clown, who can laugh at himself (Ricketts 1966:347).

My general description of the trickster among the American Indians is an extrapolation from the tales of different tribes. Tricksters in the prose narratives of individual tribes, however, either do not have all these traits or show a preponderance of a few specific traits. While the Raven trickster tales emphasize greedy hunger, the Mink trickster stories stress erotic desires. The trickster Bluejay seems primarily interested in outdoing his opponents in everything he does, and he engages in cunning and trickery (Boas 1940/1966:473). Occasionally, however, a single trickster seems to possess many of the traits that I have described, for instance, the trickster Coyote among the Indians of the Southwest or the trickster Wakdjunkaga among the Winnebago Indians. The prose narratives of a single tribe may occasionally depict several tricksters. In Klamath prose narratives Skunk, Wolf, Mink, Weasel, and Kmukampsh, an anthropomorphic figure, are all tricksters (Stern 1953:16off.). Similarly, both Wakdajunkaga and Hare are tricksters in Winnebago prose narratives.

Oceania

A trickster comparable to that in American Indian prose narratives occurs in Oceania. He is called Maui or Maui-of-a-Thousand-

Tricks. His exploits are described in a cycle of episodes that are included in the myths with many local variations. The Maui myths form one of the strongest links in the mythological chain of evidence linking the scattered inhabitants of the hundreds of island cultures in the vast area. A detailed descriptive and analytical study of Maui (Luomala 1949) constitutes the primary source for the following account.

Maui is a "happy-go-lucky young culture hero, transformer, and trickster" and is primarily a "defier of precedent, a remodeler of the world and its society, and a mischievous, adolescent trickster" (p. 28). The changes in the universe beneficial to people are achieved primarily through his scare tactics or tricks against authority. Maui is capable of changing himself into birds, insects, and animals. Maui's origin varies in the different cycles, but most frequently he is said to have originated in a clot of his mother's blood that she wrapped up and threw into the ocean. Gods and spirits of the ocean rescued Maui and treated him affectionately. He learned all kinds of magic from them, and they were awed by his success. He left the gods to seek his family and to participate in earthly life. His mother recognized him, and after he met his father, Maui was ceremonially purified to make him an acceptable member of human society (p. 52). Maui is also portrayed as the youngest of several brothers who were jealous of him. He played mean and cruel tricks on his brothers and other relatives, for example, he starved one of his grandmothers to death to get her jawbone, harassed his grandfather, and frequently frightened his brothers by performing magical acts and tricks.

Because Maui was raised by both gods and humans, his personality reflected a combination of both divine and human qualities. He was contemptuous of the gods and turned against them. He broke all taboos and had tremendous magical power. His deeds against authority included stealing the fire from an old god and bringing it to earth; thus humans acquired fire. He fished islands from the sea as a trick to frighten his brothers on fishing expeditions and thus gave land to humans. He snared the sun and thus made more light available to humans when formerly there was very little. He performed other heroic deeds such as raising the sky and bringing new plants to earth (p. 273). Most Maori tribes see in Maui a semihuman, semidivine juvenile delinquent who attempts to destroy the status quo of gods and men in order to overcome his feelings of inferiority due to his unnatural birth and unusual childhood (p. 182). In this process, however, he unwittingly helps human beings by improving their natural environment.

Among the people of Oceania, especially the Polynesians, Maui is the most widely known of all the mythological heroes. His exploits are frequently mentioned in the daily life of the islanders. The stories are not sacred and can be told at any time (p. 273). Tales of his adventures and tricks have therefore become a major form of entertainment for children and adults alike, on both festive and informal occasions. Many humorous skits based on Maui's exploits have been witnessed by ethnographers in several atolls of eastern Polynesia. Costumed actors burlesque their mythical ancestor and perform various antics to which the audience responds with laughter (p. 80). Dramas are enacted in which Maui is the principal character and the comic possibilities of the various episodes are exploited to the fullest extent (p. 83).

Hindu Myths

Over a period of two thousand years, personalities that show the typical trickster traits have waxed and waned in popularity in Vedic, Epic, and Puranic Hindu myths, most of which are in verse form. These myths reveal a combination of the most sacred and profane elements. Even the mighty gods do not escape the embarrassing consequences when they succumb to primordial desires instead of keeping them under control. An important theme that runs through many episodes is that "the excess of anything, bad or good—such as the virtue of an ascetic—poses a threat to the balance of the closed universe" (O'Flaherty 1973:282). Although many Hindu divine and semidivine figures seem to suffer at one time or another from their excesses in pleasures of food and sex, a few seem prone to such misfortunes because of their basic tricksterlike personalities. Among them are Indra, the Vedic king of gods, a sage called Narada, and Krishna, the popular hero of the epic *Mahābhārata*, especially during his childhood and adolescence.

Indra's personality as depicted in many Vedic tales combines seemingly opposite roles and attributes. He was a rowdy amoral deity fond of feasting and drinking (Basham 1959:234, 400). His birth was miraculous; he was the son of Heaven and Earth. When he was born, Indra remained concealed. He drank Soma, however, the powerful beverage that caused him to swell to such an enormous and terrifying size that Heaven and Earth flew apart to stay so forever, and Indra filled the space between them. He thus became his parents' youngest child (W. N. Brown 1961). Other gods asked Indra to be their champion in their battle against the demons, and Indra accepted the task on the condition that he would become their king. Indra then battled a mighty demon with his weapon, the lightning bolt, and killed him to take cosmic waters from his body, from which emerged the Sun (W. N. Brown 1961:282–87). Thus Indra was credited with the creation of the universe and with the presence of the sun and the water.

Indra was cowardly, however, and constantly worried that other gods, sages, and demons would usurp his power. He was especially afraid of sages practicing penance. In several episodes Indra reduced the spiritual power of the sages by turning their attention away from acquiring *tapas*, the mystical power, or omniscience. His favorite method was to entice a sage practicing penance to sexual pleasures, thus stopping him from either acquiring tapas or making him lose the power already acquired because of sexual involvement. *Apsaras*, the beautiful female entertainers from heaven, were frequently Indra's emissaries in such missions. Once a sage had "fallen" by virtue of his sexual involvement, the Apsara sent by Indra to seduce him returned to Indra's court.

Indra himself was very salacious and was a notorious adulterer. He did not hesitate to satisfy his sexual desires by cohabiting with beautiful women, whatever their status. He was willing to go to any length and to use sly and ingenious methods, including transvestism, to satisfy his lust. Many episodes describe his seduction of the beautiful wives of sages. He was not always successful, however, and, when caught, suffered serious consequences. He was cursed by the husbands of women he seduced and frequently lost his magical and spiritual power because of his deception and trickery. In one episode, he suffered by receiving a thousand eyes on his body because of his desire to see beautiful women in the nude (Meyer 1953:485). Indra's wife was "the most lascivious of women" who "boasted of her husband's sexual prowess, rejoiced in the dimensions of his sexual organ, and tried to get him drunk" (O'Flaherty 1973:85). Although Indra was a prominent trickster figure in the early Vedic literature, he appears to have lost importance in the subsequent Epic and Puranic mythological literature.

Another trickster figure in Hindu mythology was the well-known sage Narada, who often acted as a messenger among gods, sages, and demons. He was, however, a meddlesome individual and took secret pleasure in quarrels and the failure of other people. A troublemaker, he often exaggerated facts and deliberately distorted messages. Occasionally his desire to have some fun made him overzealous. The gods were offended when they found themselves in difficulties on Narada's account, and he was condemned to some lowly state or to some undesirable end. Narada too had a strong sexual drive and constantly desired beautiful women. In short, Narada was a notorious meddler and gossip-monger who acted "as a mediating agent. . ., catalysing the transition from one phase to the next by inspiring anger, jealousy or lust in characters formerly uninvolved" (O'Flaherty 1973:73). Other gods and sages were quite aware that Narada had these attributes. In one episode seven sages, while discussing Narada, remarked that any man or woman who listened to his advice was sure to leave home and become a beggar. Although Narada tried to play tricks on others for fun, he was also tricked. When he became too conceited and thought that he was as good as or even better than Shiva and Vishnu, they put him in his place to demonstrate to others that he was not superior to gods. In one episode, Narada, like Indra, had to undergo sex change because he doubted the word of Vishnu.

Krishna, the well-known hero of the epic *Mahābhārata* and the narrator of *Bhagavad-Gīta*, the sacred scripture of Hinduism, had a miraculous birth, after which he grew up in a pastoral village (W. N. Brown 1961:297–98). He was a trickster during his childhood and adolescence. He harassed milkmaids on their way to the market and frequently stole from them curd and butter, which he was especially fond of eating. He was also sexually promiscuous. He was enamored of the milkmaids and pestered them to satisfy his sexual desires. He fondled their breasts and touched their sexual organs under the pretext of finding his lost ball during games; he hid their clothing on trees when they went to the river to bathe, and he offered to return the garments only if the milkmaids came out of the water nude. His mother was constantly approached by the harassed citizens because of the antics of young Krishna and his playmates.

The pranks of young Krishna that involved food and sexual adventures became a major source of innumerable plays and prose narratives during medieval and modern times, both in Sanskrit and in the middle and modern Indic languages. In addition to the humorous overtones in which many episodes are depicted, the basic theme in much of this literature is that young Krishna's antics are manifestations of god's "play," thus emphasizing the play element in Hindu myths (Kinsley 1975). A considerable part of the later literature on Krishna's playful and sexual activities is also in poetry. Songs are sung at various festivals, especially at the spring festival of Holi, which is well known because of the freedom people have to play practical jokes and to amuse themselves at the expense of others. All such activities are said to be the enactment or imitation of young Krishna's antics (Marriott 1966/1968:207). In modern times many films have depicted Krishna's childhood and his trickster role. He is also a topic of much entertainment and humor in folk theater.

In his adult life Krishna became a celebrated culture hero and was one of the most popular incarnations of god. The culture hero role of his later life was already evident during his adolescence, when he killed several demons, including a king, to protect people from misery and misfortune.

African Prose Narratives

Animal tricksters are very common and are an integral part of many animal tales in African prose narratives. Despite the availability of many anthologies of folktales in general (see the bibliography in Finnegan 1970), anthologies and systematic studies of trickster tales have been relatively few until recently. The collection of tales pertaining to Ture, the Zande trickster (Evans-Pritchard 1967), is pioneering in this respect. Ture is a popular trickster among the Azande of East Africa. His exploits do not constitute a cycle, as they have no fixed chronological order and the tales are not connected (Evans-Pritchard 1967:19–20). Each tale is independent and self-contained and presents an episode involving one of Ture's many adventures or mishaps. The following description of Ture is based on Evans-Pritchard's anthology.

The name Ture means "spider." Ture is considered a person (p. 23), however, and appears to be an anthropomorphic figure in many tales. Ture occasionally disguises himself as a woman but generally does not change into other animal shapes or objects. Nor does he seem to have any gross physical deformities. He is thought to be immortal (p. 23); in some episodes he is killed but is brought back to life (p. 128). Ture's primary aim is to satisfy his hunger and sexual desires, and he has no scruples whatsoever in constantly pursuing these goals. Several episodes depict his efforts to obtain such foods as termites, animal meat, honey, and mushrooms. Other episodes describe his pursuit of women for intercourse.

Because he is lazy, Ture is always keen on acquiring various magical objects and formulas that he thinks will instantly satisfy his desires for food and sex. Acquisition of the formula in itself often becomes his goal, which he achieves by tricking others or by stealing magical objects. He rarely learns the formulas properly, however, because of his haste in imitating the magical acts. As a result, he never accomplishes his purpose. Instead he usually gets into trouble. Ture's failures seem inevitable because of his personality, which combines trickery and naivete. Ture has a natural proclivity for deceiving people and breaking social norms, including incest taboos. He describes himself as someone who has been fooling people all his life (pp. 22, 124). He kills his father to obtain a magical formula (pp. 139–40) and seduces his mother-in-law (pp. 144–45). In the first instance, however, he fails in using the magical formula to get food, and in the second, his incestual act is discovered because his "private parts" talk. When he finds himself in trouble, he has to run away or hide in order to prevent other people from hurting him.

All in all, then, Ture depicts such traits as childishness, selfishness, greed, treachery, foolishness, and lack of restraint. He is a liar, a cheat, a murderer, and a breaker of social rules. Still, Ture plays the role of a culture hero: he released water from the dam of an old woman who never gave it to anyone and who killed everyone who tried to get it. Ture also obtained food from a man in the sky for the people on earth, who had none, and he spread fire on earth (pp. 37–40).

Spider as a trickster appears in the prose narratives of various African cultures. Among the Limba he is Wosi and is represented as "stupid, gluttonous, selfish and irresponsible" (Finnegan 1967:37). Interestingly, Wosi is regularly outwitted by his wife, Kayi. Wosi also seems to act in "an anti-social and unfitting way" in his attempts to cheat his wife. He tells her lies, tries to take her food, and insults her mother. He is occasionally portrayed as clever and cunning and succeeds in "getting the better of bigger animals like the elephant or the leopard" (Finnegan 1967:37). He is an amusing character because of his personality and his tricks, which do not seem to work. Spider is a trickster figure also in the prose narratives in Ghana, Ivory Coast, and Sierra Leone. Among the Akan-Ashanti people he is known as Ananse (Finnegan 1970:344; Rattray 1930).

Other animals appear as tricksters in the prose narratives of some African cultures. A little hare, for example, is the trickster in the tales of the Bantu peoples of South Africa and is also common in areas of West Africa. The tortoise, antelope, squirrel, wren, weasel, and jackal also appear to play the trickster role in African folklore but are not characteristic of any specific region (Finnegan 1970:344). These animals are portrayed as wily but also as stupid, gluttonous, boastful, and generally ineffective. The tricks they use are similar from one to another. These tricksters represent human emotions in animal form. Most African trickster tales end with morals, although these do not appear to be well integrated.

Individual tricksters in the folktales of specific African cultures reflect certain traits more prominently than others, as is the case in North America. In the Bantu tales of the trickster Hare, slyness emerges as his major trait. The trickster Mantis in Bushman tales is notable for his supernatural association and unusual actions. All tricksters, however, share such opposing traits as kindness and mischief or foolishness and strength (Finnegan 1970:345).

Legba, the sky deity, and Yo are the two popular tricksters in Dahomean tales (Herskovits and Herskovits 1958). Legba is the youngest child of the female creator Mawu. He is deformed, undisciplined, and spoiled, and he has never known any punishment. Unlike his brothers, he has no kingdom to rule, knows no restraints, and is defiant of authority. So he is given the job of visiting his brothers' kingdoms and reporting the happenings to his mother. Thus he becomes the spokesman for gods and humans. Legba "loves mischief, knows no inhibition, recognizes no taboos, dares to challenge injustices, even on the part of the creator, and to expose them" (Herskovits and Herskovits 1958:36). He can do favors for others, but only if he is so disposed and only for a price. He has much knowledge, is the maker of magical charms, and is the creator of such animals as the serpent and the dog. Still, he makes his mother Mawu angry because of his undesirable activities. He often "turns the perversities of his own nature into a reproach against Mawu herself" (p. 44). Legba seems to desire sexual activity much more than food. He is willing to sleep with any woman and does so even with his mother-in-law (p. 145), his sister, and his daughter (p. 175). He frequently manages to escape punishment for his wicked deeds and does not seem to care even when cursed to bear a penis forever erect because of his incestual behavior (p. 176).

Yo is the "protagonist of the humorous tale," "the symbol of comedy" who gives his name to the tales (Herskovits and Herskovits 1958:101, 319). Yo is not a diviner or a mythic figure. He is portrayed as both a man and an animal (pp. 336–41), is immortal, and is capable of changing into different shapes (p. 343). He tricks other animals for the purpose of gaining food, and they suffer the consequences of Yo's mischief by being punished. Yo is willing to eat anything, including human beings (p. 340). Occasionally he is caught and is punished for his deeds. Unlike other tricksters, however, Yo does not display both stupidity and cleverness. He seems mostly conniving.

From an anthropological viewpoint it is desirable to determine the generality of the trickster figure. His prevalence in the folklore of world cultures depends on how the concept is defined at both the culture-specific and the general levels. While the concept has been defined in culture-specific contexts, general definitions are lacking. The term "trickster" has been used in imprecise ways, perhaps because it is believed to be self-explanatory.

In its most literal meaning, "trickster" means someone who plays tricks. Figures so labeled, however, have many other attributes in the existing descriptive accounts and analyses. One of the very few general definitions describes tricksters as "supernatural beings of semi-divine origins who may accidentally give important culture traits to the group but are not basically concerned with human welfare" (Malefijt 1968b:162). Interestingly, this definition does not even mention what others have considered to be the most crucial trait of tricksters, namely the tendency to cheat other people in order to satisfy their own primordial desires. Other definitions of the trickster based primarily on the North American Indian data merely list his "typical" physiological and psychological traits. Voegelin describes the tricksters in North American prose narratives as animal-human beings who are typically "greedy, erotic, imitative, stupid, pretentious, deceitful" and whose thievery and deceitfulness benefit people (1949:1124). Stern (1953:158) and Ricketts (1964:1) essentially agree with Voegelin's descriptive definition, although Ricketts adds that the trickster is a restless wanderer and does not distinguish between friend and foe in carrying out his pranks. According to Abrahams (1968), the trickster is the most paradoxical of all characters in traditional narratives, and his outstanding characteristic is his lack of morals. In Abraham's view the concepts of jesters, fools, clowns, and morons all basically derive from the broad, general notion of trickster.

Because most definitions and descriptive statements seem to emanate from the accounts of tricksters in the North American Indian prose narratives, they include certain attributes not necessarily shared by comparable figures in other cultures. While the American Indian tricksters appear to be mythical or divine characters, or are associated with etiological themes of the universe, such is generally not the case in African prose narratives. North American Indian tricksters are often animal-human. The same is not true of Hindu gods, who nonetheless seem to fit into the trickster role, because they are gluttonous and highly erotic and engage in many activities unbecoming to their divine nature. The situation with the Oceanic trickster Maui is similar.

The cross-cultural variations in the characteristics of the trickster and the differences of opinion concerning his nature suggest that a more comprehensive approach is necessary. The following four dimensions seem crucial in defining the theoretical concept of trickster: origin and association; identity and form; behavior and actions; and personality. Each of these dimensions in turn includes numerous traits.

Origins and Association

It appears from the prose narratives of the North American Indians that the trickster is generally associated with etiological themes of the universe, especially such elements as light, water, land, and rocks. Second, the trickster has a divine or supernatural origin. Such is also the case in the prose narratives of Oceania, in Hindu myths, and, to a limited degree, in African folktales. The trickster's acts, though not intended to be altruistic, provide many of the natural elements essential for the survival and perpetuation of humans. The trickster is also a destructive force, however. The seeming incongruity has led to considerable scholarly debate about the dual roles of some trickster figures, although not all individual tricksters embody conflict, even among the American Indians. Among the Navaho Indians, the benevolent and malevolent roles are clearly represented by two figures, one a culture hero and the other a trickster. Such is also the case in the prose narratives of the Micmac and Penobscot Indians (Boas 1940/1966:414).

Some American Indian tricksters are portrayed as having been born of virgins or of dead women (Boas 1940/1966:408). Alternatively, their birth is mysterious: they simply exist. The Oceanic trickster, Maui, in addition to having been born from a blood clot and having been picked up from the sea by the gods, is described as the last child of his parents. The Hindu god Indra is portrayed as the last child of Heaven and Earth. Similarly, Legba, the Dahomean trickster, is the last child of the female creator Mawu. Thus the causes of the tricksters' character are to be found in their unusual origins, which provide insights into their personality traits and actions. Yet not all tricksters seem to have unusual, divine, or mysterious origins. Many African animal tricksters are cases in point and differ in this respect from other tricksters. They are unusual, however, because many human qualities are associated with them despite their nonhuman existence. The Zande spider trickster, Ture, for instance, is depicted as having human emotions, desires, and abilities. Much the same is true of such other animal tricksters as Turtle, Hare, and Mantis.

Identity and Form

Tricksters frequently change form. They seem to switch back and forth from an anthropomorphic to a theriomorphic form and from one sex to another. They can also change into different objects. Such is the case with some American Indian tricksters, with the African trickster Ture, and with Indra in Hindu myths. Tricksters may also be physically grotesque, although the degree varies across cultures. The Winnebago trickster has an enormously long penis, and his intestines are wrapped around his body. In some versions the Oceanic trickster, Maui, is depicted as having eight heads (Luomala 1949:139–40). The Hindu trickster god Indra has a thousand eyes on his body. Legba, the Dahomean trickster, is cursed with a permanently erect penis. The Zande trickster, Ture, is capable of removing his intestines for cleaning.

Behavior and Actions

Tricksters are primarily preoccupied with satisfying their basal desires and with deriving pleasure. In pursuit of this goal they steal, cheat, injure, or even kill animals and humans, and they seduce women. They find enjoyment at the expense of others and take great delight in deceiving and depriving other people. In pursuit of such aims, tricksters totally disregard the established social norms. They break many taboos, and their behavior is antisocial. The tricksters often lack the ability to carry out their tasks successfully, however, and frequently act in a haphazard manner. As a result, they do not always achieve their objectives, their misdeeds are discovered, and they too suffer the injuries and pains that they try to inflict on others. They are punished for breaking taboos. Sometimes the very tricks that they try to carry out get them into trouble. To some extent, the tricksters' behavior reflects a relationship of contest with the rest of the world.

Personality

The tricksters' personalities often combine many opposing traits in an unusual way. Most tricksters are pranksters and are primarily egotistical. They are powerful, clever, selfish, cruel, deceitful, cunning, and sly. They are also boastful, foolish, lazy, and ineffective. They have no control over their basal desires and seek instant gratification. They are infantile, inordinate, lack restraint, and ignore social responsibilities. Tricksters are prone to blunder and have no ability to distinguish between good and evil, between themselves and others, and between objects and organisms. Within the Freudian conceptual framework, the tricksters have psychopathic personalities that are dominated by Id without the control of the Super Ego. Thus impulse has the upper hand over control and conscience, and the pleasure principle reigns supreme.

The traits pertaining to the theoretical concept of trickster as extracted from the relevant prose narratives in different cultures and included in each of the four dimensions are presented in table 4. The traits listed under each dimension are not ranked. Under the dimension "Behavior and Actions," incestual acts are considered specific manifestations of the general behavior of gratification of sexual desire and the two are therefore treated as part of the same trait. Under "Origin and Association," different juxtapositions of human and animal forms and qualities are treated as part of the same trait because the emphasis is on the unusual combination.

Although all four dimensions are necessary for formulating the theoretical concept of trickster, the number of traits under each dimension exhibited by tricksters in individual cultures may vary. A few tricksters possess more than other tricksters, and some traits are more common than others. A majority of tricksters appear to be males and either have unusual origins or seem to juxtapose animal form and human qualities. On the other hand, few tricksters engage in deliberate self-punishment. Because of the cross-cultural variation, it is difficult to specify a minimum number of traits necessary for identifying tricksters in individual culture. Rather the

Table 4. Dimensions of the conceptualization of the trickster and the traits involved

Origin and association	Identity and form	Behavior and actions	Personality
1. Divine origin	1. Male	1. Trickery	1. Extremely egotistical and selfish
2. Mysterious origin	2. Animal	2. Imitation of others' behavior	2. Gluttonous
3. Accidental origin	3. Human	3. Gratification of hunger	3. Highly erotic
4. Association with supernatural elements	4. Unusual anatomical features	4a. Gratification of sexual desire	4. Lacking in self-control and discretion, thus infantile; immoderate
5. Association with etiological themes of the universe	5. Abnormal physiological traits, i.e., constant hunger and eroticism	4b. Incestuous acts	5. Clever, cunning and cruel
		5. Foolish acts	
6a. Association with human qualities (if animal form)	6. Ability to change from anthropomorphic to theriomorphic form and vice versa	6. Excessive and/or incorrect use of magical formulas	6. Cowardly and foolish
6b. Association with animal qualities (if human form)	7. Ability to change sex	7. Participation in all kinds of competitions	7. Naive, ineffective
	8. Ability to change into inanimate objects	8. Acts of hurting or killing others	8. Competitive nature
		9. Self-punishment	9. Braggart

discussion of traits listed in table 4 and their classification into four major dimensions should primarily constitute a general framework within which culture-specific tricksters can be identified and analyzed.

THE TRICKSTER AS A SOURCE OF HUMOR

Although the trickster has long been a topic of anthropological and folkloristic research, investigators have primarily focused on understanding why a culture hero and a trickster have been combined in one personage. The trickster is recognized to be a major stimulus of humor,[10] but there is little systematic analysis explaining why and how. What fundamental humor themes do tricksters represent, and what functions do they serve through humor? These matters need to be discussed.

Incongruity Theories

Theories that see humor as a consequence of incongruency or discrepancy best explain why tricksters and their antics are amusing, although other theories also seem relevant in limited ways. Many scholars have proposed theories of humor in which incongruity figures prominently.[11] McGhee takes the position that incongruity is central to all humor. By "incongruity" he means that "something unexpected, out of context, inappropriate, unreasonable, illogical, exaggerated and so forth must serve as the basic vehicle for humor of an event, even though additional elements like sex and aggression maximize funniness" (1979:10).

The trickster concept appears to merge biological, psychological, behavioral, and sociocultural incongruities—juxtapositions of elements that are considered unexpected, inappropriate, and illogical in the sociocultural reality of most human beings. In addition, the degree of divergence from cultural expectations in these incongruities is often extreme. As we have seen, no single trickster figure embodies all possible incongruities. It is nevertheless useful to recapitulate them, providing the context within which the concept of the trickster and the humor associated with him at the culture-specific level may be explained and understood.

A fundamental incongruity inherent in the trickster concept is the combination of the opposing roles and functions of a culture hero and a selfish buffoon, a "giver of culture" and a "destroyer of culture." On the one hand, the trickster is associated with the "origin of culture" (Carroll 1981; Lévi-Strauss 1955), while on the other, he is associated with excessive indulgence in and gratification of primordial desires in ways that are generally associated with the "destruction of culture."

The tricksters in general have extraordinary circumstances associated with their birth that defy the senses of reason, order, or logic and thus represent an incongruous aspect of their character. Other such aspects include tricksters' anatomical and physiological features that have extraordinary or exaggerated forms and functions and their juxtapositions of opposing personality traits. Rarely are individuals with such opposing traits to be found in human societies. Tricksters thus appear to be disorderly, chaotic personalities. They also manifest extremely inappropriate and socially deviant behavior and actions. Their acts are aberrant by any cultural standards, making the tricksters misfits in human societies because of their refusal to abide by the established sociocultural norms. Finally, not only the tricksters' actions but sometimes also the consequences of such actions present incongruities. The incongruities associated with tricksters, in other words, are biological, psychological, and sociocultural.

Other Theories

Theories of vicarious pleasure, cathartic release of tension, and superiority can help explain why tricksters provide humor stimuli. The trickster's activities, involving his gratification of infantile hunger and eroticism while he flouts social norms, appeal to most individuals' suppressed desires and provide vicarious pleasure. Freud (1905, 1928), the major exponent of this theory, argued that human beings have strong sexual and aggressive impulses at the unconscious level that need to be vented. Because society does not allow individuals to express these impulses directly, humor, especially of the type associated with tricksters, provides cathartic release and also the vicarious triumph of the pleasure principle. At the same time, the numerous punishments that are meted out to the trickster, the undesirable consequences of his outrageous actions, and his overall stupidity make the listeners feel superior.[12]

THE TRICKSTER AND NARRATIVE

Verbal narration of tales is a major contributing factor in trickster-related humor. Accompanied by gestures, facial expressions,

movements, and mimicking, such narration constitutes performance that provides a crucial context for the available text (Ben-
Amos 1971:5). Trickster tales, like any other genre of verbal art,
are generally presented orally to an audience by an accomplished
storyteller-cum-performer, who provides the additional audiovis-
ual stimuli of humor. In many African cultures talented storytellers
are much in demand because of their narrative style and mimicking
abilities (Scheub 1975). The story tellers "live" and "act" the tales
rather than just repeating them, and no written version could re-
produce the real atmosphere of the actual narration. The animal
tricksters and their amusing antics are described vividly in terms
of their appearance, behavior, and calls. "Mimicry of a humorous
and satirical kind seems most common" in the case of animal trickster stories (Finnegan 1970:384). In addition, the tone of voice,
gestures, the musical quality of the chants, and mimicry all emphasize what is being said (Evans-Pritchard 1967:18–19). The humor in trickster tales clearly depends on the use of verbal and visual
modalities and on social collectivity and interaction. Unfortunately,
even in the case of American Indian prose narratives, little attention
has been given in the past to context, function, and performance
of verbal art, while texts are overemphasized in folklore research
(Brunvand 1972:2).

THE TRICKSTER AND RELIGIOUS IDEOLOGY

Much controversy has surrounded the so-called incongruent
combination of opposing roles as "destroyer of culture" and "culture hero," or transformer. The term "transformer" is used in this
context because the trickster transformed the nature of the world
by acquiring numerous natural elements so that people could live
on this earth.

Although the debate about the duality of the trickster figure has
often centered on the North American trickster tales, the situation
is similar in the folktales of other culture areas. Maui, the Oceanic
trickster, for instance, also transformed the world by obtaining fire
and pulling islands from the sea. Indra, the Hindu trickster-deity,
obtained cosmic waters. Ture, the African trickster, obtained fire
and water. The issue of this duality is significant because it has
broader implications. It suggests that humor bears a close relationship to the ideological aspects of religion, and the traditional
distinction between myths and folktales that was emphasized by

early folklorists and anthropologists seems to blur. Several theories have been proposed to explain how the trickster came to be both culture hero and destroyer.[13]

Part of the problem in the debate lies with the unfortunate use of the phrase "culture hero." Tricksters are not culture heroes in the sense in which the term is commonly used. They are not noble, generous, caring, far-sighted, or altruistic. They certainly lack both a broad vision of the ultimate good of human societies and a motivation to act for it. As Boas (1898:7) rightly noted, the fact that the tricksters' acts benefited humans is simply incidental, an unintentional by-product of the quest for self-gratification or trouble. One reason for the scholarly controversy is to be found in the monotheistic religious perspective of Christianity, which does not approve of vulgar elements. In keeping with the Judaeo-Christian religious tradition, scholars felt that religious ideology had to be solemn. Vulgar, outlandish, and humorous elements had no place in it. In addition, scholars in the nineteenth and early twentieth centuries were influenced by ethnocentric viewpoints, which prompted them to subscribe to a unilinear evolutionary theory of human culture and to distinguish between primitive and civilized religious systems by inferring a difference in cultural sophistication. An implicit assumption in some early theories seems to be that only in the primitive psyche or religion can the sacred and the vulgar be juxtaposed.[14]

The primary assumption implicit in the extensively debated issue of the duality of the trickster, namely that humor and religious ideology are not consonant with each other, has been rejected by some scholars (Trueblood 1964; Webster 1960), who have tried to demonstrate, with reference to the Bible, that Christ used humor to preach to the masses. In such other major world religions as Hinduism and Zen Buddhism, the sacred and the profane are sufficiently mixed to indicate that these elements were combined without any awareness of contradiction. In Hindu mythology there is much emphasis on *līlā* (play) of the gods, which includes both humor and laughter as well as indulgence for its own sake (Kinsley 1975). In addition, there are Hindu gods who are both transformers on the one hand and gluttons and buffoons on the other. Similarly, the ancient Zen masters' clownish activities and their tricksterlike behavior suggests that "concentration upon enlightenment often takes forms closer to pure clowning" (Willeford 1969:233).

In general, then, the premise that trickster-related humor is an integral part of religion appears consonant with the many theoretical positions of scholars, namely, that there is a parallel between religion and humor because both allow humans to dispose of much that seems unpredicted, capricious, and out of place in life (Allport 1950:92), that mythology bridges the gap between the psychological and cognitive aspects of religion by the use of humor (O'Flaherty 1976:15), or that the "religious values" of humor are important and if "they are lost or forgotten, heroic religion is deprived of one of its principal techniques for meeting life's defeats" (Ricketts 1966:348).

PROBLEMS OF SEMANTIC BOUNDARIES

The concept of the trickster is closely related to other concepts represented by such terms as "fool," "clown," "buffoon," "moron," and "numskull." They all overlap semantically and have been used as synonyms in both generic and specific senses by anthropologists and folklorists as well as by other scholars. They are also used interchangeably to denote judgment pronounced upon certain types of individuals in contemporary societies and cultures. Willeford (1969) makes the problem explicit when he comments that he is using the terms "fool" and "clown" "sometimes synonymously, sometimes not, in a compromise between current and earlier usage" (p. 240). Towsen's (1976) book is entitled *Clowns*, while the first chapter is called "Fools: Natural and Artificial." Zucker (1967) uses the term "clown" in a generic sense inclusive of the concepts of fool and trickster in his discussion of its artistic, behavioral, religious, and mythological underpinnings. It is therefore necessary to examine the nature of interrelationships among these concepts, taking into consideration the inclusive, intersecting, contrastive and common-core semantic attributes of the terms in order to distinguish between them in some way. The problem is a complex one, and the solution presented here is tentative at best.

It appears that all such terms as "trickster," "fool," "clown," "buffoon," "moron," and "numskull" share a common-core meaning involving lack of common sense and social propriety, love of imitation, at least an outward manifestation of stupidity, a chaotic or disorderly nature, and an incongruous juxtaposition of traits generally assumed to be contradictory. Beyond this shared meaning, however, each term needs to be separated from others by additional semantic attributes.

It appears that the terms "fool" and "buffoon" do not really have additional semantic attributes associated with them and can therefore be used generically, to include all the other terms, or specifically, without any additional connotations. Such is not the case with other terms. The term "clown" has a strong behavioristic connotation and the context of social reality. It is applied to individuals who act in an absurd manner because they "naturally" lack common sense and social propriety or intentionally pretend to do so, sometimes as part of a profession or performance.

Various subcategories of the concept of clown can be recognized on contextual bases. The existing literature already specifies them, using such labels as "ritual clown," of much interest to anthropologists, "circus clowns," "stage clowns," "stand-up clowns," and "royal clowns" (Towsen 1976). The last subcategory is also identified by the term "jester," which historically seems associated with the royal courts, in which the clown was generally a companion of kings or other similar figures of authority. A jester is generally intelligent but often deformed. He entertains his master and courtesans by absurd behavior but can and often does outwit them if the need arises. He is good at scapegoating others, and his master is no exception.

The terms "moron" and "numskull" generally seem to denote individuals in contemporary societies around whom numerous jokes and tales cluster. Such figures become popular for their utter stupidity, and new jokes are continually being associated with them. The terms also become attached to members of socioeconomically disadvantaged ethnic or occupational groups who are stereotypically viewed as displaying stupidity and other related and uncouth traits. Thus the popularity of the so-called Polish moron or numskull jokes and jokes at the expense of "Aggies," students at Texas A and M University.

The term "trickster" has by and large a textual, expecially folkloristic, basis and is separated from the other terms by four characteristics. First, the trickster usually has an unusual origin or association. He seems embedded in antiquity and often, though not always, has some divine or mythical background. Other terms do not seem to have this connotation. The trickster also appears to be primordial. Second, the trickster's activities usually have etiological implications. He is frequently considered responsible for the shape and nature of the universe as it is today, most often because he transformed it, though unintentionally, by the acquisition of natural elements such as fire, water, sun, and rocks for his own use. Other terms do not have this semantic attribution.

234

Third, the trickster can be either theriomorphic or anthropo-morphic, while the other terms are used generally to refer to human characters. The trickster is also capable of transforming himself into any animal, object, or human being of either sex. The other terms do not imply this capacity. When the trickster is anthromorphic, he is either enfant terrible, as seems to be the case with the Da-homean Legba, the Oceanic Maui, and Krishna in Hindu mythol-ogy, or he is an "old man," as he is among many North American Indian tribes. The other terms generally imply an adult human being. The clown, though an adult, may make himself small in appearance or may have a physical deformity—note the prepon-derance of dwarfs and midgets as clowns (Towsen 1976:5, 34) and the number of actors of normal size who move about in a squatting position to pretend to be dwarfs. (Dwarfs are quite popular as circus clowns.)

Fourth, the figures to which the label "trickster" has been applied in the extensive folkloristic literature seem finite, most having been enumerated and taken into account in the study of the folklore of cultures around the world. Edmonson (1971:142) provides an ex-tensive list of trickster figures recognized in various cultural tra-ditions. It is unlikely, for instance, that, among the numerous American Indian groups, any new animal will acquire the status of trickster, since Coyote, Mink, Weasel, Bluejay, Raven, Hare, and a few other animals have already been established as tricksters. In other words, trickstermaking is not a continuous process, nor is it a social one. On the other hand, new individuals continue to emerge as clowns, fools, buffoons, and so on, primarily because fool making is a continuing social process.[15] Individuals may un-wittingly fall into the role of a fool or buffoon or may become so professionally. In American mass media, for example, especially in movies and on television, Steve Martin achieved recognition as a fool.

THEORETICAL PROPOSITIONS

The following cross-culturally significant theoretical propositions emerge from the discussion of the trickster.

The biological, psychological, behavioral, and sociocultural incongruities shape the trickster's personality, making him a major humor-generating stimulus in the oral literature of many societies.

235

The dimensions of origin and association, identity and form, behavior and action, and personality are crucial in establishing a cross-cultural conceptual framework for identifying tricksters.

Trickster tales are popular because they provide vicarious outlets for infantile aggression and for sexual desires while enabling the listener to feel superior because of the trickster's stupidity.

Humor in trickster tales has a normative function, because the tales reinforce self-control as a prerequisite for membership in social groups.

Narration is of great importance in trickster-related humor. There is much scope for dramatizing the trickster's personality by imitation and action. Trickster tales depend for their humor on the use of both verbal and visual modalities.

Trickster tales demonstrate that humor is indeed an integral part of religious ideology in many cultures of the world.

PART III

BEHAVIORAL RESPONSES
TO HUMOR

8

Laughter and Smiling: Evolutionary and Biosocial Aspects

The term "laughter" has been used extensively and in many ways in most studies on humor. It has been used as a synonym for "humor" by some individuals and as a criterion to define the overall domain of humor by others.[1] In any case, researchers recognize the intimate connection between humor and laughter; the two seem to have a cause-effect or a stimulus-response relationship in many social situations. Not every instance of laughter, however, results from humor, nor does every humorous event necessarily produce laughter.[2] Laughter, besides being linked to humor, appears to express the primordial human emotion of sheer joy.

There is considerable diversity within and across cultures in the kinds of stimuli that evoke laughter. Sociocultural and psychological factors affecting individuals within a culture also lead to differential responses to potential laughter-producing stimuli. In one study (Valentine 1942, as quoted in Flugel 1954:710), it was found that young children respond with laughter to, among other things, delight, the laughter or smile of another person, the sight of a bright or pleasing object, tickling, mild shock or surprise, social play, and incongruity in words or ideas. Many of these stimuli can also produce laughter or smiling in adults.

In this chapter I shall examine laughter and smiling from biological, evolutionary, and sociocultural perspectives, focusing on the following topics: laughter as a physiological process; causes of laughter within the context of human emotions and their expressions (I shall examine the evolutionary aspects of "laughter" and "smiling" expressions among mammals, particularly among the higher primates—in short, their phylogenetic development); the ontogeny of laughter and smiling in *Homo sapiens*; the phonetics

239

and sound symbolism of laughter; and sociocultural factors affecting laughter and smiling in human behavior.

Homo sapiens has often been defined as a laughing animal because laughter and smiling are considered uniquely human attributes,[3] together with such other traits as language and tool making. The higher primates come close to being like humans in language and tool making, but do not have the human capacity of producing diverse varieties of laughter and smiling and of associating them with social, psychological, and symbolic values. Although scholars of diverse disciplinary interests have studied the phenomenon of laughter from many different perspectives, no single theory has satisfactorily explained the origins of laughter and smiling. A survey of the extensive research on laughter and facial expressions undertaken during the hundred years since Darwin's famous study on the subject was published in 1872 (Ekman 1973) indicates that notable advances over Darwin's findings and theories are only now being made.

Darwin (1872/1965:196) stated that laughter seemed primarily to express mere joy and cited as evidence the fact that idiots and imbeciles laughed in quite a senseless manner without any external stimuli. He claimed that such individuals merely "feel pleasure and express it by laughter or smiles." He relied on his own observations and on those of his contemporaries in discussing various causes of laughter. He considered tickling, crying, and other nonjoyous emotions also to be the causes of laughter (pp. 198–99). The current view among scholars that laughter occurs for a variety of reasons, not all of which are necessarily due to humor, is basically a continuation of Darwin's views.

One of the earliest physiological theories is that of Spencer (1860), who viewed laughter as resulting from the release of excess nervous energy that could not be dissipated through another emotional action. Izard (1971:41) has labeled Spencer's theory mechanical and purely physiological. Although the physiologically beneficial effects of laughter have generally been recognized, little light has been thrown on the origin of laughter from the physiological perspective (Flugel 1954:712). Whatever the physiological causes of laughter, it is at times an involuntary reflex action and at times occurs intentionally. Individuals in different cultures are intuitively able to recognize whether or not laughter and smiling are genuine. Yet no criteria have been established for distinguishing between spontaneously occurring natural laughter and laughter that is deliberate, artificial, and acquired as part of the socialization process.

The organs involved in the production of laughter are primarily facial, although other parts of the body can also be involved, depending on the intensity of the laughter. The mouth is the most important part of the face, but eyes, eyebrows, cheeks, tongue are also used. The mouth is opened widely or narrowly, depending on the degree of laughter, with its corners drawn backward and a little upward. The upper lip is somewhat raised, and teeth are bared. The eyes are partially closed and often sparkle, while the eyebrows are generally lowered. The cheeks are drawn upward too, and wrinkles appear under the eyes. A nasolabial fold is formed that runs from the outer side of each nostril to the corner of the mouth. The lower jaw frequently moves up and down. If the laughter is sufficiently intense, tears may come to the eyes, and the whole face may become red. Breathing may become rapid. Laughter generally involves the articulation of sounds that are usually short, staccato, and often interrupted by the abrupt closing of the vocal bands.

In order to create a genuine expression of laughter, some coordination of the facial organs is necessary, especially between eye, cheek, and lip muscles. A lack of such coordination may create the impression that laughter is false or artificial or that laughter is being expressed together with some other emotion. It is not clear how much coordination is necessary, nor is there sufficient evidence to indicate whether only a single facial feature is needed for laughter to be recognized. In many cultures, the greeting expression includes both smiling and "eyebrow flashes," a very rapid eyebrow-raising movement. A mere smile without eyebrow flashes suggests recognition but also aloofness rather than a friendly attitude (Eible-Eibesfeldt 1972:299).

Recently a Facial Action Code (FAC) has been devised by Ekman and Friesen (1975, 1976) to measure facial movements. It supposedly provides a comprehensive guide for identifying all visually distinguishable and possible facial movements that underlie expressions of emotions. It includes single action units that refer separately to brows, forehead, eyelids, lips, cheeks, nasolabial folds, and so forth. The elaboration of this system suggests that various combinations of these single action units result in what the investigators have called "blends," that is, expressions that convey two or more emotions simultaneously. It is also obvious from the published discussions and from the accompanying photos that coordination of a minimum number of such single action units of facial movements is necessary to signify not only the blends but also the primary emotions, including laughter.

As the intensity of laughter increases, the upper limbs of the body may be set in motion, so that hand movements may occur, the torso may be swung back and forth, and the head may be thrown back. It is difficult, however, to determine with any degree of precision how many bodily features may be involved in any particular degree or state of laughter, just as it is difficult to distinguish clearly between moderate and intense laughter.

EVOLUTION

In analyzing laughter and other similar facial expressions from the comparative and evolutionary viewpoints, the crucial question is: how did facial displays become the mode of communicating different emotions in *Homo sapiens* and other animals? According to ethologists and primatologists, expressions of joy and affection that involve opening the mouth, baring the teeth, and making noises occur among primates. The vocal organs seem to give many animals the most efficient way of expressing emotions, but the kinds of sounds produced vary considerably. Animals also use numerous bodily displays, for example, the involuntary erection of hair, the ruffling of feathers, the expansion of throat pouches, the enlargement of the body, and the drawing back of ears, to express different emotions.

Together with other bodily displays, facial expressions acquired communicative functions during the evolutionary process. Most animals have some form of social organization, and because of the need to coordinate social behavior, many bodily displays begin to serve as signals when they are frequently accompanied by a certain state of arousal or activity on the part of members of specific social groups. Thus "expressive movements are behavioral patterns that have become differentiated into signals" (Eible-Eibesfeldt 1970:91). Expressive movements did not, however, have the same communicative functions throughout the evolutionary process. Not only do the functions change over a period of time, but often the displays may occur without antecedent stimuli or subsequent responses. Many animals continue to behave in particular ways that related to survival at one point in evolution but not at the present time. Some bodily displays continue to occur as reflex actions.

The probable sequence in the evolution of facial expressions can be described as follows. Originally, facial expressions, like other bodily displays, probably accompanied functional activities or were reflex responses to stimuli from the environment. Andrew (1963, 1965) argues that various processes involving the environment or other organisms activated specific responses to protect vulnerable areas, especially sense organs. Among animals that fight with their teeth, for example, ear flattening could be considered a response action to protect the ears from being torn by antagonists. Any startling change in the environment that suggests the possibility of attack may lead such animals to flatten their ears. In the evolutionary process such response actions were perpetuated by natural selection and became exaggerated displays because of their newly acquired communicative value (Andrew 1965:4). Darwin made essentially the same point much earlier (1872/1965:356) when he alluded to the fact that many inherited expressive movements were at first voluntarily performed for a specific purpose, soon became habitual, and eventually were hereditary. It appears, then, that expressions originally accompanied functional activities or reflex responses to certain stimuli, that they were originally not innate expressions of emotions, and that through evolutionary processes facial expressions came to represent not only intentions but also emotional states.

Despite general agreement on such points, there are differing views on the evolutionary development of laughter and smiling in *Homo sapiens*. Among the primates two major types of displays appear to be morphologically similar to the expressive movements of laughter and smiling among humans. They are "grin face," which Van Hooff (1972:212) further classifies into "silent bared-teeth" and "vocalized bared-teeth" displays, and "play face," or "relaxed open-mouth," display (Andrew 1963, 1965; Van Hooff 1972). Various intentions have been attributed to the grin face display. A grin, for instance, could occur as a preliminary to the action of biting hard at food or in defense; it could also occur as a protective response, either to a startling stimuli or when the animal's face is in close proximity to an unknown or dangerous object (Andrew 1963).

The grin face display among the primates involves not only retraction of the lips but also the baring of teeth. Van Hooff argues that both types of grin face displays are characterized by "fully retracted mouth-corners and lips, so that an appreciable part of the gum is bared; closed or only slightly opened mouth; inhibited body movements and eyes that are widely or normally open and can be directed straight or obliquely towards an interacting partner" (1972:213). The only difference between the silent bared-teeth displays and the vocalized bared-teeth displays is that the latter are accompanied by mostly high-pitched and loud vocalizations, which can be roughly described as screams, squeals, and barks.

The vocalized bared-teeth display is phylogenetically one of the oldest facial expressions, according to Van Hooff, and occurs not only in all primates but also in most other mammals. Vocalized and silent bared-teeth displays are produced when primates confront some threat or strong aversive stimulation. These displays essentially express fear and occur in a situation of defense when the actor shows a strong tendency to flee or when the actor cannot flee but is nonetheless threatened. Both Van Hooff (1972) and Andrew (1963) claim that many of the individual display elements, such as strong expiration and lip retraction, are protective measures triggered by aversive stimulation of the face and of the esophagus. The widely opened mouth and the baring of the teeth, usually accompanied by shrill barks or hisses, may be regarded as indicating readiness to bite in case the attacker suddenly advances. During the evolutionary process, the silent bared-teeth display has come to mean other things. The silent bared-teeth display, for example, is a submissive gesture in higher primates, but in a few species a dominant animal may also display before a subordinate one. The context suggests that the display may sometimes function as a reassuring signal or even as a sign of attachment in these species (Van Hooff 1972:215).

The play face display, which seems to occur primarily among the primates, is characterized by a wide open mouth, lips that cover much of the teeth, free and easy eye and body movements, and quick and shallow staccato breathing. According to Loizos (1967), the relaxed open-mouth, or play face, display accompanies social play involving mock fighting and chasing in primates.

Similarities between human smiling and primate silent bared-teeth display on the one hand and between human laughter and primate relaxed open-mouth display on the other reflect a phylo-genetic relationship (Van Hooff 1967). Morphologically, human laughter is considered to be an intermediate stage between the classical primate relaxed open-mouth display and the silent bared-teeth face, the human smile being its weaker form (Van Hooff

1972:226). Thus the human smile and laughter, though of different phylogenetic origin, began to converge and to overlap considerably.

It appears, then, that in the evolutionary process leading from nonprimate mammals to primates, and finally to *Homo sapiens*, the meaning of the teeth-baring display broadened. While it was originally a part of the mainly defensive or protective behavior mechanism, it became a signal of submission and nonhostility. In some species, the nonhostility signal probably became predominant, so that finally a signal indicating friendliness could evolve. Among primates, the bared-teeth display overlapped with the lip-smacking display, while human smiling appears to have resulted from the combination of both, very nearly replacing the latter.

According to Chevalier-Skolnikoff, "Darwin would probably be surprised to discover that we now consider the human smile to have derived from what was originally a primate fear expression which the 'grin' certainly is in lemur and monkeys" (1973:82). She, however, voices the sentiments of other scholars in feeling that major theoretical advances have not been made in explaining the evolutionary development of facial expressions, although the knowledge of the anatomical structure of the face has increased since Darwin's time.

THE CASE OF HOMO SAPIENS

In discussing the development of laughter and smiling in humans, either as expressions of emotions or as responses to humor, we need to examine issues that fall into two major domains: similarities and differences between laughter and smiling, and ontogeny of laughter and smiling. Regarding the first domain, the following questions need to be answered. Is there a difference between laughter and smiling, and if so, is it qualitative or quantitative in nature? What type of criteria can be and are used by laymen and scholars to identify a particular expression as either smiling or laughter? If laughter and smiling are polar expressions of the same emotions, is there a need to recognize intermediate stages?

Other questions are germane to the second domain. Are laughter and smiling innate to humans, or are they learned? Is one innate and the other learned? At what age do expressions of smiling and laughter occur among infants, and what is their sequential order?

Do both occur at approximately the same age, or does one precede the other?

Laughter and Smiling Compared

While there is a general agreement that smiling and laughter are different, scholars disagree as to whether they are qualitatively or merely quantitatively different, because both involve the same facial movements.[4] The most notable difference between smiling and laughter in the view of many investigators is that vocalization accompanies the latter, while it is generally absent in the former. Such a view, however, is based mostly on casual observation, and variations in other facial movements are ignored. Whether vocalization alone is sufficient to define a particular expression as laughter is a moot question. Even if vocalization is the distinguishing criterion, it is difficult to determine what degree is crucial for a distinction between smiling and laughter. That vocalization alone does not always permit us to make a clear-cut distinction between the two expressions is obvious from the cautious view expressed by Darwin (1872/1965:208).

Van Hooff (1972) believes that features other than vocalization, such as the degree to which the mouth is opened, help distinguish between smiling and laughter. He suggests that only a multidimensional model in which such expressive elements as head posture, eye, and vocalization can vary independently is adequate for describing the variations in the smiling-laughter continuum. Andrew (1972), however, questions the usefulness of such a model. It appears that, while polar expressions of grin face and play face among primates represent quite different states of emotions, they have converged to a considerable extent in humans, especially in adults; they have amalgamated to the point where their separate identities on purely physiological grounds have been reduced considerably. Part of the problem in distinguishing between smiling and laughter is that there are numerous varieties of both, so that it is difficult to separate them from purely anatomical and physiological perspectives. Researchers who believe that the two expressions are qualitatively separate use functional and attitudinal criteria to make such a distinction. If any intermediate stages between smiling and laughter need to be recognized, only sociocultural factors can help identify them. As a result, the recognition of any intermediate stages will vary cross-culturally.

Human beings label expressions of happiness and responses to humor in numerous ways. Such labeling is unconsciously affected by many cultural and contextual factors, chief among which may be the existing linguistic categories in a culture. It is not clear, for instance, to what degree the debate among English-speaking scholars about the differences between smiling and laughter can be attributed to the two well-established words themselves. How many other languages make the same distinction? In other languages a single linguistic term may describe all shades of facial expressions labeled as smiling or laughter by English speakers. On the other hand, some languages may have more than two linguistic terms to describe different stages of the facial expressions. Cognition of varieties of laughter and smiling may conceivably be influenced by the available ready-made linguistic categories in a given language, and speakers of the language may be unconscious of the influence of the linguistic system on cognition and classification (Mandelbaum 1958:157–59; Whorf 1956/1964:213–14). Any studies undertaken to determine which criteria are used to distinguish smiling from laughter within and across cultures should take into account the existing vocabularies categorizing facial expressions of joy.

The Ontogeny of Laughter and Smiling

Whether laughter and smiling are innate or learned has been a controversial topic. Considerable research has been undertaken to gather substantive data and to prove or disprove empirically the differing views. The innateness issue can be best resolved by studying the behavior of very young infants and children, and toward this end many studies have been conducted,[5] several of which conclude that the motor pattern of smiling is instinctive and that babies produce spontaneous and reflex smiling right from birth. Such does not seem to be the case with laughter. Facial movements among infants that morphologically resembled smiling, for example, were observed within two to twelve hours after their birth (Wolff 1963) but appear to be void of any accompanying emotional state and seem to be closely related to internal events that occur mostly during irregular sleep or drowsiness. Such facial movements seldom occur during regular sleep or when the infant is alert and attentive (Wolff 1963:116–17; 1966). Despite Wolff's assertions, it is difficult to judge whether the infants dream or experience pleasant sensations at such an early stage; if they do so, smiling expressions may prove to be linked with these sensations. Without further extensive experimental and observational studies, the question of whether smilelike facial expressions in very young infants are devoid of any accompanying emotional state cannot be satisfactorily answered.

The initial phase of smiling, if it can be so labeled, lasts for about five weeks. The second phase, the "social smile," does not develop until sometime during the second to fourth month and seems to be accompanied by gaze fixation on a person's face during its occurrence. Considerable age variation exists, however, regarding the end of the first phase and the onset of the second. Any generalizations must therefore necessarily be tentative and broad. Wolff (1963:119–21) observed that a clear-cut broad social smile appeared in the third week in response to a high-pitched human voice. Other observers have noted that, in the early growth period of the infants, such auditory and visual stimuli as high-pitched human voices and human faces produce a smile. Touch or contact and other tactile stimuli also produce a smile. Few studies that distinguish between a simple smiling reflex and a social smile, however, explicitly state what is understood by the latter term, nor are the requirements for a social smile always spelled out (Charlesworth and Kreutzer 1973:106).

There is a general consensus among scholars[6] that laughter occurs later than smiling. Various empirical studies indicate that laughter can begin as early as five weeks of age and as late as twelve to sixteen weeks. Wolff (1963) observed, for instance, that, in response to a pat-a-cake game, infants in their fifth week frequently gurgle or coo with an open-mouthed grin and at times become so excited that their vocalizaitons resemble a chortling laughter. The recorded responses of these expressions were judged by adults to be laughter. Darwin, on the other hand, observed "incipient" laughter in his child at the age of 113 days. Many of these studies indicate that laughter occurs primarily as a response to specific auditory, tactile, social, or visual stimuli. It appears that tactile stimuli, especially tickling carried out by a familiar person, arouse most of the laughter expressed by four- to six-month-old infants. As they grow older, however, infants seem to respond more to social and visual stimulation.

Ambrose (1963) has argued that the occurrence of laughter in infants essentially manifests ambivalent motivation and is caused by stimulus situations that elicit simultaneously both stimulus-maintaining tendencies and stimulus-terminating tendencies, with the former predominating. He believes that the infants' capacity for ambivalence is not fully developed until the age of four months, which explains why laughter first occurs around that age. Ambrose's hypothesis is not substantiated by Wolff's study (1963), discussed above, in which he was able to elicit laughter in five-week-old infants. That smiling occurs without any external stimuli and is innate to humans has been demonstrated by studies of congenitally blind and deaf infants, who produce expressions of smiling although they are not exposed to external visual and auditory stimuli (D. G. Freedman 1964, 1965; J. Thompson 1941). These studies do not, however, make clear whether such is the case with laughter.

Scholars are divided as to whether the expressions of smiling are voluntary or involuntary. Some studies (Fraiberg 1968; F. L. Goodenough 1932) indicate that blind children are deficient in producing voluntary emotional expression as compared with normal, sighted children. Yet it has also been claimed (Eible-Eibesfeldt 1972:305–306; 1973; Fulcher 1942) that the blind are not deficient in showing voluntary emotional expressions. Charlesworth and Kreutzer (1973), after surveying many studies, concluded that, when expressions were spontaneous, many of the facial expressions of the blind did not vary significantly from those of people with sight but that differences became obvious when emotions were acted out or were voluntary. The question of whether smiling and laughter are conditioned responses has been resolved variously by different scholars. Washburn's (1929) observations indicated that laughing was not as learned or conditioned a response as smiling by the end of the first year, because the average number of smiling responses, but not laughing responses, increased markedly after three months.

In general, then, it appears that smiling is innate, involuntary, and occurs in infants right from birth. Whether smiling indicates any expression of joy at that stage, however, is uncertain. From the age of three weeks the smile becomes social because of the interaction between the infant and other individuals, especially the mother. The question of whether laughter is innate has not been satisfactorily answered. It appears from empirical studies that laughter associated with vocalization is originally induced by numerous kinds of stimuli, especially tactile ones. Laughter response can be elicited from the fifth week onward, although it is most readily elicited at approximately four months of age. Once social smiling and laughter have appeared during the succeeding stages, up to twelve months, infants show preferences for different kinds of stimuli, and at twelve months social and visual stimuli induce the most laughter. Laughter thus does not appear to be an innate expression.

The Phonetics of Laughter

Little attention has been paid to the phonetics of laughter, despite the considerable focus on the physiological and anatomical aspects of smiling and laughter. Nor have sounds of laughter been included in phonological analyses of individual languages. The reason for such neglect is that linguists do not consider laughter an integral part of any linguistic system. Although individuals in all cultures intuitively perceive that a variety of meaningful messages are communicated by different kinds of laughter, these meanings are neither as precise nor as amenable to rigorous analysis as the rest of the language system.

Despite the marginal position of laughter as a mode of communication (the grunt, cough, belch, weeping, and moaning are also marginal in this sense), attempts have been made to account for its communicative potential. Communicatively marginal vocalizations are grouped under the label of "paralanguage," and some systematic efforts to analyze them by using the established phonetic symbols of the International Phonetic Association or by creating additional phonetic symbols have been made.[7] Writers of popular fiction have also attempted to transcribe laughter and smiling. Languages have many onomatopoeic words to describe different kinds of laughter and smiling. The sounds of laughter are produced by a deep inspiration, followed by short interrupted, expiration due to spasmodic contractions of the chest, especially of the diaphragm. Most people when laughing produce repetitive sounds that can last for some time, until much of the breath of air taken in has been expirated. Thus the physiological necessity of producing long laughter requires that the inspiration be prolonged.

Few discussions of laughter have gone beyond some basic observations about the production of vocalizations during laughter. Various issues need to be discussed in the study of phonetics of laughter. Is the phonetics of laughter more limited than that of speech? Does the phonology of a language condition the sounds of laughter made by its speakers? Is the intensity of laughter closely linked to its duriation and pitch? Do such factors as sex and age affect differences in laughter? Does the co-occurrence of laughter and speech result in their mutual distortion? The following gen-

eralizations are quite tentative. They are based on my own observations and need to be verified by systematic cross-cultural linguistic
analyses of laughter.

Comparison of the Sounds
of Laughter and Speech

Even to a casual observer it should be obvious that the sounds
of speech and of laughter are similarly articulated, by obstructing
the outgoing flow of air from the chest cavity through the larynx,
pharynx, and the oral and nasal passages. Both speech and laughter
are perceived to be linear concatenations of sound segments. Regardless of the language they speak, however, individuals apparently do not use all the sounds in their language in producing
laughter. Different types of stops and laterals, for example, rarely,
if ever, occur in laughter. On the other hand, vowels are regularly
used in laughter and in general are much more frequently articulated than consonants, with the notable exception of the glottal
fricative consonant [h], which is frequently used in laughter and
either precedes or follows different vowels. It can be voiced or
voiceless, depending on its position.

Another consonant commonly found in laughter is the glottal
stop [ʔ]. It should be noted that this consonant is not really a sound
in the usual sense but merely represents the abrupt and sharp cut
in the flow of outgoing air through the mouth. In laughter a sequence of the same vowel can be produced, each utterance being
abruptly interrupted by total silence, created by the sudden complete closure and quick separation of vocal cords. This silence is
labeled in phonetics the "glottal stop." Although some other consonants may be occasionally used in producing sounds of laughter,
on the whole consonants used in laughter are more limited in
number than those used in speech. Vowel sounds used in laughter
can be quite varied, ranging from the high front vowel [i] through
[e], [æ], [ə], [a], [ɔ], [o] to the back high vowel [u]. All combinations
of tongue and lip movements used in the articulation of vowels in
speech can theoretically occur in producing laughter. I would guess,
however, that those vowels in the articulation of which the front
part of the tongue is raised while lips are rounded are less likely
to occur. The general tendency appears to be to start with a particular vowel and to repeat it throughout the laughter, with either
a glottal stop or a glottal fricative interrupting several times. Occasionally laughter may consist of merely an extended uninter-

rupted articulation of a single vowel. Few diphthongs seem generally to occur in laughter.

Sounds of laughter are described in ordinary language as musical, the reason being that they are chiefly voiced vowels, that is, vowels with pitch. Although it can be produced, whispered laughter seems far less common, in contrast to whispered speech, which commonly occurs in many social situations. Even in whispered speech and laughter, vowel sounds stand out because of their inherent loudness. Children can be observed producing whispered laughter as they experiment with different kinds of voice and noise productions. Very few adults, however, produce whispered laughter voluntarily. On the whole, it appears that the phonetics of laughter is more restricted than the phonetics of human speech, since fewer sounds are used in the articulation of laughter than are used in speech.

Phonological Constraints

Generally, human laughter is not subject to the same constraints that are imposed on human speech. In order to be understood, any speech utterance must conform to the phonological and grammatical rules of a language of which it is a token. Laughter in this sense is not an instance of a fixed linguistic code, however, because it does not have recurring patterns like those of language that are significant for communication. Most languages have a finite number of different types of units, and these units are combined in a limited number of ways, following specific phonological, morphological, and syntactic rules of conjoining and constraints. As a result speech utterances may to some degree be predicted. Such is not the case with laughter. In this sense, then, laughter, like many other paralinguistic features, is not closely integrated into the phonological and grammatical structure of utterances (Lyons 1972:53).

Individuals undoubtedly tend to use similar patterns of laughter and thus can generally be identified on the basis of pattern. But the same is also true of the voice quality of individuals. Most people can recognize a caller on the telephone by the idiosyncratic features of the speaker's voice. This overall voice quality is not a part of the referential meaning of the actual utterance, however, and neither is laughter. In general, then, laughter is not restricted by either the linguistic or the cultural codes of the laugher. Individuals of diverse linguistic and cultural backgrounds can and do laugh in similar ways. Conversely, individual speakers of the same language can and do laugh quite differently. Individuals may also articulate sounds in their laughter that are not part of the phonological system of their native language.

Because laughter of different linguistic and ethnic populations cannot be distinguished, it is ludicrous to treat laughter as one of the many ethnic or linguistic attributes characteristic of a particular group. This very fact, however, can be used as a basis for creating humor, because such identification imputes all stereotypic and other qualities associated with a particular group label—a commonly observed phenomenon in all cultures. A humorous cartoon that appeared in the daily *Boston Globe* for March 29, 1979, during the gasoline crunch in the United States, suggested the resentment Americans felt toward the people they believed to be responsible for the shortage. The cartoon depicted a middle-aged American couple standing in front of their big car, marked "Guzzler." The husband appeared to be talking to his wife while simultaneously listening to the noise from under the hood, his one ear toward it and his hand cupped over his ear. The wife looked puzzled and angry. The text underneath read: "Can you hear it . . . from inside the hood? Uncontrolled laughter—in Arabic!"

The Duration, Pitch, and Intensity of Laughter

Laughter varies considerably not only among speakers of a single language but even in a single laugher. Depending on the situation, the nature of the stimulus that provokes laughter, and the mental state of the laugher, laughter can be either soft or loud, short or extended. The parameters of both mild and intense laughter may vary from person to person. It is generally true, however, that short and soft laughter characterized by an overall low pitch is considered mild, while laughter characterized by a sustained high or rising pitch, inherent loudness, considerable duration, and a number of head and body movements is intense.

The Effects of Sex and Age on Laughter

Such factors as age and sex physiologically affect a person's laughter. Women's laughter, like their speech, generally has a higher overall pitch than men's. Physiological abnormalities may sometimes produce cases that do not fit these general conditions. The overall high pitch of children's and women's laughter creates the impression that it is more "musical" than men's. Age and sex do not seem to condition the use of consonant and vowel sounds in laughter. Whether psychophysiological conditions affect the tempo of an individual's laughter in term of the number of vowels, consonants, or syllables uttered per second is difficult to determine.

Just as the voice quality of a person can change during certain periods of life, so can laughter. While physiological factors may cause the change in the former, sociocultural factors may be responsible for the change in the latter. The generally high-pitched voice of young boys, for instance, begins to change during puberty and becomes increasingly bass. On the other hand, socialization pressures may impose constraints on the uncontrolled, intense laughter of children, especially of girls as they reach puberty, particularly in societies that regard loud, intense, uncontrolled laughter as unbecoming and inappropriate in social interactions in the public domain. The change in the male voice is involuntary, while a change in laughter due to social pressure is voluntary. An individual may therefore use laughter as an indicator of rebellion against societal norms.

Simultaneous Laughter and Speech

Laughter occurring simultaneously with speech distorts it, but no systematic analyses of the nature of such distortions have been made. Do the effects of laughter on speech vary across languages, or does the speech distortion show some universal features? Speech cannot distort laughter, because there are no norms about laughter other than the broad cultural ones that I have mentioned and because laughter does not convey messages as linguistic utterances do. While commenting on laughter's general influence on speech, Trager (1961:19) noted that laughter could break up or otherwise distort vowel nuclei but that the influence of the nature of vowel nucleus on the manner of distortion was not known.

Laughter cannot be regarded as being on par with such suprasegmental features as stress, pitch, and duration. The suprasegmental features as they are generally defined by linguists are essential for the articulation of normal speech. Such is not the case with laughter. Speech can and does occur much of the time without laughter, which is not essential for articulation of sounds.

Most languages seem to have words that describe the sounds of laughter and smiling. Depending on the structural disposition of individual languages, the number of such words may be relatively large or small. Languages that are characterized by reduplication processes and have onomatopoeic words for all kinds of noises and actions are also likely to have many words to describe different types of laughter and smiling.

The languages of South Asia have a strong cultural and structural disposition toward developing onomatopoeic words and include many such words. Speakers readily create new ones. These languages also have many words that describe different kinds of laughter and designate various motives and emotions associated with them. The following are some onomatopoeic words given in transliteration for different types of laughter from Marathi, a language spoken by some forty million people in Western India.

Word	*Meaning*
khudukhudu	Soft, pleasant laughter of an infant
khadākhadā	Loud laughter of an infant
phidīphidī	Vulgar and obscene laughter
khaskhas	Mild appreciative laughter
khokho; hoho	Loud uproarious laughter
khikhi	Horselike laughter
phisphis	Derogatory laughter
hyāhyā	Superficial polite laughter

Most of these words are used as adverbs and usually accompany the verb *has*, meaning "to laugh or to smile"; some can also be used as verbs, in which case they include both the action of laughing and the other meanings.

Sometimes onomatopoeic words describing a particular kind of laughter become associated with specific roles or personality types and thus come to identify a character. In English, for example, "ho, ho, ho" is universally associated with Santa Claus and is considered to be a belly laugh, while the word "haha" is associated with facetiousness. To what degree onomatopoeic words representing different kinds of laughter also carry other connotations is difficult to determine. A great deal depends on contextual cues, and individuals often have different associations with different kinds of laughter, depending on their sociocultural background. Any generalizations about the connotations of different onomatopoeic words that represent laughter for the majority of speakers of a language are therefore difficult to make. At best such generalizations are educated guesses unless they are backed by experimental and empirical research. Writers and scholars have nevertheless made such generalizations (Berne 1973:338–39).

CROSS-CULTURAL PERSPECTIVES

Darwin (1872/1965:211) concluded that laughter and smiling were universal human expressions of joy; he analyzed responses he received from individuals around the world to whom he had sent a list of sixteen questions, two of which dealt specifically with laughter and smiling. A similar approach was used by Klineberg (1954), a social psychologist, who contended that emotional expressions are primarily determined socioculturally. Although Darwin can perhaps be faulted for his somewhat "unscientific" methods, he deserves credit for having initiated cross-cultural research into the facial expression of emotions. Despite Darwin's conclusions, the view that certain facial expressions are universal and represent the same emotions in all cultures has for many reasons been controversial among behavioral scientists, especially social psychologists and anthropologists. The few anthropologists interested in studying facial expressions and body gestures (Birdwhistell 1970; Douglas 1971; La Barre 1947) have generally rejected the notion that laughter and smiling are universal expressions of joy, instead considering them culture-specific.

There has been a failure to distinguish between facial expressions of emotions on the one hand and gestures on the other. The impression that facial expressions are culture-specific may have been created because norms and expectations concerning the occurrence, display, and control of facial expressions vary across cultures. Much of the evidence presented has been anecdotal (Eible-Eibesfeldt 1972; Ekman 1973:174ff.). Some anthropologists, like Birdwhistell (1970:34), have merely asserted, without presenting any conclusive evidence, that facial expressions, especially smiling and laughter, are culture-specific. On the basis of experiments conducted by social psychologists in different cultures, Ekman concluded that "the same facial features are associated with the same emotions regardless of culture or language" (1973:219). He acknowledged, however, that there is cross-cultural variation regarding the events that elicit an emotion.

In order to develop any anthropologically relevant generalizations about laughter and smiling, it is necessary to determine whether similar stimuli produce a response of laughter and smiling across cultures, whether societies share similar ideas about the appropriateness of laughter and smiling in comparable social situations, and whether societies share similar attitudes toward laughter and smiling and value or discredit them in similar ways. Unless cross-cultural comparisons are undertaken to answer these and other, related questions, the finding that the same facial expressions represent the same emotions across cultures is of little value in studies of humor and laughter.

CULTURAL VALUES

Existing ethnographic data indicate that there is much diversity across cultures regarding the emotional states that are favored and valued and those that are looked down upon. Such attitudes in individual cultures are likely to affect the overall occurrence of certain facial expressions of emotions. This applies equally well to expressions of laughter and smiling, which are not valued equally across cultures. Among the Dobuans of New Guinea, for instance, dourness is a virtue, while laughter is negatively valued (Benedict 1934/1946:150). On the other hand, the Pygmies of Central Africa are readily given to laughter and express their joy without inhibitions (Turnbull 1961). In public the Saluteaux and other Ojibwa Indians of northeast America severely restrain almost all emotions except laughter (Driver 1969:443; Hallowell 1967:145). Even in cultures that value laughter and smiling positively, there exist norms regarding the appropriateness of these expressions that are closely related to the nature of social situations; the participants and their background, including age, sex, and socioeconomic status; the stimuli that generate laughter and smiling; and cultural values associated with different types of social interaction.

Laughter seems more susceptible than smiling to scrutiny in connection with sociocultural norms because laughter is perceived to reflect less controlled—and more marked—behavior. In many situations where smiling, however inappropriate, may be tolerated, laughter is not. In the Thai culture of Southeast Asia, hilarious laughter falls in the same category as acts that are considered vulgar, for example, touching another person's head, calling attention to one's feet by kicking, the use of uncouth language, and loud speech (Haas 1957b). In the upper classes of nineteenth-century British society, the manner in which women laughed was obviously of considerable importance, judging from Mrs. Murphy's words in her book *Manners for Women*, published in 1897.

> Laughing should, if its expression does not come by nature, be carefully taught.... The only thing to be guarded against is that the inculcated laugh is apt to grow stereotyped, and few things are more irritating than to hear it over and over again, begin on the same note, run down the same scale, and consequently express no more mirth than the keys of the piano.
>
> There is no greater ornament to conversation than the ripple of silvery notes that form the perfect laugh. It makes the person who evokes it feel pleased with himself, and invests what he has said with a charm of wit and humour which might not be otherwise observed. [Quoted in Douglas 1973:126]

This carefully cultivated laughter contrasts greatly with the totally unrestrained laughter shown by the Pygmies of Central Africa. "The Pygmy is not in the least self-conscious about showing his emotions; he likes to laugh until tears come to his eyes and he is too weak to stand. He then sits down or lies on the ground and laughs still louder" (Turnbull 1961:56). When Pygmies laugh, the whole body becomes involved: they "slap their sides, snap their fingers and go through all manner of physical contortions" (p. 44). Among the urban blacks of America, several types of laughter are quite common. They involve all sorts of bodily actions and gestures, such as waving of the hands and arms, staggering, the shaking of the whole body in a synchronized motion, and even the embracing of another person, and two people's support of each other while they laugh (M. D. Williams 1981:114–15).

Laughter is more subject than a smile to restraint in accordance with norms of appropriateness because it often has derogatory and aggressive connotations that smiling lacks. For this reason laughter cannot be substituted for smiling in many social situations. In American culture, as in many others, smiling is appropriate during a greeting, because it indicates a welcome or the affirmation of established bonds. Laughter on such an occasion, however, may suggest an insult or mockery at the expense of the person greeted, who may feel uneasy or apprehensive and may suspect that something is wrong in his appearance or demeanor (Howell 1973:5). For the same reasons, however, a ritualized form of greeting may develop among very close friends; mocking and insults accompanied by hilarious laughter may be common and favored. Such seems to be the case among Punjabi men in North India. When two close friends meet after a long interval, each will slap the other and will engage in horseplay accompanied by all kinds of vile verbal insults, name calling, and loud laughter (Shonek 1974).

Positive or negative attitudes toward laughter and smiling are also unalterably fused with specific role models for different sex and age groups. Culturally differential standards are thus used to judge good or bad behavior in relation to laughter and smiling, depending on who the laugher is. In societies where ideal sex-role models for women emphasize modesty, passivity, and politeness, it is considered unbecoming for women to laugh in an unrestrained manner, while men are free to express their joy or amusement quite freely. Among the Sarakatsani shepherds of Greece, women rarely, if ever, laugh in public and in front of their affinal relatives; such laughter is incompatible with the self-discipline and modesty that are essential traits of ideal womanhood (Campbell 1974:154, 169).[8] By and large, restraints on laughter seem more stringent for young or middle-aged women and for people of high socioeconomic status. On the other hand, peasant women seem relatively free in their laughter in many societies.[9]

In some cultures, loud, unrestrained laughter is considered incommensurate with norms of deferential behavior toward one's elders and superiors. Respect for elders is often an important aspect of cultural values, and loud laughter signifies disrespect. In rural India, for instance, ideal norms of behavior for young men prohibit their laughing loudly, smoking, playing with their children, or speaking to their wives in front of their parents.[10]

THEORETICAL PROPOSITIONS

The following theoretical propositions are based on the discussion of phylogenetic, ontogenetic, and sociocultural aspects of laughter and smiling.

Smiling among humans probably evolved from an expression of fear among primates.
Laughter and smiling are evoked by different stimuli both across and within cultures.

The expressions of laughter and smiling need to be differentiated by sociocultural, linguistic, and contextual criteria, because anatomical and physiological criteria are inadequate for this purpose.

The innate, involuntary smiling that occurs in infants right from birth becomes social smiling as a result of interaction with adults.

The nature and form of laughter are not determined by either the linguistic or the cultural code of the laugher.

Laughter is generally more susceptible than smiling to restraint in accordance with sociocultural norms of propriety because laughter has more apparent derogatory and aggressive connotations.

Cultural norms regarding the appropriateness of laughter and smiling depend on many factors, such as the social situation, age, sex, and social status of participants and their relationship.

Societies characterized by sexual inequality and gerontocracy generally emphasize cultural values of modesty in women and respect for elders. Excessive laughter by women in the presence of men and by young people in the presence of elders is therefore considered inappropriate because it symbolizes lack of modesty in women and disrespect for elders on the part of young people.

Postscript

In this book I have suggested that humor is a culturally shaped individual cognitive experience, culturally determined because sociocultural factors are the primary trigger mechanisms leading to its occurrence. Humor provides the best evidence of the psychic unity of mankind; healthy individuals who have not enjoyed mirthful laughter as a consequence of humorous experiences are probably nonexistent. Yet the antecedents of such experiences are culture-specific, especially if they involve symbols, language, and other, similar stimuli.

Humor is also social and functions both as a lubricant to smooth social interactions and as a means of expressing hostility and aggression. Conceptions of humor across cultures are quite diverse, as are the norms concerning its occurrence and use. It mirrors sociocultural systems, often in topsy-turvy ways but on occasion also in realistic ways. Nevertheless, not all humor is socioculturally relevant, and it should not be expected always to be so. At the personal cognitive level, humor may be sporadic and may lack the context of social interaction. For an individual, it may be an "act of creation," full of fantasy, aesthetically pleasing, intellectually stimulating, and uniquely personal. It needs no sociocultural explanation or justification. Such humor is not, however, really the subject of this book. Rather I have focused on institutionalized and patterned humor developed through well-recognized techniques that is appreciated collectively by the people who experience it.

Three factors reflect the cultural bases of humor and are necessary for its institutional development: shared cultural knowledge, shared rules for interpreting it, and agreement on the cultural appropriateness of the incongruence and exaggeration involved. Language underlies all three of these factors; not only is much humor verbal, but language predetermines the categories of humor for members of a culture and provides opportunities to elaborate the rules governing both interpretation and cultural appropriateness. Because humor is based on culture, it becomes a significant criterion for measuring cultural homogeneity. As societies become more heterogeneous, complex, and pluralistic, the three shared factors refer no longer to the society at large but to smaller subcultural and social groups within it that are bound by occupation, social status, education, regional and dialectal affiliations, religion, and so on. Unless there is a strong unifying force, such as powerful mass media, humor increasingly becomes a subcultural collectivity as societies move from a small-scale, homogeneous state to a heterogeneous, large-scale, and complex one.

The notion of culturally appropriate incongruity is applicable at all levels, extending from the individual to the society at large. Because of differences in background and socialization, two individuals may disagree as to whether or not certain potential humor stimuli reflect a culturally appropriate incongruity. One may experience humor, while the other may feel anger, frustration, shock, or displeasure. Disagreement regarding the cultural appropriateness of incongruity can thus occur between individuals, groups, and even societies; ethnic humor provides a prime example of such a phenomenon.

The criterion of cultural appropriateness applies not only to the incongruity underlying humor but also to its form, substance, and techniques. Much cross-cultural variation occurs in this respect. Joking relationships may be prominent in one culture, ritual humor in another, puns and riddles in a third, and verbal duels in a fourth. In most cultures many types and techniques of humor are culturally appropriate. The greatest intracultural diversity is likely to occur with respect to incongruities; despite shared cultural knowledge, rules for interpreting potential humor stimuli may vary from individual to individual and also from one social context to another.

Are all cultures equal with regard to the development of institutionalized humor? This question is likely to create much controversy. It could be argued that societies that value a sense of humor more highly develop more varieties of institutionalized humor. The problem lies, of course, in defining a "sense of humor." Like other anthropological concepts, this one is difficult to define and to quantify etically. In addition, the issue of cultural equality in humor is related not merely to the attitudes toward humor but also to such other factors as the development of technology, the spread of literacy, the increasing complexity of life, the leisure time available to individuals for pleasure-seeking activities, and so forth.

If we follow the lead of contemporary linguistic theory, we might argue that all societies are equal in that each develops humor that adequately meets the psychological and sociocultural needs of its members. In view of the difficulty of defining the concept of humor, the diverse disciplinary orientations manifested in analyses of its development, nature, dissemination and appreciation, and the current state of cross-cultural research on humor, however, the notion that societies are equal in this respect cannot be empirically validated, nor can it be stated with confidence that certain techniques and forms of humor occur in all societies, although intuitively such a notion seems viable.

The main thesis of this book is that culture constitutes the contextual, textual, and technical bases of humor. In conclusion I shall discuss some issues that arise from this premise but have not been addressed in previous chapters. An exploration of these issues could provide additional evidence of the cultural bases of humor. The observations used for illustrations are impressionistic and do not result from systematic research. These issues could provide a challenge to anthropologists for future investigations of the interconnections between humor and culture.

If humor depends on the nature of sociocultural systems, then as societies change, so should humor. Similarly, culture contact should lead to mutual borrowing of form, technique, type, and content of humor. In this context I shall raise several questions, but I shall discuss only a couple of them. What has been or is likely to be the impact of literacy on the nature of humor in traditional and preliterate societies? How has technological development affected humor? Does humor show a growing relationship with economic transactions and political systems? Has humor become a salable commodity? How can the sociocultural bases of humor be linked to the process of acculturation?

Impact of Literacy

The consequences of literacy in preliterate and traditional societies have been discussed in detail by anthropologists (Goody 1968). As people learn to read and write, they are exposed to many kinds of knowledge, including humor accumulated in written works such as anthologies of jokes, tales, rhymes, riddles, cartoons, and so on. A major aspect of humor in the oral tradition, namely performance, loses its significance with the advent of literacy. Such a change also reduces the shared and public aspects of humor, because individuals can enjoy humor by reading rather than by listening to it in social gatherings. New genres of humor, however, such as jokes, comic strips, and satire, may be introduced as a result of literacy. According to Goody and Watt (1968), the past in preliterate societies is interpreted in the context of the present, and anything not relevant for the present is forgotten. In other words, the past is perceived not objectively, as distinct from the present, but rather subjectively, through the present. In such a situation, remembering and forgetting become important tools of cultural knowledge. Once literacy is introduced, jokes, proverbs, rhymes, and stories, become a matter of record. The point, then, is that humor in order to survive in preliterate societies must be constantly relevant to the existing culture milieu—forever contemporaneous and never obsolete. What is not recited, told, or performed is lost. On the other hand, in literate societies humor by way of anthologies, collections, and so forth survives. In order to understand and appreciate humor, we must return to the sociocultural conditions that existed at the time of its creation. The obsoleteness of humor with respect to time must be seen as the consequence of literacy.

The Effects of Technological Development

In any cross-cultural studies of humor, anthropologists need to examine the impact of technological development, especially the mass media, on the development, nature, and dissemination of humor. In the Western world, the advent, first, of newspapers and periodicals, then of radio, movies, and television, has opened vast avenues for the dissemination of humor. In this respect, it appears that the mass media have made humor ubiquitous and diverse. New forms and topics are being constantly developed, ranging from magazines devoted exclusively to humor to humorous bumper stickers, greeting cards, and jokes about computers and space ships (Winick 1961). In the United States humor appears to have pervaded every walk of life. Comedy shows dominate television programs; newspapers abound with cartoons and comic strips; cartoon characters and comic slogans appear on shirts, toys, playing cards, dishes, watches, and other commercial products; and humor columnists are syndicated in large numbers of newspapers. Technology has even reached the point where humor is available on a twenty-four hour basis: people can simply dial a joke. There appears to be a relationship between the mass media, which are responsible for this expansion of humor, and the increasingly complex nature of life. People have more leisure time, because technological development has freed them from working long hours—and more leisure time means more entertainment and pleasure, of which humor has become an important part.

My rather cursory discussion emphasizes the relationship between sociocultural change and the nature of humor. I am convinced that in studying humor intraculturally and interculturally, anthropologists need both synchronic and diachronic perspectives. Societies are not static, because there is always interaction both between individuals within societies and between societies. Similarly, humor, as part of this interactional dynamics, goes through transformations regarding its form, technique, and function. Anthropologists should therefore ideally analyze not only specific societies at particular times but also diversity across cultures and through time.

CONCLUSION

In this work I have analyzed humor within the holistic and comparative theoretical framework so crucial to anthropological research. I have sought to provide new theoretical insights into several aspects of humor, some studied by anthropologists in the past and others investigated here for the first time. In addition, I have offered systematic analyses of the multifaceted nature of humor as it is linked to different aspects of sociocultural systems. I have evaluated and synthesized existing research in anthropology pertinent to the topics discussed. Finally, I have used previously scattered ethnographic data to illustrate the analytical insights presented.

I have offered no comprehensive global theory of humor in these pages. I do not believe that a global anthropological theory of humor and laughter is possible until many minitheories have been developed. The reason is simply that the relationship between humor and sociocultural systems is too complex and too multifaceted to conform to a global theory. Past theories that sought to explain humor by a single factor were primarily psychological and philosophical in nature. They cannot satisfactorily explain institutionalized humor and its sociocultural roots, however, because they are likely to falter in the face of diverse ethnographic data.

Hence the need to gather ethnographic data pertaining to various aspects of humor more systematically, to analyze different facets of humor and their linkage to sociocultural factors, to synthesize existing research regarding the interconnections between humor and particular attributes of human cultural systems, and to formulate theoretical propositions at the micro level. My book has taken the first step in this direction.

Notes

1. Wit and laughter were discussed by Aristotle (*Poetics*) and Plato (*Philebus*) and later by Hobbes, Kant, Schopenhauer and other writers. Theorizing reached its peak in the nineteenth century and in the first half of the twentieth. See Keith-Spiegel (1972) for a historical overview of humor theories.

2. The first international conference on humor, held in Wales in 1976, was followed by others in 1979 and 1982 in the United States and in 1984 in Israel. The papers read at the first two conferences have been published in Chapman and Foot (1977) and Mindess and Turek (n.d.), respectively.

3. For a discussion of definitions of humor, see Bergler (1956:viff.), Chapman and Foot (1976), Keith-Spiegel (1972), and McGhee (1979:4–8, 42–43).

4. For a discussion of the biologically beneficial effects of humor and laughter see the discussions in Keith-Spiegel (1972), Darwin (1872/1965), Dearborn (1900), Menon (1931), and Spencer (1860).

5. An etic framework is a conceptual model of universal categories developed by an investigator as a methodological aid to research. It is an observer-oriented as opposed to an emic, or actor-oriented, conceptual framework. For further elaboration of etic versus emic frameworks and categories, see Pike (1954).

6. For a discussion of an anthropological perspective, see Apte (1983). For an integrative approach to the study of culture, see Malinowski (1944). For the comparative approach in anthropology, see Naroll and Cohen (1970, pt. 5). For a history of anthropology, see Harris (1968).

7. The following are just a few of the important studies on the topic of humor that have been written in the twentieth century: Bergler (1956),

Bergson (1911), Charney (1978), Eastman (1921), Fry (1963), Goldstein and McGhee (1972), Leacock (1935, 1937), J. Levine (1969), McGhee (1979), F. C. Miller (1967), Mindess (1971), Monro (1951), Morreall (1983), and Piddington (1933/1963). For the latest addition to the ever-increasing number of publications on humor see McGhee and Goldstein (1983).

1. JOKING RELATIONSHIPS

1. The following publications, among others, describe and analyze the joking relationship among the various African ethnic populations and show either a particularistic or a generalistic orientation: Beidelman (1966), Christensen (1963), Colson (1953), J. Freedman (1977), Goody (1959), Griaule (1948), Gulliver (1957, 1958), Hammond (1964), Labouret (1929), Mayer (1950, 1951), J. C. Mitchell (1956), Moreau (1941, 1943), Radcliffe-Brown (1940 and 1949/1965), Reynolds (1958), A. I. Richards (1937), Rigby (1968), Sharman (1969), Spies (1943), Stefaniszyn (1950), Stevens (1978), Tew (1951), White (1957, 1958), and Wilson (1957).

2. See Alford (1981), Bradney (1957), Coser (1960), Handelman and Kapferer (1972), Howell (1973), Loudon (1970), Lundberg (1969), Malefijt (1968a), Pilcher (1972), and Sykes (1966).

3. See Hammond (1964), Mayer (1951), Rigby (1968), Stevens (1978), and White (1958).

4. Children of siblings of the opposite sex are cross-cousins. The child of a person's father's sister or of a person's mother's brother, for example, is that individual's cross-cousin.

5. Two notable exceptions are the studies of Beidelman (1966) and Brukman (1975).

6. A few anthropologists, such as Goldschmidt (1972:71–72), Howell (1973:3), and Sharman (1969), seem aware that detailed ethnographic accounts of the substantive nature of the actual joking activity itself are lacking.

7. More than fifty different phrases and terms have been used by scholars to describe the many aspects of this phenomenon. They refer to prerequisites of, or conditions coexisting with, the phenomenon; to its patterned, institutionalized, formal, and substantive nature; to its various types; and to the activities associated with it.

8. Lineal relatives of a person are individuals related to him or her through the direct line of descent. A person's father, mother, grandfather, grandmother, son, daughter, grandson, and granddaughter are lineal relatives. Collateral relatives are individuals not in the direct line of descent. A person's mother's and father's brothers and sisters, a person's brother's and sister's children, and a person's cousins are collateral relatives.

9. Individuals are considered classificatory relatives by virtue of their membership in such kinship units as lineages of more than five or six

generations, clans, moieties, and so forth. They may be distant blood relatives or not relatives at all.

10. See Colson (1953), Cunnison (1959), Kennedy (1970), Mayer (1951), Rigby (1968), Sharman (1969), Stevens (1978), Turner (1957), and White (1957). Murdock (1949:278) states that a joking relationship of this sort occurs in many societies and that it involves a high frequency of permissive joking, although Murdock does not define "permissive."

11. For ethnographic literature on interclan joking relationships, see Beidelman (1966), Christensen (1963), Colson (1953), Fortes (1945), Moreau (1943), A. I. Richards (1937), Rigby (1968), Stefaniszyn (1950), and Tew (1951). For intertribal joking relationships, see Christensen (1963), Gulliver (1958), Moreau (1941), White (1957), and Wilson (1957).

12. For a discussion of utani in African cultures, see Beidelman (1966), Christensen (1963), Gulliver (1957), Moreau (1941, 1943), Pedler (1940), Reynolds (1958), Rigby (1968), and Wilson (1957).

13. Hammond (1964), Mayer (1951), Rigby (1968), and White (1958).

14. Parenthetical page numbers throughout this discussion refer to Radcliffe-Brown (1952/1965).

2.   SEXUAL INEQUALITY IN HUMOR

1. See the special issue "Sex Roles in Cross-Cultural Perspective," *American Ethnologist* 2 (1975); also see D'Andrade (1966), Farrer (1975), Friedl (1975), Martin and Voorhies (1975), and Quinn (1977), especially the extensive bibliography, and Schlegel (1972, 1977).

2. Cantor (1976), Cantor and Zillman (1973), Chapman and Gadfield (1976), La Fave (1972), J. B. Levine (1976), and Losco and Epstein (1975).

3. Black and white American teenagers (Abrahams 1962; Ayoub and Barnett 1965; Dollard 1939; and Labov 1972a:297–353), Chamula Indians (Gossen 1976), Eskimos (Balikci 1970:140–41, 186; and Rasmussen 1931:345–49, 515–16, as reported in Briggs 1970:342–43), Puerto Ricans (Lauria 1964), and Turkish boys and men (Dundes, Leach, and Özkök 1972).

4. Hermes in Greek mythology (Kerényi 1951:162–80); Hindu mythological figures such as Indra (Basham 1959:234, 400–401; O'Flaherty 1973:81ff., 1976:369), Narada (O'Flaherty 1973:74, 300ff.), or Krishna (Kinsley 1975); Maui-of-a-Thousand Tricks among the island cultures of Oceania (Luomala 1949); Nasruddin Hodja among the various cultures in the Middle East (Barnham 1924; Kelsey 1943; Rosenthal 1956); and Wakdajunkaga and Hare among the Winnebago Indians (Radin 1956/1969).

5. For other examples, see Gumperz and Hymes (1972:45) and Jolly (1979:198).

6. For other examples, see Gillison (1977:128–29), Sharman (1969), and B. B. Whiting (1963:189).

7. For other examples, see Fortune (1932:245) and B. B. Whiting (1963:81).

3. Children's Humor

1. Burling (1966, 1970), Farb (1975), McDowell (1979), Sanches and Kirshenblatt-Gimblett (1976), Schwartzman (1976), Sutton-Smith (1972), and Wolfenstein (1954).
2. Burling (1970:136), Conklin (1956, 1959), Haas (1957a, 1969), Sherzer (1976), Vatuk (1968).
3. For other examples, see Jolly (1979) and Price and Price (1976).
4. Cheska (1981), Lancy and Tindall (1976), Loy (1982), Manning (1983), Salter (1978), Schwartzman (1980), and Stevens (1977b).
5. Caillois (1961), Edwards (1973), Huizinga (1944/1955), Mouledoux (1976), Norbeck (1969, 1971, 1974, 1976), and Piaget (1962).
6. For examples of the absence of competitive play, see Ager (1976), Draper (1976), Sutton-Smith (1972:297), and B. B. Whiting (1963:834).
7. Gorer (1949), DuBois (1960), Honigmann (1954:257–58), La Barre (1945), and Mead (1949).
8. Abrahams (1962, 1963/1970b, 1972b), Ayoub and Barnett (1965), Dollard (1939), Dundes et al. (1972), Gossen (1976), Kochman (1972), Labov (1972a), Mitchell-Kernan and Kernan (1975), Sutton-Smith (1972:123–39), and Vatuk (1968).
9. For other examples, see Alland (1975:123) and Sutton-Smith (1959).
10. For additional examples, see Ammar (1970:230–31) and Stone and Church (1957:153).
11. For another example, see Wolfenstein (1954:194–95).
12. For other examples, see Dube (1955:193) and Siskind (1973:108).
13. For another example, see B. B. Whiting (1963:838).
14. Barry, Bacon, and Child (1957), Roberts and Sutton-Smith (1962), Sutton-Smith and Roberts (1972), and Whiting and Edwards (1973).
15. Chapman (1972, 1973, 1975, 1976), Groch (1974), McGhee (1971b, 1974b, 1976a, 1979), Shultz (1972, 1976), Shultz and Horide (1974), and Ziegler, Levine, and Gould (1966b, 1967). McGhee (1979) and McGhee and Chapman (1980) are the latest and the most extensive discussions on the subject of children's humor.

4. Humor, Ethnicity, and Intergroup Relations

1. Abrahams (1970a), Abrahams and Dundes (1969), Arnez and Anthony (1968), Barron (1950), Burma (1946), Dundes (1971, 1975, 1977), Ehrlich (1979), La Fave (1972, 1977), La Fave, Haddad, and Marshall (1975), La Fave, McCarthy, and Haddad (1973), R. Middleton (1959), Obrdlik (1942), Oring (1973, 1982), Paredes (1966, 1973), Rinder (1965), Rosenberg and Shapiro (1959), and Zenner (1970).
2. Gadfield et al. (1979), La Fave (1972), La Fave et al. (1973), La Fave et al. (1975), Issar et al. (1977), Mutuma et al. (1977), Wolff, Smith and Murray (1934).

3. Abrahams (1970a), Barron (1950), Brandes (1980), Clements (1969), Cray (1964), Dundes (1971, 1975), Kravitz (1977), Rinder (1965), Rosenberg and Shapiro (1959), and Zenner (1970).

4. Abrahams and Dundes (1969), Barrick (1970), Birnbaum (1971), Brunvand (1970), Clements (1969), Cray (1964), Dundes (1971, 1975, 1977), Ferris (1970), Klymasz (1970), Kravitz (1977), Paredes (1973), and D. C. Simmons (1963).

5. See references in Glazer and Moynihan (1963, 1975), Gordon (1964), LeVine and Campbell (1972), Schermerhorn (1970), and Shibutani and Kwan (1965).

6. Barth (1969), Fried (1975), Hymes (1968), Leach (1954), Moerman (1965, 1968).

7. Allport (1954/1958:144), Dundes (1971, 1975), Ferris (1970), Klymasz (1970), Kravitz (1977), Mintz (1977), and D. C. Simmons (1963).

8. Ethnic groups with humor studies pertinent to each: Anglo-Americans (Paredes 1966, 1973), blacks (Abrahams 1970a; Abrahams and Dundes 1969; Arnez and Anthony 1968; Burma 1946; Dundes 1977; Ferris 1970; A. Greenberg 1972; Lomax 1961; Podair 1956; and Prange and Vitols 1963), Gypsies (Brandes 1980), Italian Americans (D. C. Simmons 1966), Jews (Dundes 1971; Ehrlich 1979; A. Greenberg 1972; Oring 1973, 1981; Rosenberg and Shapiro 1959; and Rovit 1966–67), Mexican Americans (Paredes 1973), Mormons (Brunvand 1970), Newfoundlanders (Klymasz 1970), Pakistanis (Kravitz 1977), Polish Americans (Barrick 1970; Clements 1969; Dundes 1971; Welsch 1967), and West Indians (Kravitz 1977).

9. Arnez and Anthony (1968), Cray (1964), Dundes (1971, 1975), Ehrlich (1979), A. Greenberg (1972), R. Middleton (1959), Prange and Vitols (1963), and Rosenberg and Shapiro (1959).

10. See the feature article in *Newsweek*, May 3, 1982.

5. Humor in Religion

1. Bricker (1973), Charles (1945), Codere (1956), Crumrine (1969), Hieb (1972), Honigmann (1942), Howard (1962), J. Levine (1961), Makarius (1970), Norbeck (1961, 1963, 1974), Parsons and Beals (1934), Radin (1914), Ray (1945), Titiev (1975). See Steward (1931) for a good summary of clowns and their antics as reported in many early ethnographic studies of American Indian tribes.

2. For Africa, see Beidelman (1966), Evans-Pritchard (1929), Gluckman (1963), Nadel (1946, 1947, 1954); Norbeck (1963) has the most extensive survey of ethnographic materials on ritual humor in Africa. For North India and Sri Lanka, see Amarasingham (1973), Marriott (1966/1968), D. B. Miller (1973). For Europe, see Cox (1969/1972), Norbeck (1974), Van den Berghe (1963), Welsford (1935). For cross-cultural studies of ritual humor, see Norbeck (1961, 1963, 1974), and Van den Berghe (1963).

3. For additional examples, see Gorer (1935:36), Herskovits (1938:26), Krige (1937:105), Norbeck (1963), B. B. Whiting (1963:189).

4. For additional examples, see Grinnell (1923:2, 204–10, as quoted in Steward 1931:203), Harrington (1921:156), and Kroeber (1902–1907:192, as quoted in Makarius 1970:63), Norbeck (1963:1269), Parsons and Beals (1934:503), Ray (1945:93), Seligman and Seligman (1950:356).

5. For other examples, see E. O. Henry (1975), Marriott (1966/1968), D. B. Miller (1973), Parsons and Beals (1934:493), Sharman (1969:106).

6. For other examples, see Fewkes (1900:128–29, as quoted in Steward 1931:193), Hitchcock (1966:47), D. B. Miller (1973:18), F. F. Williams (1930:251).

7. For examples, see Alland (1975:138), Crumrine (1969:7), Marriott (1966/1968:204), Nadel (1946:396), Steward (1931:193–94).

8. For other examples of scatological aspects of ritual humor, see Crumrine (1969:7), Marriott (1966/1968:203).

9. For other examples, see Bourke (1891:5), Chambers (1909[2]:266–70), Crumrine (1969:7), Parsons (1936, as quoted in Honigmann 1942:221), Parsons and Beals (1934:491), Stirling (1942:33, 37, 65, as quoted in Makarius 1970:53).

10. For more examples, see Evans-Pritchard (1929:313), Goody (1957:91), Herskovits (1937/1971:211), Horowitz (1967:76–77), Kennedy (1970:41), B. B. Whiting (1963:623).

11. For examples, see E. O. Henry (1975), Jacobson (1977), Marriott (1966/1968), D. B. Miller (1973), Steward (1931).

12. For other examples, see Steward (1931:199–200).

13. The following research deals with different theories of ritual humor. Psychological and social psychological: Charles (1945), Crumrine (1969), Gluckman (1954, 1959, 1963), Honigmann (1942), J. Levine (1961), Spicer (1954). Sociological: Bricker (1973), Codere (1956), Norbeck (1974). Cyclical: Van den Berghe (1963). Symbolic: Makarius (1970). Theological: Zucker (1967). Historical: Bricker (1973), Parsons and Beals (1934), Ray (1945). Some scholars have proposed several theories each of which belongs to a different type mentioned above. Parsons and Beals, for instance, propose both psychological and historical theories of ritual humor.

6. Humor and Language

1. Puns have been analyzed in Annamese (Emeneau 1948), Mixteco (Pike 1945, 1946), Navaho (Sapir 1932), Vietnamese (Hoa 1955), and Winnebago (Susman 1941).

2. Esar (1952), Espy (1972), Hockett (1967, 1972), Milner (1972), Quirk (1951).

3. For other examples of interlingual puns, see Espy (1972:195), Hieb (1972:24), and Leslau (1959:105–107).

4. For other examples of such humor, see Hockett (1958:425–26; 1967:932–33), Jesperson (1922:122), and Rosten (1972:13).

5. For other examples, see P. Suzuki (1977:424, 429).

6. For another example, see Trudgill (1974:21).

7. For other examples, see H. A. Bowman (1937:71).

8. For a general discussion of ethnosemantics, see Frake (1962), W. H. Goodenough (1956), Sturtevant (in Spradley 1972), and Burling (in Tyler 1969). For analyses of specific domains in individual languages, see Conklin (1955, 1964), Frake (1961), Wallace and Atkins (1960), and several other papers in Spradley (1972) and Tyler (1969).

7. THE TRICKSTER IN FOLKLORE

1. The term "folklore" is used to mean oral traditional texts, following the views of Bascom (1953), Dorson (1959), and Utley (1961).

2. Whether or not folktales and myths are distinct categories in folklore has been a controversial issue much discussed by scholars. See Bascom (1957, 1965), Hyman (1955), Raglan (1949), S. Thompson (1955).

3. The term "prose narrative" is used in the sense of a "category of verbal art which includes myths, legends, and folktales" (Bascom 1965:3).

4. An excellent bibliography of early American Indian folklore texts appears in Ricketts (1964).

5. For collections or analyses of trickster tales in specific tribes, see Hill and Hill (1945), Opler (1940), Stern (1953).

6. For descriptive, definitional, analytical, and theoretical studies of American Indian tricksters, see Abrahams (1968), Boas (1898, 1914), Brinton (1896), Carroll (1981), Lévi-Strauss (1955), Lowie (1909), Makarius (1973), Parabola (1979), Radin (1914, 1937, 1956/1969), Ricketts (1964, 1966), S. Thompson 1946, 1929/1966), and Voegelin (1949).

7. On Ash'ab, a fool figure in early Islamic literature in Arabic, see Rosenthal (1956), on Nasruddin Hodja, a traditional popular fool figure in Turkey, see Barnham (1924), Kelsey (1943), and Shah (1972). On Shakespearean fools, see Barber (1959), Busby (1923), Bush (1956), Goldsmith (1963), Hotson, (1952), and Swain (1932). For modern comedians and clowns, see Cohen (1967) and Kofsky (1974) on Lenny Bruce; W. D. Bowman (1931/1974), Cotes and Niklaus (1951), Huff (1951), and McCabe (1978) on Charlie Chaplin; Coursodon (1973) on Buster Keaton; Barr (1968), Everson (1967), and McCabe (1966) on Laurel and Hardy; and Adamson (1973) on the Marx Brothers.

8. Charles (1945), Daniels and Daniels (1964), Disher (1925), Kern (1980), Klapp (1949–50), Swain (1932), Towsen (1976), Welsford (1935), Willeford (1969), and Zucker (1967).

9. Boas (1940/1966), Radin (1956/1969), Ricketts (1964, 1966), and S. Thompson (1929/1966).

10. Evans-Pritchard (1967:18–19), Finnegan (1970:350), Luomala (1949:80), Radin (1956/1969:148, 151), Skeels (1954), and Voegelin (1949:1124).

11. Clark (1970), Koestler (1964), McGhee (1979), Nerhardt (1976), and Suls (1983). For a general summary of incongruity theories, see Keith-Spiegel (1972:8–9).

12. For superiority theories, see La Fave et al. (1975), Leacock (1935), Rapp (1947, 1949), Sidis (1913), and Wallis (1922).

13. Boas (1898), Brinton (1896), Lowie (1909), Radin (1914:352ff.), and Ricketts (1964, 1966).

14. See C. G. Jung in Radin (1956/1969). For a comparable explanation regarding the phasing out of the trickster-clown Ash'ab from sacred Islamic literature, which had occurred by the medieval period, see Rosenthal (1956).

15. For the social process of fool making and the social functions of a fool, see Daniels and Daniels (1964) and Klapp (1949–50).

8.   LAUGHTER AND SMILING: EVOLUTIONARY AND BIOSOCIAL ASPECTS

1. Edmonson (1952:2) and Koestler (1964:31) use laughter as a criterion to define the broad domain of humor. Armstrong (1928), Grotjahn (1957), Hertzler (1970), and Piddington (1933/1963) use the terms "laughter" and "humor" synonymously.

2. Berlyne (1969), Chapman and Foot (1976:3–4), and Potter (1954).

3. Geertz (1964:37), Hertzler (1970:27), Huizinga (1944/1955:6), and Lorenz (1967:285).

4. Buytendijk (1947, 1948), Eible-Eibesfeldt (1967), and Plessner (1950, 1953), all treat smiling and laughter as qualitatively different. Van Hooff (1972) considers them only quantitatively different.

5. Ambrose (1961, 1963), Blurton-Jones (1967), Charlesworth and Kreutzer (1973), Spitz and Wolf (1946), Washburn (1929), and Wolff (1963, 1966, 1969).

6. Charlesworth and Kreutzer (1973:109), Darwin (1872/1965), Washburn (1929:527), and Wolff (1963).

7. Crystal (1974), Lieberman (1967), Pittenger, Hockett, and Danehy (1960), Scherer (1972), Trager (1958, 1961), and Williams and Stevens (1972).

8. For other examples of restraints, see Murphy and Murphy (1974:106) and Wiser and Wiser (1930/1965:73).

9. For examples, see Osgood (1951:99) and Embree (1939:177).

10. For another ethnographic example, see Mead (1949:116).

References

Abrahams, R. 1962. Playing the Dozens. Journal of American Folklore 75:209–20.

——. 1968. Trickster, the Outrageous Hero. *In* Our Living Traditions: An Introduction to American Folklore, Tristram P. Coffin, ed. New York: Basic. Pp. 170–78.

——. 1970a. The Negro Stereotype. Journal of American Folklore 83:229–49.

——. 1970b. Deep Down in the Jungle. Chicago: Aldine. Rev. ed. (First published in 1963.)

——. 1972a. Stereotyping and Beyond. *In* Language and Cultural Diversity in American Education, Roger D. Abrahams and Rudolph C. Troike, eds. Englewood Cliffs, N. J.: Prentice-Hall. Pp. 19–29.

——. 1972b. Joking: The Training of the Man of Words in Talking Abroad. *In* Rappin' and Stylin' Out: Communication in Urban Black America, Thomas Kochman, ed. Urbana: University of Illinois Press. Pp. 215–40.

Abrahams, R. D., and A. Dundes. 1969. On Elephantasy and Elephanticide. Psychoanalytic Review 56:225–41.

Abrams, D. 1977. A Developmental Analysis of the Trickster from Folklore. *In* Studies in the Anthropology of Play, Phillip Stevens, Jr. ed. West Point, N.Y.: Leisure. Pp. 145–54.

Adams, H. E. 1937. Minority Caricatures on the American Stage. *In* Studies in the Science of Society, George P. Murdock, ed. New Haven: Yale University Press. Pp. 1–27.

Adams, J. 1975. Ethnic Humor. New York: Manor.

Adamson, J. 1973. Groucho, Harpo, Chico, and Sometimes Zeppo. New York: Simon & Schuster.

Ager, L. P. 1976. The Reflection of Cultural Values in Eskimo Children's Games. *In* The Antropological Study of Play: Problems and Prospects, David F. Lancy and B. Allan Tindall, eds. Cornwall, N.Y.: Leisure. Pp. 79–86.

275

Ahenakew, E. 1929. Cree Trickster Tales. Journal of American Folklore 42:309–53.

Albert, E. M. 1972. Culture Patterning of Speech Behavior in Burundi. *In* Directions in Sociolinguistics, John J. Gumperz and Dell Hymes, eds. New York: Holt, Rinehart & Winston. Pp. 72–105.

Alford, F. 1981. The Joking Relationship in American Society. American Humor: Interdisciplinary Newsletter 8:1–8.

Alland, A., Jr. 1975. When the Spider Danced: Ethnography of the Abron of the Ivory Coast. Garden City, N.Y.: Anchor.

Allport, G. W. 1950. The Individual and His Religion. New York: Macmillan.

———. 1958. The Nature of Prejudice. Garden City, N.Y.: Doubleday. (Originally published in 1954.)

Altman, S. 1971. The Comic Image of the Jew: Explorations of a Pop Culture Phenomenon. Teaneck, N.J.: Fairleigh Dickinson University Press.

Amarasingham, L. R. 1973. Laughter as Cure: Joking and Exorcism in a Singhalese Curing Ritual. Doctoral dissertation, Cornell University.

Ambrose, J. A. 1961. The Development of the Smiling Response in Early Infancy. *In* Determinants of Infant Behaviour, B. M. Foss, ed. London: Methuen. Pp. 179–95.

———. 1963. The Age of Onset of Ambivalence in Early Infancy: Indications from the Study of Laughing. Journal of Child Psychology and Psychiatry and Allied Disciplines 4:167–84.

Ammar, H. 1970. The Aims and Methods of Socialization in Silwa. *In* From Child to Adult: Studies in the Anthropology of Education, John Middleton, ed. Garden City, N.Y.: Natural History. Pp. 226–49.

Anderson, E. N., Jr. 1967. Prejudice and Ethnic Stereotypes in Rural Hong Kong. Kroeber Anthropological Society Papers 37:90–107.

Andrew, R. J. 1963. Evolution of Facial Expression. Science 142, no. 3595:1034–41.

———. 1965. The Origins of Facial Expressions. Scientific American 213(4):88–94.

———. 1972. Comments on J. A. R. A. M. Van Hooff's paper "A Comparative Approach to the Phylogeny of Laughter and Smiling." *In* Non-verbal Communication, Robert A. Hinde, ed. London: Cambridge University Press. Pp. 239–41.

Apte, M. L. 1983. Humor Research, Methodology, and Theory in Anthropology. *In* Handbook of Humor Research, Paul E. McGhee and Jeffrey H. Goldstein, eds. New York: Springer. Pp. 183–212.

Armstrong, M. 1928. Laughing: An Essay. New York: Harper.

Arnez, N. L., and C. B. Anthony. 1968. Contemporary Negro Humor as Social Satire. Phylon 29:339–46.

Arnott, D. W. 1957. Proverbial Lore and Word-play of the Fulani. Africa 27:379–96.

Aufenanger, H. 1958. Children's Games and Entertainments among the Kumongo Tribe in Central New Guinea. Anthropos 53:575–84.

References

Ayoub, M., and S. A. Barnett. 1965. Ritualized Verbal Insults in White School Culture. Journal of American Folklore 78:337–44.

Baldwin, J. D., and J. I. Baldwin. 1977. The Role of Learning Phenomena in the Ontogeny of Exploration and Play. *In* Primate Bio-social Development: Biological, Social, and Ecological Determinants, Suzanne Chevalier-Skolnikoff and Frank E. Poirier, eds. New York: Garland. Pp. 343–406.

———. 1978. The Primate Contribution to the Study of Play. *In* Play: Anthropological Perspectives, Michael A. Salter, ed. West Point: Leisure. Pp. 53–68.

Balikci, A. 1970. The Netsilik Eskimo. Garden City, N.Y.: Natural History.

Barber, C. L. 1959. Shakespeare's Festive Comedy. Princeton: Princeton University Press.

Barnett, W. K. 1970. An Ethnographic Description of Sanlei Ts'un, Taiwan, with Emphasis on Women's Roles Overcoming Research Problems Caused by the Presence of a Great Tradition. Doctoral dissertation, Michigan State University.

Barnham, H. D. 1924. The Khoja: Tales of Nasr-ed-Din. New York: Appleton.

Barr, C. 1968. Laurel and Hardy. Berkeley: University of California Press.

Barrick, M. E. 1970. Racial Riddles and the Polack Joke. Keystone Folklore Quarterly 15:3–15.

Barron, M. L. 1950. A Content Analysis of Intergroup Humor. American Sociological Review 15:88–94.

Barry, H. III, M. K. Bacon, and I. L. Child. 1957. A Cross-cultural Survey of Some Sex Differences in Socialization. Journal of Abnormal and Social Psychology 55:327–32.

Barth, F. ed. 1969. Ethnic Groups and Boundaries. Boston: Little, Brown.

Bascom, W. R. 1953. Folklore and Anthropology. Journal of American Folklore 66:283–90.

———. 1955. Verbal Art. Journal of American Folklore 68:245–52.

———. 1957. The Myth-Ritual Theory. Journal of American Folklore 70:104–14.

———. 1965. The Forms of Folklore: Prose Narratives. Journal of American Folklore 78:3–20.

Basham, A. L. 1959. The Wonder That was India. New York: Grove.

Basso, K. 1970. To Give Up on Words: Silence in the Western Apache Culture. Southwestern Journal of Anthropology 26:213–30.

———. 1979. Portraits of "The Whiteman." New York: Cambridge University Press.

Bauman, R., and J. Sherzer, eds. 1974. Explorations in the Ethnography of Speaking. New York: Cambridge University Press.

Beals, R. 1953. Acculturation. *In* Anthropology Today: An Encyclopedic Inventory, prepared under the chairmanship of A. L. Kroeber. Chicago: University of Chicago Press. Pp. 621–41.

Beck, P., and A. L. Walters. 1977. The Sacred: Ways of Knowledge, Sources of Life. Tsaile, Ariz., Navajo Nation: Navajo Community College.

Beidelman, T. O. 1963. Some Kaguru Riddles. Man 63:158–60.

———. 1964. Intertribal Insult and Opprobrium in an East African Chiefdom (Ukaguru). Anthropological Quarterly 37:33–52.

———. 1966. *Utani*: Some Kaguru Notions of Death, Sexuality, and Affinity. Southwestern Journal of Anthropology 22:354–80.

Bell, R. R. 1981. Worlds of Friendship. Beverly Hills, Calif.: Sage.

Ben-Amos, D. 1971. Toward a Definition of Folklore in Context. Journal of American Folklore 84:3–15.

———. 1973. The "Myth" of Jewish Humor. Western Folklore 32(2):112–31.

Benedict, R. 1946. Patterns of Culture. New York: New American Library. (Originally published in 1934.)

Berger, A. A. 1976. Anatomy of the Joke. Journal of Communication 26(3):113–15.

Berger, P., and T. Luckman. 1967. The Social Construction of Reality. Garden City: Doubleday, Anchor. (Originally published in 1966.)

Bergler, E. A. 1956. Laughter and the Sense of Humor. New York: Intercontinental Medical.

Bergson, H. 1911. Laughter: An Essay on the Meaning of the Comic. New York: Macmillan.

Berlyne, D. E. 1969. Laughter, Humor, and Play. *In* Handbook of Social Psychology, G. Lindsey and E. Aronson, eds. 2d ed. Vol. 3. Reading, Mass.: Addison-Wesley. Pp. 705–852.

Bernard, H. R. 1975. The Human Way: Readings in Anthropology. New York: Macmillan.

Bernard, H. R., and J. S. Pedraza, eds. 1976. Otomi Parables, Folktales, and Jokes. International Journal of American Linguistics Native American Texts Series, vol. 1, no. 2. Chicago: University of Chicago Press.

Berne, E. 1973. What Do You Say After You Say Hello? New York: Bantam.

Bhat, G. K. 1959. The Vidusaka. Ahmedabad, India: New Order.

Birdwhistell, R. L. 1970. Kinesics and Context. Philadelphia: University of Pennsylvania Press.

Birnbaum, M. D. 1971. On the Language of Prejudice. Western Folklore 30:247–68.

Bloch, M., ed. 1975. Political Language and Oratory in Traditional Society. New York: Academic.

Blom, J., and J. J. Gumperz. 1972. Social Meaning in Linguistic Structures: Code-Switching in Norway. *In* Directions in Sociolinguistics, John J. Gumperz and Dell Hymes, eds. New York: Holt, Rinehart & Winston. Pp. 407–34.

Blurton-Jones, N. G. 1967. An Ethological Study of Some Aspects of Social Behavior of Children in Nursery School. *In* Primate Ethology, D. Morris, ed. London: Weidenfeld & Nicolson. Pp. 347–68.

References

------. 1972. Ethological Studies of Child Behavior. London: Cambridge University Press.

Boas, F. 1898. Introduction. Traditions of the Thompson River Indians of British Columbia, by James Teit. Memoirs of the American Folklore Society, vol. 6. Pp. 1–18. New York: Houghton Mifflin.

------. 1914. Mythology and Folktales of the North American Indians. Journal of American Folklore 27:374–410.

------. 1966. Race, Language, and Culture. New York: Free Press. (Originally published in 1940.)

Bogardus, E. S. 1950. Stereotypes versus Sociotypes. Sociology and Social Research 34:286–91.

Bolinger, D. 1968. Aspects of Language. New York: Harcourt, Brace & World.

Bourke, J. G. 1891. Scatologic Rites of All Nations. Washington, D.C.: Lowdermilk.

Bowen, Elenore S. 1964. Return to Laughter. Natural History Library. Garden City, N.Y.: Doubleday.

Bowman, H. A. 1937. The Humor of Primitive Peoples. *In* Studies in the Science of Society, George P. Murdock, ed. New Haven: Yale University Press. Pp. 67–83.

Bowman, W. D. 1974. Charles Chaplin: His Life and Art. New York: Haskell House. (Reprint of 1931 edition.)

Bradney, P. 1957. The Joking Relationship in Industry. Human Relations 10:179–87.

Brandes, S. 1980. Metaphors of Masculinity: Sex and Status in Andalusian Folklore. Publications of the American Folklore Society, n.s., vol. 1. Philadelphia: University of Pennsylvania Press.

Brant, C. S. 1948. On Joking Relationships. American Anthropologist, n.s., 50:160–62.

Bricker, V. R. 1973. Ritual Humor in Highland Chiapas. Austin: University of Texas Press.

------. 1974. The Ethnographic Context of Some Traditional Mayan Speech Genres. *In* Explorations in the Ethnography of Speaking. R. Bauman and J. Sherzer, eds. New York: Cambridge University Press. Pp. 368–88.

Briggs, J. L. 1970. Never in Anger: Portrait of an Eskimo Family. Cambridge: Harvard University Press.

Brigham, J. C. 1971. Ethnic Stereotypes. Psychological Bulletin 76:15–38.

Brinton, D. G. 1896. The Myths of the New World. 3d ed. Philadelphia: McKay.

Brown, R. 1958. Words and Things. Glencoe: Free Press.

------. 1965. Social Psychology. New York: Free Press.

Brown, W. N. 1961. Mythology of India. *In* Mythologies of the Ancient World, Samuel N. Kramer, ed. Garden City: N.Y.: Doubleday. Pp. 277–330.

279

Brukman, J. 1975. "Tongue Play": Constitutive and Interpretive Properties of Sexual Joking Encounters among the Koya of South India. *In* Sociocultural Dimensions of Language Use, Mary Sanches and B. Blount, eds. New York: Academic. Pp. 235–69.

Brunvand, J. H. 1970. As the Saints Go Marching By. Journal of American Folklore 83:53–60.

———. 1972. The Study of Contemporary Folklore: Jokes. Fabula 13:1–19.

Burling, R. 1966. The Metrics of Children's Verse: A Cross-linguistic Study. American Anthropologist 68:1418–41.

———. 1970. Man's Many Voices: Language in Its Cultural Context. New York: Holt, Rinehart & Winston.

Burma, J. H. 1946. Humor as a Technique in Race Conflict. American Sociological Review 11:710–15.

Busby, O. M. 1923. Studies in the Development of the Fool in Elizabethan Drama. New York: Oxford University Press.

Bush, G. 1956. Shakespeare and the Natural Condition. Cambridge: Harvard University Press.

Buytendijk, F. J. J. 1947. De eerste glimlach van het kind. Nijmegen: Dekker, Vegt.

———. 1948. Algemene theorie der menselijke houding en beweging. Utrecht: Het Spectrum.

Caillois, R. 1961. Man, Play and Games. Trans. from the French by Meyer Barash. Glencoe, Ill.: Free Press.

Cameron, W. B. 1963. Informal Sociology. New York: Random House.

Campbell, D. T., and R. A. LeVine. 1961. A Proposal for Cooperative Cross-cultural Research on Ethnocentrism. Journal of Conflict Resolution 5:82–108.

Campbell, J. K. 1974. Honour, Family, and Patronage. London: Oxford University Press.

Cantor, J. R. 1976. What Is Funny to Whom? The Role of Gender. Journal of Communication 26(3):164–72.

Cantor, J. R., and D. Zillman. 1973. Resentment toward Victimized Protagonists and Severity of Misfortune They Suffer as Factors in Humor Appreciation. Journal of Experimental Research in Personality 6:321–29.

Carroll, M. P. 1981. Lévi-Strauss, Freud, and the Trickster: A New Perspective upon an Old Problem. American Ethnologist 8:301–13.

Chagnon, N. 1968. Yanomamo: The Fierce People. New York: Holt, Rinehart & Winston.

Chambers, E. K. 1909. The Mediaeval Stage. 2 vols. Oxford: Clarendon Press.

Champion, S. G. 1938. Racial Proverbs. London: Routledge.

Chapman, A. J. 1972. Some Aspects of the Social Facilitation of "Humorous Laughter" in Children. Doctoral dissertation, University of Leicester.

———. 1973. Social Facilitation of Laughter in Children. Journal of Experimental Social Psychology 9:528–41.

———. 1975. Humorous Laughter in Children. Journal of Personality and Social Psychology 31:42–49.

———. 1976. Social Aspects of Humorous Laughter. *In* Humour and Laughter: Theory, Research, and Applications, Antony J. Chapman and Hugh C. Foot, eds. New York: Wiley. Pp. 155–86.

Chapman, A. J., and H. C. Foot, eds. 1976. Humour and Laughter: Theory, Research, and Applications. New York: Wiley.

———, eds. 1977. It's a Funny Thing, Humour. New York: Pergamon.

Chapman, A. J., and N. J. Gadfield. 1976. Is Sexual Humor Sexist? Journal of Communication 26(3):141–53.

Charles, L. H. 1945. The Clown's Function. Journal of American Folklore 58:25–34.

Charlesworth, W. R., and M. A. Kreutzer. 1973. Facial Expressions of Infants and Children. *In* Darwin and Facial Expression: A Century of Research in Review, Paul Ekman, ed. New York: Academic. Pp. 91–168.

Charney, M. 1978. Comedy High and Low. New York: Oxford University Press.

Cheska, A., ed. 1981. Play as Context. West Point: Leisure.

Chevalier-Skolnikoff, S. 1973. Facial Expression of Emotion in Nonhuman Primates. *In* Darwin and Facial Expression, Paul Ekman, ed. New York: Academic. Pp. 11–89.

Chomsky, N. 1965. Aspects of the Theory of Syntax. Cambridge: MIT Press.

Christensen, J. B. 1963. Utani: Joking, Sexual License, and Social Obligations among the Luguru. American Anthropologist 65:1314–27.

Cicourel, A. V. 1974. Cognitive Sociology. New York: Free Press.

Clark, M. 1970. Humor and Incongruity. Philosophy 45:20–32.

Clements, W. M. 1969. The Types of the Polack Jokes. Folklore Forum. Bibliographic and Special Series, 3. Bloomington: Folklore Institute, Indiana University.

Codere, H. 1956. The Amiable Side of Kwakiutl Life: The Potlatch and the Play Potlatch. American Anthropologist 58:334–51.

Cohen, J., ed. 1967. The Essential Lenny Bruce. New York: Bell.

Cohen, R., and J. Middleton. 1970. From Tribe to Nation in Africa: Studies in Incorporation Processes. Scranton: Chandler.

Colson, E. 1953. Clans and the Joking-Relationship among the Plateau Tonga of Northern Rhodesia. Kroeber Anthropological Society Papers 10:45–60.

Conklin, H. C. 1955. Hanunoo Color Categories. Southwestern Journal of Anthropology 11:339–44.

———. 1956. Tagalog Sppech Disguise. Language 32:136–39.

———. 1959. Linguistic Play in Its Cultural Context. Language 35:631–36.

——. 1964. Ethnogenealogical Method. *In* Explorations in Cultural Anthropology, Ward Goodenough, ed. New York: McGraw-Hill. Pp. 25–55.

Coser, R. L. 1960. Laughter among Colleagues: A Study of Social Functions of Humor among the Staff of a Mental Hospital. Psychiatry 23:81–95.

Cotes, P., and T. Niklaus. 1951. The Little Fellow: The Life and Work of Charles Spencer Chaplin. New York: Philosophical Library.

Coursodon, J. 1973. Buster Keaton. Paris: Seghers.

Cox, H. 1972. The Feast of Fools. Perennial Library. New York: Harper & Row. (Originally published in 1969.)

Craig, D. R. 1971. Education and Creole English in the West Indies: Some Sociolinguistic Factors. *In* Pidginization and Creolization of Languages, Dell Hymes, ed. New York: Cambridge University Press. Pp. 371–87.

Cray, E. 1964. The Rabbi Trickster. Journal of American Folklore 77:331–45.

Cronin, C. 1977. Illusion and Reality in Sicily. *In* Sexual Stratification, A. Schlegel, ed. New York: Columbia University Press. Pp. 67–93.

Crumrine, N. R. 1969. Čapakoba, the Mayo Easter Ceremonial Impersonator: Explanations of Ritual Clowning. Journal for the Scientific Study of Religion 8:1–22.

Crystal, D. 1974. Paralinguistics. *In* Current Trends in Linguistics, vol. 12 (pts. 1–2), Thomas A. Sebek, ed. The Hague: Mouton. Pp. 265–95.

Cunnison, I. 1959. The Luapula Peoples of Northern Rhodesia. Manchester, England: Manchester University Press.

Dandekar, G. N. 1973. Smaranagāthā. Bombay: Majestic Book Stall.

D'Andrade, R. 1966. Sex Differences and Cultural Institutions. *In* The Development of Sex Differences, E. Maccoby, ed. Stanford, Calif.: Stanford University Press. Pp. 174–204.

Daniels, A. K., and R. R. Daniels. 1964. The Social Function of the Career Fool. Psychiatry 27:219–29.

Darwin, C. 1965. The Expression of the Emotion in Man and Animals. Chicago: University of Chicago Press. (Originally published in 1872.)

Dearborn, G. V. N. 1900. The Nature of the Smile and the Laugh. Science 9:851–56.

Devereux, G. 1947. Mohave Orality. Psychoanalytic Quarterly 16:519–46.

Disher, M. W. 1925. Clowns and Pantomimes. London: Constable.

Dollard, J. 1939. The Dozens: Dialectic of Insult. American Imago 1:3–24.

Dorson, R. 1959. American Folklore. Chicago: University of Chicago Press.

——. 1960. Jewish-American Dialect Jokes on Tape. *In* Studies in Biblical and Jewish Folklore, Raphael Patai, Francis L. Utley, and Dov Noy, eds. Indiana University Folklore Series, Monograph 13. Bloomington: Indiana University Press. Pp. 111–74.

——. 1961. More Jewish Dialect Stories. Midwest Folklore 10:133–46.

References

Douglas, M. 1968. The Social Control of Cognition: Some Factors in Joke Perception. Man 3:361–76.

——. 1971. Do Dogs Laugh? A Cross-cultural Approach to Body Symbolism. Journal of Psychosomatic Research 15-387–90.

——. 1973. Rules and Meanings: The Anthropology of Everyday Knowledge. Harmondsworth, England: Penguin.

Dozier, E. P. 1961. Rio Grande Pueblos. *In* Perspectives in American Indian Culture Change, E. H. Spicer, ed. Chicago: University of Chicago Press. Pp. 94–186.

Draper, P. 1976. Social and Economic Constraints on Child Life among the !Kung. *In* Kalahari Hunter-Gatherers, Robert Lee and I. Devore, eds. Cambridge: Harvard University Press. Pp. 199–217.

Driver, H. E. 1969. Indians of North America. 2d ed. rev. Chicago: University of Chicago Press.

Dube, S. C. 1955. Indian Village. London: Routledge & Kegan Paul.

DuBois, C. 1960. The People of Alor: A Social-Psychological Study of an East Indian Island. Cambridge: Harvard University Press. (Originally published in 1944.)

Dundes, A. 1971. A Study of Ethnic Slurs: The Jew and the Polack in the United States. Journal of American Folklore 84:186–203.

——. 1975. Slurs International: Folk Comparisons of Ethnicity and National Character. Southern Folklore Quarterly 39:15–38.

——. 1977. Jokes and Covert Language Attitudes: The Curious Case of the Wide-Mouth Frog. Language in Society 6:141–47.

Dundes, A., J. W. Leach, and B. Özkök. 1972. The Strategy of Turkish Boys' Verbal Dueling Rhymes. *In* Directions in Sociolinguistics, John J. Gumperz and Dell Hymes, eds. New York: Holt, Rinehart & Winston. Pp. 130–60.

Dwyer, B. 1971. Dictionary for Yankees and Other Uneducated People. Highland: Merry Mountaineers.

Eastman, M. 1921. The Sense of Humor. New York: Scribners.

Edmonson, M. 1952. Los Manitos: Patterns of Humor in Relation to Cultural Values. Doctoral dissertation, Harvard University.

——. 1971. Lore: An Introduction to the Science of Folklore and Literature. New York: Holt, Rinehart & Winston.

Edwards, H. 1973. Sociology of Sports. Homewood: Dorsey.

Eggan, F. 1955. The Cheyenne and Arapaho Kinship System. *In* Social Anthropology of North American Tribes, Fred Eggan, ed. Chicago: University of Chicago Press. Pp. 35–98. (Originally published in 1937.)

Ehrlich, H. J. 1979. Observations on Ethnic and Intergroup Humor. Ethnicity 6:383–98.

Eible-Eibesfeldt, I. 1967. Grundriss der vergleichenden Verhaltensforschung. Munich: Piper.

——. 1970. Ethology: The Biology of Behavior. New York: Holt, Rinehart & Winston.

283

——. 1972. Similarities and Differences between Cultures in Expressive Movements. *In* Non-verbal Communication, Robert A. Hinde, ed. London: Cambridge University Press. Pp. 297–312.

——. 1973. The Expressive Behaviour of the Deaf-and-Blind Born. *In* Social Communication and Movement, M. Von Cranach and I. Vine, eds. London: Academic. Pp. 163–94.

Ekman, P. 1973. Darwin and Facial Expression. New York: Academic.

Ekman, P., and W. V. Friesen. 1975. Unmasking the Face. Englewood Cliffs: Prentice-Hall.

——. 1976. Measuring Facial Movement. Environmental Psychology and Non-verbal Behavior 1:56–75.

Eliason, M. 1974. Israeli Humor Grisly in the Wake of War. Durham [N.C.] Morning Herald, February 6.

Embree, J. F. 1939. Suye Mura: A Japanese Village. Chicago: University of Chicago Press.

Emeneau, M. B. 1948. Homonyms and Puns in Annamese. Language 23:239–44.

Emerson, R. 1960. From Empire to Nation. Cambridge: Harvard University Press.

Epstein, A. L. 1968. Linguistic Innovation and Culture on the Copperbelt, Northern Rhodesia. *In* Readings in the Sociology of Language, Joshua A. Fishman, ed. The Hague: Mouton. Pp. 320–39.

Esar, E. 1952. The Humor of Humor. New York: Bramhall House.

Espy, W. R. 1972. The Game of Words. New York: Grosset & Dunlap.

Evans-Pritchard, E. E. 1929. Some Collective Expressions of Obscenity in Africa. Journal of the Royal Anthropological Institute of Great Britain and Ireland 59:311–31.

——. 1965. The Position of Women in Primitive Societies and Other Essays in Social Anthropology. New York: Free Press.

——. 1967. The Zande Trickster. London: Oxford University Press.

Everson, W. K. 1967. The Films of Laurel and Hardy. New York: Citadel.

Falk, J. S. 1973. Linguistics and Language. Lexington: Xerox College Publishing.

Fallers, L. A. 1974. The Social Anthropology of the Nation-State. Chicago: Aldine.

Farb, P. 1975. Word Play. New York: Bantam. (originally published in 1973).

Farrer, C. R. 1975. Introduction. *In* Women and Folklore, Claire R. Farrer, ed. Journal of American Folklore, special issue, 88(347):i–xv.

Feinberg, L., ed. 1971. Asian Laughter: An Anthology of Oriental Satire and Humor. New York: Weatherhill.

Ferguson, C. A. 1959. Diglossia. Word 15:325–40.

——. 1964. Baby Talk in Six Languages. American Anthropologist 66(2)(pt. 2):103–14.

——. 1968. Myths about Arabic. *In* Readings in the Sociology of Language, Joshua A. Fishman, ed. The Hague: Mouton. Pp. 375–81.

References

———. 1976. The Structure and Use of Politeness Formulas. Language in Society 5:137–51.

Fernea, E. 1969. Guests of the Sheikh: An Ethnography of an Iraqi Village. New York: Doubleday. (Originally published in 1965.)

Ferris, W. R., Jr. 1970. Racial Stereotypes in White Folklore. Keystone Folklore Quarterly 15:188–98.

Fewkes, J. W. 1900. The New Fire Ceremony at Walpi: American Anthropologist, n.s., 2:80–138.

Fine, G. A. 1976. Obscene Joking across Cultures. Journal of Communication 26:134–40.

Finnegan, R. 1967. Limba Stories and Story-telling. London: Oxford University Press.

———. 1970. Oral Literature in Africa. London: Oxford University Press.

Fischer, J. L. 1963. The Sociopsychological Analysis of Folktales. Current Anthropology 4:235–95.

Fishman, J. A., ed. 1968. Readings in the Sociology of Language. The Hague: Mouton.

Flugel, J. C. 1954. Humor and Laughter. In Handbook of Social Psychology, vol. 2, G. Lindzey, ed. Reading, Mass.: Addison-Wesley. Pp. 709–34.

Foot, H. C., and A. J. Chapman, 1976. The Social Responsiveness of Young Children in Humorous Situations. In Humour and Laughter: Theory, Research, and Applications, Antony J. Chapman and Hugh C. Foot, eds. New York: Wiley. Pp. 187–214.

Ford, C. S. 1967. On the Analysis of Behavior for Cross-Cultural Comparisons. In Cross-cultural Approaches, C. S. Ford, ed. New Haven: HRAF Press. Pp. 3–21.

Ford, C. S., and F. A. Beach. 1951. Patterns of Sexual Behavior. New York: Harper.

Fortes, M. 1945. The Dynamics of Clanship among the Tallensi. London: Oxford University Press.

———. 1949. The Web of Kinship among the Tallensi. London: Oxford University Press.

Fortune, R. F. 1932. The Sorcerers of Dobu. New York: Dutton.

Fox, G. 1977. "Nice Girl": Social Control of Women through Value Construct. Signs 2(4):805–17.

Fraiberg, S. 1968. Parallel and Divergent Patterns in Blind and Sighted Infants. Psychoanalytic Study of the Child 23:264–300.

Frake, C. O. 1961. The Diagnosis of Disease among the Subanun of Mindanao. American Anthropologist 63:113–32.

———. 1962. The Ethnographic Study of Cognitive Systems. In Anthropology and Human Behavior, T. Gladwin and W. C. Sturtevant, eds. Washington: Anthropological Society of Washington, D.C. Pp. 72–85, 91–93.

Franklyn, J. 1960. A Dictionary of Rhyming Slang. London: Routledge & Kegan Paul.

Freedman, D. G. 1964. Smiling in Blind Infants and the Issue of Innate versus Acquired. Journal of Child Psychology and Psychiatry 5:171–84.
——. 1965. Hereditary Control of Early Social Behavior. *In* Determinants of Infant Behavior, vol. 3, B. M. Foss, ed. London: Methuen. Pp. 149–56.

Freedman, J. 1977. Joking, Affinity, and the Exchange of Ritual Services among the Kiga of Northern Rwanda: An Essay on Joking Relationship Theory. Man, n.s., 12:154–65.

Freud, S. 1905. Jokes and Their Relation to the Unconscious. (Der Witz und seine Beziehung zum Unbewussten.) Leipzig: Deuticke.
——. 1928. Humor. International Journal of Psychoanalysis 9:1–6.

Fried, M. H. 1965. A Four-Letter Word That Hurts. Saturday Review, October 2.
——. 1975. The Notion of Tribe. Menlo Park, Calif.: Cummings.

Friedl, E. 1975. Women and Men: An Anthropologist's View. New York: Holt, Rinehart & Winston.

Fromkin, V. A. 1973. Slips of the Tongue. Scientific American 229(6):110–17.

Fry, W. F., Jr. 1963. Sweet Madness: A Study of Humor. Palo Alto: Pacific.

Fulcher, J. S. 1942. "Voluntary" Facial Expression in Blind and Seeing Children. Archives of Psychology 38(272):5–49.

Gadfield, N. J., H. Giles, R. Y. Bourhis, and H. Tajfel. 1979. Dynamics of Humor in Ethnic Group Relations. Ethnicity 6:373–82.

Gardner, P. M. 1966. Symmetric Respect and Memorate Knowledge: The Structure and Ecology of Individualistic Culture. Southwestern Journal of Anthropology 22:389–415.

Geertz, C. 1960. The Religion of Java. Glencoe: Free Press.
——. 1963. The Integrative Revolution. *In* Old Societies and New States, Clifford Geertz, ed. Glencoe, Ill.: Free Press. Pp. 105–57.
——. 1964. The Transition to Humanity. *In* Horizons of Anthropology, Sol Tax, ed. Chicago: Aldine. Pp. 37–49.
——. 1973. The Interpretation of Cultures. New York: Basic.

Gibbs, J. L., Jr. 1969. Law and Personality: Sign Posts for a New Direction. *In* Law in Culture and Society, Laura Nader, ed. Chicago: Aldine. Pp. 176–207.

Gilbert, W. H., Jr. 1955. Eastern Cherokee Social Organization. *In* Social Anthropology of North America Tribes, Fred Eggan, ed. Chicago: University of Chicago Press. Pp. 283–338. (Originally published in 1937.)

Gillison, G. 1977. Fertility Rites and Sorcery in a New Guinea Village. National Geographic 152(1):124–46.

Girling, F. K. 1957. Joking Relationships in a Scottish Town. Man 57:102.

Glacken, C. J. 1955. The Great Loochoo: A Study of Okinawan Village Life. Berkeley: University of California Press.

Glazer, N., and D. P. Moynihan. 1963. Beyond the Melting Pot. Cambridge: MIT Press.

——, eds. 1975. Ethnicity: Theory and Experience. Cambridge: Harvard University Press.

Gluckman, M. 1954. Rituals of Rebellion in South-East Africa. Manchester, England: Manchester University Press.

——. 1959. Custom and Conflict in Africa. Glencoe, Ill.: Free Press.

——. 1963. The Role of the Sexes in Wiko Circumcision Ceremonies. *In* Social Structure, Meyer Fortes, ed. New York: Russell & Russell.

Goldschmidt, W. 1972. An Ethnography of Encounters: A Methodology for the Enquiry into the Relation between the Individual and Society. Current Anthropology 13:59-78.

Goldsmith, R. H. 1963. Wise Fools in Shakespeare. East Lansing, Mich.: Michigan State University Press.

Goldstein, J. H., and P. E. McGhee, eds. 1972. The Psychology of Humor. New York: Academic.

Goodale, J. C. 1971. Tiwi Wives: A Study of the Women of Melville Island, N. Australia. Seattle: University of Washington Press.

Goodenough, F. L. 1932. Expressions of the Emotions in a Blind-Deaf Child. Journal of Abnormal Social Psychology 27:328-33.

Goodenough, W. H. 1956. Componential Analysis and the Study of Meaning. Language 32:195-216.

Goody, J. R. 1956. The Social Organisation of the LoWiili. London: Her Majesty's Stationery Office.

——. 1957. Fields of Social Control among the Lo Dagaba. Journal of the Royal Anthropological Institute 87:75-104.

——. 1959. The Mother's Brother and the Sister's Son in West Africa. Journal of the Royal Anthropological Institute 89:61-88.

——, ed. 1968. Literacy in Traditional Societies. London: Cambridge University Press.

——. 1969. Comparative Studies in Kinship. Stanford: Stanford University Press.

Goody, J. R., and I. Watt. 1968. The Consequences of Literacy. *In* Literacy in Traditional Societies, J. Goody, ed. London: Cambridge University Press. Pp. 27-68.

Gordon, M. M. 1964. Assimilation in American Life. New York: Oxford University Press.

Gorer, G. 1935. Africa Dances. New York: Knopf.

——. 1949. Themes in Japanese Culture. *In* Personal Character and Cultural Milieu, D. G. Haring, ed. Rev. ed. Syracuse: Syracuse University Press. Pp. 273-90.

Gossen, G. H. 1974. To Speak with a Heated Heart: Chamula Canons of Style and Good Performance. *In* Explorations in the Ethnography of Speaking, Richard Bauman and Joel Sherzer, eds. London: Cambridge University Press. Pp. 389-413.

——. 1976. Verbal Dueling in Chamula. *In* Speech Play, Barbara Kirshenblatt-Gimblett, ed. Philadelphia: University of Pennsylvania Press. Pp. 121-46.

Greenberg, A. 1972. Form and Function of the Ethnic Joke. Keystone Folklore Quarterly 27:144–61.

Greenberg, J. H. 1968. Anthropological Linguistics: An Introduction. New York: Random House.

Greenough, J. B., and G. L. Kittredge. 1961. Words and Their Ways in English Speech. New York: Macmillan. (Originally published in 1900–1901.)

Greenway, J. 1965. The Primitive Reader. Hatboro, Pa.: Folklore Associates.

Gregor, T. 1977. Mehinaku: The Drama of Daily Life in a Brazilian Indian Village. Chicago: University of Chicago Press.

Griaule, M. 1948. L'alliance cathartique. Africa 18:242–58.

Grinnell, G. B. 1923. The Cheyenne Indians: Their History and Ways of Life. 2 vols. New Haven: Yale University Press.

Groch, A. S. 1974. Joking and Appreciation of Humor in Nursery School Children. Child Development 45:1098–1102.

Gross, E., and G. P. Stone. 1964. Embarrassment and the Analysis of Role Requirements. American Journal of Sociology 70:1–15.

Grotjahn, M. 1957. Beyond Laughter. New York: McGraw-Hill.

Gulliver, P. H. 1957. Joking Relationships in Central Africa. Man 57:176.

———. 1958. Joking Relationships in Africa. Man 58:145.

Gumperz, J. J., and D. Hymes, eds. 1972. Directions in Sociolinguistics. New York: Holt, Rinehart & Winston.

Haas, M. 1957a. Thai Word Games. Journal of American Folklore 70:173–75.

———. 1957b. Interlingual Word Taboo. American Anthropologist 53:338–41.

———. 1969. Burmese Disguised Speech. Bulletin of the Institute of History and Philology. (Academia Sinica 39[2]:227–85.)

Hall, E. T. 1968. The Silent Language. New York: Fawcett. (Originally published in 1959.)

Halliday, M. A. K. 1968. The Users and Uses of Language. In Readings in the Sociology of Language, Joshua Fishman, ed. The Hague: Mouton. Pp. 139–69.

Hallowell, A. I. 1967. Culture and Experience. New York: Schocken.

Hammond, P. B. 1964. Mossi Joking. Ethnology 3:259–67.

Handelman, D., and B. Kapferer. 1972. Forms of Joking Activity: A Comparative Approach. American Anthropologist 74:484–517.

Hanson, F. A. 1970. Rapan Lifeways: Society and History on a Polynesian Island. Boston: Little, Brown.

Harding, J. 1968. Stereotypes. In International Encyclopedia of the Social Sciences, David Sills, ed., vol. 15. New York: Macmillan, Free Press. Pp. 259–62.

Harrington, M. R. 1921. Religion and Ceremonies of the Lenape. Indian Notes and Monographs, 19. New York: Museum of the American Indian Heye Foundation.

Harris, M. 1968. The Rise of Anthropological Theory. New York: Crowell.

Hart, C. W. M. 1970. Fieldwork among the Tiwi, 1928–1929. *In* Being an Anthropologist, G. D. Spindler, ed. New York: Holt, Rinehart & Winston. Pp. 142–63.

Henry, E. O. 1975. North Indian Wedding Songs: An Analysis of Functions and Meanings. Journal of South Asian Literature 11:61–93.

Henry, J. 1949. The Social Function of Child Sexuality in Pilaga Indian Culture. *In* Psychosexual Development in Health and Disease, P. H. Hock and J. Zubin, eds. New York: Grune & Stratton. Pp. 91–101.

Henry, J. and Z. Henry. 1944. Doll Play of Pilaga Indian Children. Research Monograph 4. New York: American Orthopsychiatric Association.

Herskovits, M. J. 1938. Dahomey, an Ancient West African Kingdom. 2 vols. New York: J. J. Augustin.

———. 1971. Life in a Haitian Valley. New York: Doubleday. (Originally published in 1937.)

Herskovits, M. J., and F. S. Herskovits. 1958. Dahomean Narrative. Evanston: Northwestern University Press.

Hertzler, J. O. 1970. Laughter: A Socio-scientific Analysis. New York: Exposition.

Hieb, L. A. 1972. The Hopi Ritual Clown: Life as It Should Not Be. Doctoral dissertation, Princeton University.

Hill, W. W. 1943. Navaho Humor. General Series in Anthropology, 9. Menasha: George Banta.

Hill W. W., and Dorothy W. Hill. 1945. Navaho Coyote Tales and Their Position in the Southern Athabascan Group. Journal of American Folklore 58:317–43.

Hitchcock, J. T. 1966. The Magars of Banyan Hill. New York: Holt, Rinehart & Winston.

Hoa, N. D. 1955. Double Puns in Vietnamese: A Case of "Linguistic Play." Word 11:237–44.

Hocart, A. M. 1915. Chieftainship and the Sister's Son in the Pacific. American Anthropologist 17:631–46.

Hockett, C. F. 1958. A Course in Modern Linguistics. New York: Macmillan.

———. 1960. The Origin of Speech. Scientific American 203:89–96.

———. 1967. Where the Tongue Slips, There Slip I. *In* To Honor Roman Jakobson. Janua Linguarum, Series Maier, no. 32:910–36.

———. 1972. Jokes. *In* Studies in Linguistics in Honor of George L. Trager, M. Estellie Smith, ed. The Hague: Mouton. Pp. 153–78.

Holmberg, A. R. 1969. Nomads of the Long Bow: The Siriono of Eastern Bolivia. Garden City: American Museum of Natural History. (Originally published in 1950.)

Honigmann, J. J. 1942. An Interpretation of the Social-Psychological Functions of the Ritual Clown. Character and Personality 10:220–26.

———. 1944. A Cultural Theory of Obscenity. Journal of Criminal Psychopathology 5:715–34.

——. 1954. Culture and Personality. New York: Harper & Row.

Horowitz, M. 1967. Morne-Payson: Peasant Village in Martinique. New York: Holt, Rinehart & Winston.

Hotson, L. 1952. Shakespeare's Motley. New York: Oxford University Press.

Howard, J. H. 1962. Peyote Jokes. Journal of American Folklore 75:10–14.

Howell, R. W. 1973. Teasing Relationships. Reading, Mass.: Addison-Wesley.

Huff, T. 1951. Charlie Chaplin. New York: Schuman.

Huizinga, J. 1955. Homo Ludens. Boston: Beacon (Originally published in German in 1944.)

Huntingford, G. W. B. 1953. The Southern Nilo-Hamites. East Central Africa, pt. 8. London: International African Institute, Ethnographic Survey of Africa.

Hyers, M. C. 1973. Zen and the Comic Spirit. Philadelphia: Westminster Press.

Hyman, S. E. 1955. The Ritual View of Myth and the Mythic. Journal of American Folklore 68:462–72.

Hymes, D. 1962. The Ethnography of Speaking. In Anthropology and Human Behavior, T. Gladwin and W. C. Sturtevant. eds. Washington: Anthropological Society of Washington, D.C. Pp. 13–53.

——, ed. 1964. Language in Culture and Society. New York: Harper & Row.

——. 1967. Models of the Interaction of Language and Social Setting. Journal of Social Issues 23(2):8–28.

——. 1968. Linguistic Problems in Defining the Concept of "Tribe." In Essays on the Problem of Tribe, June Helm, ed. Seattle: University of Washington Press. Pp. 23–48.

——. 1972. Models of the Interaction of Language and Social Life. In Directions in Sociolinguistics, John J. Gumperz and Dell Hymes, eds. New York: Holt, Rinehart & Winston. Pp. 35-71.

——. 1974. Foundations in Sociolinguistics. Philadelphia: University of Pennsylvania Press.

Isajiw, W. W. 1974. Definitions of Ethnicity. Ethnicity 1:111–24.

Issar, N., S. Y. W. Tsang, L. La Fave, A. Guilmette, and K. Issar. 1977. Ethnic Humour as a Function of Social-Normative Incongruity and Ego-Involvement. In It's a Funny Thing, Humour, Antony J. Chapman and Hugh C. Foot, eds. New York: Pergamon. Pp. 281–82.

Izard, C. E. 1971. The Face of Emotion. New York: Appleton-Century-Croft.

Jacobs, M. 1959. The Content and Style of an Oral Literature. Chicago: University of Chicago Press.

——. 1960. Humor and Social Structure in an Oral Literature. In Culture in History: Essays in Honor of Paul Radin, S. Diamond, ed. New York: Columbia University Press. Pp. 180–89.

———. 1964. Pattern in Cultural Anthropology. Homewood, Ill: Dorsey.

Jacobson, D. W. 1977. Purdah in India: Life behind the Veil. National Geographic 152(2):270–86.

Jansen, W. H. 1959. The Esoteric-Exoteric Factor in Folklore. Fabula 2:205–11.

Jesperson, O. 1922. Language. London: Allen & Unwin.

Jolly, G. 1979. Social Mobility and Specialization in Language Use. *In* Language and Society: Anthropological Issues, William C. McCormack and S. A. Wurm, eds. New York: Mouton. Pp. 195–205.

Joos, M. 1967. The Five Clocks. New York: Harcourt, Brace & World. (Originally published in 1961.)

Jordan, D. 1973. Anti-American Children's Verses from Taiwan. Western Folklore 32(3):205–209.

Kalčik, S. 1975. ". . . Like Ann's Gynecologist; or, The Time I Was Almost Raped": Personal Narratives in Women's Rap Groups. Journal of American Folklore 88(347): 3–11.

Kardiner, A. 1939. The Individual and His Society. New York: Columbia University Press.

Keesing, R. M. 1975. Kin Groups and Social Structure. New York: Holt, Rinehart & Winston.

Keith-Spiegel, P. 1972. Early Conceptions of Humor: Varieties and Issues. *In* The Psychology of Humor, Jeffrey H. Golstein and Paul E. McGhee, eds. New York: Academic. Pp. 3–39.

Kelsey, A. G. 1943. Once the Hodja. New York: Longmans, Green.

Kennedy, J. G. 1970. Bonds of Laughter among the Tarahumara Indians: Toward the Rethinking of Joking Relationship Theory. *In* The Social Anthropology of Latin America, W. Goldschmidt and H. Hoijer, eds. Los Angeles: Latin American Studies Center, University of California. Pp. 36–38.

Kerényi, K. 1951. The Gods of the Greeks. New York: Thames & Hudson.

———. 1969. The Trickster in Relation to Greek Mythology. *In* The Trickster, Paul Radin, ed. New York: Greenwood. Pp. 173–91. (Originally published in 1956.)

Kern, E. 1980. The Absolute Comic. New York: Columbia University Press.

Kessler, E. 1974. Anthropology: the Humanizing Process. Boston: Allyn & Bacon.

Kiefer, T. M. 1968. Institutionalized Friendship and Warfare among the Tausug of Jolo. Ethnology 7(3):225–44.

King, A. R. 1979. North American Indian Clowns and Creativity. *In* Forms of Play of Native North Americans, Edward Norbeck and Claire R. Farrer, eds. 1977 Proceedings of the American Ethnological Society. New York: West. Pp. 143–51.

Kinsley, D. R. 1975. The Sword and the Flute: Kālī and Kṛṇśa. Berkeley: University of California Press.

Kirshenblatt-Gimblett, B., ed. 1976. Speech Play. Philadelphia: University of Pennsylvania Press.

Kirtley, M., and A. Kirtley. 1979. The Inadan Artisans of the Sahara. National Geographic 156:282–98.

Klapp, O. E. 1949–50. The Fool as a Social Type. American Journal of Sociology 55:157–62.

Klineberg, O. 1950. Tensions Affecting International Understanding: A Survey of Research. Bulletin 62. New York: Social Science Research Council.

———. 1954. Social Psychology. Rev. ed. New York: Holt.

Klymasz, R. B. 1970. The Ethnic Joke in Canada Today. Keystone Folklore Quarterly 15:167–73.

Kochman, T., ed. 1972. Rappin' and Stylin' Out. Urbana: University of Illinois Press.

Koestler, A. 1964. The Act of Creation. New York: Macmillan.

Kofsky, F. 1974. Lenny Bruce: Comedian as Social Critic and Secular Moralist. New York: Anchor Foundation, Monad Press.

Kravitz, S. 1977. London Jokes and Ethnic Stereotypes. Western Folklore 36(4):275–301.

Kreitler, H., and S. Kreitler. 1970. Dependence of Laughter on Cognitive Strategies. Merrill-Palmer Quarterly 16:163–77.

Krige, E. J. 1937. Individual Development. In The Bantu-Speaking Tribes of South Africa, I. Schapera, ed. London: Routledge & Kegan Paul. Pp. 95–118.

Kroeber, A. L. 1902–1907. The Arapaho. Bulletin 18. New York: American Museum of Natural History.

La Barre, W. 1945. Some Observations on Character Structure in the Orient: The Japanese. Psychiatry 8:319–42.

———. 1947. The Cultural Basis of Emotions and Gestures. Journal of Personality 16:49–68.

Labouret, H. 1929. La parenté à plaisanateries en Afrique Occidentale. Africa 2:244–54.

Labov, W. 1972a. Language in the Inner City: Studies in the Black English Vernacular. Philadelphia: University of Pennsylvania Press.

———. 1972b. Sociolinguistic Patterns. Philadelphia: University of Pennsylvania Press.

La Fave, L. 1972. Humor Judgments as a Function of Reference Group and Identification Classes. In The Psychology of Humor, Jeffrey H. Goldstein and Paul E. McGhee, eds. New York: Academic. Pp. 195–210.

———. 1977. Ethnic Humor: From Paradoxes towards Principles. In It's a Funny Thing, Humour, Anthony J. Chapman and Hugh C. Foot, eds. New York: Pergamon. Pp. 237–60.

La Fave, L., J. Haddad, and N. Marshall. 1975. Humor Judgments as a Function of Identification Classes. Sociology and Social Research 58:184–94.

La Fave, L., K. McCarthy, and J. Haddad. 1973. Humor Judgments as a Function of Identification Classes: Canadian versus American. Journal of Psychology 85:53–59.

References

La Fontaine, J. S. 1959. The Gisu of Uganda. East Central Africa, pt. 10. London: International African Institute, Ethnographic Survey.

Lakoff, R. 1975. Language and Woman's Place. New York: Harper & Row.

Lancy, D. F., and B. A. Tindall, eds. 1976. The Anthropological Study of Play: Problems and Prospects. Proceedings of the First Annual Meeting of the Association for the Anthropological Study of Play. Cornwall: Leisure.

Landes, R. 1937. The Ojibwa of Canada. *In* Cooperation and Competition among Primitive Peoples, Margaret Mead, ed. New York: McGraw-Hill. Pp. 87–127.

Landtman, G. 1927. The Kiwai Papuans of British New Guinea. London: Macmillan.

Langacker, R. W. 1973. Language and Its Structure. 2d ed. New York: Harcourt Brace Jovanovich.

Lanham, R. A. 1974. Style: An Anti-text Book. New Haven: Yale University Press.

La Pierre, R. T. 1936. Type-rationalization of Group Anti-play. Social Forces 15:232–37.

Larkin, R. T., ed. 1975. The International Joke Book. New York: Leisure.

Lauria, A., Jr. 1964. "Respeto," "Relajo," and Inter-Personal Relations in Puerto Rico. Anthropological Quarterly 37:53–67.

Leach, E. R. 1954. Political Systems of Highland Burma. London: Bell.

Leach, M., and J. Fried. 1949. Funk & Wagnalls Standard Dictionary of Folklore, Mythology, and Legend. New York: Funk & Wagnalls.

Leacock, S. B. 1935. Humour: Its Theory and Technique. New York: Dodd, Mead.

———. 1937. Humor and Humanity. London: Butterworth.

Lee, R. B. 1969. Eating Christmas in the Kalahari. Natural History 78(10):14–22, 60–63.

Legman, G. 1968. Rationale of the Dirty Joke: 1st ser. New York: Grove.

———. 1975. No Laughing Matter: Rationale of the Dirty Joke: 2d ser. New York: Breaking Point.

Leighton, D., and C. Kluckhohn. 1974. Children of the People: The Navaho Individual and His Development. New York: Farrar, Straus & Giroux.

Leis, P. E. 1972. Enculturation and Socialization in an Ijaw Village. New York: Holt, Rinehart & Winston.

Leslau, W. 1959. Taboo Expressions in Ethiopia. American Anthropologist 61:105–107.

Lessa, W. A. 1966. Ulithi: A Micronesian Design for Living. New York: Holt, Rinehart & Winston.

Levine, Jacob. 1961. Regression in Primitive Clowning. Psychoanalytic Quarterly 30:72–83.

———. 1969. Motivation in Humor. New York: Atherton.

Levine, Jacob, and F. C. Redlich. 1955. Failure to Understand Humor. Psychoanalytic Quarterly 24:560–72.

Levine, Joan B. 1976. The Feminine Routine. Journal of Communication 26(3):173–75.

LeVine, R. A., and D. T. Campbell. 1972. Ethnocentrism: Theories of Conflict, Ethnic Attitudes, and Group Behavior. New York: Wiley.

Lévi-Strauss, C. 1943. The Social Use of Kinship Terms among Brazilian Indians. American Anthropologist 45:398–409.

———. 1955. The Structural Study of Myth. Journal of American Folklore 28:428–42.

Levy, A. 1976. Poland's Polish Jokes. New York Times Magazine, August 8.

Leyton, E. 1974. The Compact: Selected Dimensions of Friendship. New-foundland Social and Econcomic Paper No. 3. Toronto: Memorial University of Newfoundland, University of Toronto Press.

Lieberman, P. 1967. Intonation, Perception, and Language. Cambridge: MIT Press.

Linden, E. 1981. Apes, Men, and Language. New York: Penguin.

Linton, R. 1937. One Hundred Percent American. American Mercury 40:427–29.

Lippmann, W. 1922. Public Opinion. New York: Harcourt, Brace.

Lips, J. E. 1966. The Savage Hits Back. Trans. from the German by Vincent Benson. New Hyde Park, N.Y.: University Books. (Originally published in 1937.)

Loizos, C. 1967. Play Behaviour in Higher Primates: A Review. In Primate Ethology, D. Morris, ed. London: Weidenfeld & Nicholson. Pp. 176–218.

Lomax, L. E. 1961. The American Negro's New Comedy Act. Harper's Magazine 122:41–46.

Lorenz, K. 1967. On Aggression. New York: Bantam.

Losco, J., and S. Epstein. 1975. Humor Preference as a Subtle Measure of Attitudes toward the Same and the Opposite Sex. Journal of Personality 43:321–34.

Loudon, J. B. 1970. Teasing and Socialization on Tristan de Cunha. In Socialization: The Approach from Social Anthropology, Philip Mayer, ed. Association of Social Anthropologists Monograph 8. London: Tavistock. Pp. 293–332.

Lowie, R. H. 1909. The Hero-Trickster Discussion. Journal of American Folklore 22:431–33.

———. 1914. Rapid Speech Puzzles in Crow. Journal of American Folklore 27:330–31.

———. 1961. Primitive Society. New York: Harper Torchbooks. (Originally published in 1920.)

Loy, J., ed. 1982. Play as Paradox. West Point: Leisure.

Lundberg, G. C. 1969. Person-Focused Joking: Pattern and Function. Human Organization 28:22–28.

Luomala, K. 1949. Maui-of-a-Thousand-Tricks: His Oceanic and European Biographers. Bulletin 198. Honolulu: Bernice P. Bishop Museum.

References

Lyons, J. 1972. Human Language. *In* Non-verbal Communication, Robert A. Hinde, ed. London: Cambridge University Press. Pp. 49–85.

McCabe, J. 1966. Mr. Laurel and Mr. Hardy. New York: Grosset & Dunlap.

———. 1978. Charlie Chaplin. Garden City: Doubleday.

McDowell, J. H. 1979. Children's Riddling. Bloomington: Indiana University Press.

McGhee, P. E. 1971a. Development of the Humor Response: A Review of the Literature. Psychological Bulletin 76:328–48.

———. 1971b. Cognitive Development and Children's Comprehension of Humor. Child Development 42:123–38.

———. 1971c. The Role of Operational Thinking in Children's Comprehension and Appreciation of Humor. Child Development 42:733–44.

———. 1972. Methodological and Theoretical Considerations for a Cross-Cultural Investigation of Children's Humor. International Journal of Psychology 7:13–21.

———. 1974a. Cognitive Mastery and Children's Humor. Psychological Bulletin 81:721–30.

———. 1974b. Development of Children's Ability to Create Joking Relationship. Child Develpment 45:552–56.

———. 1976a. Children's Appreciation of Humor: A Test of the Cognitive Congruency Principle. Child Development 47:420–26.

———. 1976b. Sexual Differences in Children's Humor. Journal of Communication 26:176–89.

———. 1977a. Children's Humour: A Review of Current Research. *In* It's a Funny Thing, Humour, Antony J. Chapman and Hugh C. Foot, eds. New York: Pergamon. Pp. 199–209.

———. 1977b. A Model for the Origins and Early Development of Incongruity-based Humour. *In* It's a Funny Thing, Humour, Antony J. Chapman and Hugh C. Foot, eds. New York: Pergamon. Pp. 27–36.

———. 1979. Humor: Its Origins and Development. San Francisco: Freeman.

McGhee, P. E., and A. J. Chapman, eds. 1980. Children's Humour. New York: Wiley.

McGhee, P. E., and Jeffrey H. Goldstein, eds. 1983. Handbook of Humor Research. New York: Springer.

McIlwraith, T. F. 1948. The Bella Coola Indians. Toronto: University of Toronto Press.

Makarius, L. 1970. Ritual Clowns and Symbolic Behaviour. Diogenes 69:44–73.

———. 1973. The Crime of Manabozo. American Anthropologist 75:663–75.

Malefijt, A. M. deW. 1968a. Dutch Joking Patterns. Transactions of the New York Academy of Sciences, ser. 2, 30:1181–86.

———. 1968b. Religion and Culture. New York: Macmillan.

Malinowski, B. 1926. Crime and Custom in Savage Society. London: Kegan Paul, Trench, Trubner.

———. 1941. An Anthropological Analysis of War. American Journal of Sociology 46:521–50.

——. 1944. A Scientific Theory of Culture and Other Essays. Chapel Hill: University of North Carolina Press.

Mandelbaum, D. G. 1958. Selected Writings of Edward Sapir in Language, Culture and Personality. Berkeley: University of California Press.

Manning, F., ed. 1983. The World of Play. West Point, N.Y.: Leisure.

Marriott, M. 1968. The Feast of Love. *In* Krishna: Myths, Rites, and Attitudes, Milton Singer, ed. Chicago: University of Chicago Press. Pp. 200–12. (Originally published in 1966.)

Martin, M. K., and B. Voorhies. 1975. Female of the Species. New York: Columbia University Press.

Matthews, W. 1938. Cockney Past and Present. New York: Dutton.

Mayer, P. 1950. Privileged Obstruction of Marriage Rites among the Gusii. Africa 20:113–25.

——. 1951. The Joking of "Pals" in Gusii Age-sets. African Studies 10:27–41.

Mead, M. 1949. Male and Female. New York: Morrow.

Mencken, H. L. 1942. A New Dictionary of Quotations. New York: Knopf.

Menon, V. K. 1931. A Theory of Laughter. London: Allen & Unwin.

Messenger, J. D. Jr. 1960. Anang Proverb Riddles. Journal of American Folklore 73:225–35.

Meyer, J. J. 1953. Sexual Life in Ancient India. New York: Barnes & Noble.

Middleton, J., ed. 1970. From Child to Adult: Studies in the Anthropology of Education. Garden City: Natural History.

Middleton, R. 1959. Negro and White Reactions to Racial Humor. Sociometry 22:175–83.

Middleton, R., and J. Moland. 1959. Humor in Negro and White Subcultures: A Study of Jokes among University Students. American Sociological Review 24:61–69.

Miller, D. B. 1973. Holi-Dulhendi: Licensed Rebellion in a North Indian Village. South Asia 3:15–22.

Miller, F. C. 1967. Humor in a Chippewa Tribal Council. Ethnology 6:263–71.

Milner, G. B. 1971. The Quartered Shield: Outline of a Semantic Taxonomy. *In* Social Anthropology and Language, Edwin Ardener, ed. Association of Social Anthropologists Monograph 10. London: Tavistock. Pp. 243–69.

——. 1972. Homo Ridens: Towards a Semiotic Theory of Humor and Laughter. Semiotica 5:1–30.

Mindess, H. 1971. Laughter and Liberation. Los Angeles: Nash.

Mindess, H., and J. Turek, eds n.d. The Study of Humor. Los Angeles: Antioch University.

Mintz, L. E. 1977. Ethnic Humour: Discussion. *In* It's a Funny Thing, Humour, Antony J. Chapman and Hugh C. Foot, eds. New York: Pergamon. Pp. 287–89.

Mitchell, C. A. 1977. The Sexual Perspective in the Appreciation and Interpretation of Jokes. Western Folklore 36(4):303–29.

Mitchell, J. C. 1956. The Kalela Dance. Manchester, England: Rhodes-Livingstone Institute, Manchester University Press.

Mitchell, S. 1976. How to Speak Southern. New York: Bantam.

Mitchell-Kernan, C. 1972. Signifying and Marking: Two Afro-American Speech Acts. *In* Directions in Sociolinguistics, John J. Gumperz and Dell Hymes, eds. New York: Holt, Rinehart & Winston. Pp. 161–79.

Mitchell-Kernan, C., and K. T. Kernan. 1975. Children's Insults: America and Samoa. *In* Sociocultural Dimensions of Language Use, Mary Sanches and B. G. Blount, eds. New York: Academic. Pp. 307–15.

Moerman, M. 1965. Ethnic Indentification in a Complex Civilization: Who Are the Lue? American Anthropologist 67:1215–30.

——. 1968. Being Lue: Uses and Abuses of Ethnic Identification. *In* Essays on the Problem of Tribe, J. Helm, ed. Seattle: University of Washington Press. Pp. 153–69.

Monro, D. H. 1951. Argument of Laughter. Melbourne: Melbourne Universtiy Press.

Montagu, A., ed. 1964. The Concept of Race. Glencoe: Free Press.

Moreau, R. E. 1941. The Joking Relationship (Utani) in Tanganyika. Tanganyika Notes and Records 12:1–10.

——. 1943. Joking Relationships in Tanganyika. Africa 14:386–400.

Morreall, John. 1983. Taking Laughter Seriously. Albany: State University of New York Press.

Morris, D., P. Collett, P. Marsh, and M. O'Shaughnessy. 1979. Gestures: Their Origins and Distribution. New York: Stein & Day.

Morrison, C. 1972. A Comparative Study of Urban Castes. Journal of the Indian Anthropological Society 5:47–63.

Mouledoux, E. C. 1976. Theoretical Considerations and a Method for the Study of Play. *In* The Anthropological Study of Play: Problems and Prospects, David F. Lancy and B. Allan Tindall, eds. Cornwall, N.Y.: Leisure. Pp. 38–50.

——. 1977. The Development of Play in Childhood: An Applicaton of the Classifications of Piaget and Caillois in Development Research. *In* Studies in the Anthropology of Play, Phillip Stevens, Jr., ed. West Point, N.Y.: Leisure. Pp. 196–209.

Murdock, G. P. 1949. Social Structure. New York: Macmillan.

Murphy, Mrs. 1897. Manners for Women. N.p.: James Bowden.

Murphy, R. F., and B. Quain. 1955. The Trumai Indians of Central Brazil. American Ethnological Society 24. New York: J.J. Augustin.

Murphy, Y., and R. F. Murphy. 1974. Women of the Forest. New York: Columbia University Press.

Mutuma, H., L. La Fave, R. Mannell, and A. M. Guilmette. 1977. Ethnic Humor Is No Joke. *In* It's a Funny Thing, Humour, Antony J. Chapman and Hugh C. Foot, eds. New York: Pergamon. Pp. 277–80.

Myrdal, G. 1944. An American Dilemma. New York: Harper.

Nadel, S. F. 1946. A Black Byzantium. London: Oxford University Press.

——. 1947. The Nuba: An Anthropological Study of the Hill Tribes in Kordofan. London: Oxford University Press.

——. 1954. Nupe Religion. London: Routledge & Kegan Paul.

Nader, L. 1962. A Note on Attitudes and the Use of Language. Anthropological Linguistics 6:24–29.

Naroll, R., and R. Cohen, eds. 1970. A Handbook of Method in Cultural Anthropology. New York: Natural History.

Nerhardt, G. 1976. Incongruity and Funniness: Toward a New Descriptive Model. *In* Humor and Laughter: Theory, Research, and Application, Antony J. Chapman and Hugh C. Foot, eds. London: Wiley. Pp. 55–62.

Newman, E. 1974. Strictly Speaking. New York: Bobbs-Merrill..

Newsweek. 1982. Richard Pryor Busts Loose. May 3:48–54.

Nimmo, H. A. 1970. Bajau Sex and Reproduction. Ethnology 9:251–62.

Norbeck, E. 1961. Religion in Primitive Society. New York: Harper.

——. 1963. African Rituals of Conflict. American Anthropologist 65:1254–79.

——. 1969. Human Play and Its Cultural Expression. Humanities 5:43–55.

——. 1971. Man at Play. Natural History, special supp., December:48–53.

——. 1974. Religion in Human Life: Anthropological Views. New York: Holt, Rinehart & Winston.

——. 1976. The Study of Play—John Huizinga and Modern Anthropology. *In* The Anthropological Study of Play: Problems and Prospects, David F. Lancy and B. Allan Tindall, eds. Cornwall, N.Y.: Leisure. Pp. 1–10.

Nurge, E. 1965. Life in a Leyte Village. Seattle: University of Washington Press.

Obrdlik, J. 1942. "Gallows Humor"—A Sociological Phenomenon. American Journal of Sociology 47:709–16.

O'Flaherty, W. D. 1973. Ascetism and Eroticism in the Mythology of Śiva. London: Oxford University Press.

——. 1976. The Origins of Evil in Hindu Mythology. Berkeley: University of California Press.

Oliver, D. L. 1967. A Solomon Island Society: Kinship and Leadership among the Siuai of Bougainville. Boston: Beacon. (Originally published in 1955.)

Opler, M. E. 1940. Myths and Legends of Lipan Apache Indians. Memoirs of the American Folklore Society, vol. 36. New York: J. J. Augustin.

Oring, E. 1973. "Hey, You've Got No Character": Chizbat Humor and the Boundaries of Israeli Identity. Journal of American Folklore 86:358–66.

——. 1975. Everything Is a Shade of Elephant: An Alternative to a Psychoanalysis of Humor. New York Folkore 1:149–59.

——. 1981. Israeli Humor: The Content and Structure of the Chizbat of the Palmah. Albany: State University of New York Press.

Osgood, C. 1951. The Koreans and Their Culture. New York: Ronald.

Parabola. 1979. The Trickster. Vol. 4, no. 1, special issue.

References

Paredes, A. 1966. The Anglo-American in Mexican Folklore. *In* New Voices in American Studies, Ray B. Browne, Donald M. Winkelman, and Allen Hayman, eds. Purdue University Studies. Lafayette: Purdue Research Foundation.

———. 1973. Folk Medicine and the Intercultural Jest. *In* Introduction to Chicano Studies, L. I. Duran and H. R. Bernard, eds. New York: Macmillan. Pp. 261–75.

Parsons, E. C. 1936. Mitla: Town of the Souls and Other Zapotaco-Speaking Pueblos of Oaxaca, Mexico. Chicago: University of Chicago Press.

Parsons, E. C., and R. L. Beals. 1934. The Sacred Clowns of the Pueblo and Mayo-Yaqui Indians. American Anthropologist 36:491–514.

Partridge, E. 1970. A Dictionary of Slang and Unconventional English. 7th ed. New York: Macmillan. (Originally published in 1937.)

Pedler, F. J. 1940. Joking Relationships in East Africa. Africa 13:170–73.

Peristiany, J. G., ed. 1966. Honour and Shame: The Values of Mediterranean Society. Chicago: University of Chicago Press.

Peshkin, A. 1972. Kanuri Schoolchildren: Education and Social Mobilization in Nigeria. New York: Holt, Rinehart & Winston.

Philips, S. U. 1976. Some Sources of Cultural Variability in the Regulation of Talk. Language in Society 5:81–96.

Piaget, J. 1962. Play, Dreams, and Imitation in Childhood. London: Routledge & Kegan Paul.

———. 1972. Play, Dreams, and Imitation in Childhood. New York: Norton.

Piddington, R. 1963. The Psychology of Laughter: A Study in Social Adaptation. 2d ed. New York: Gamut. (Originally published in 1933.)

Pien, D., and M. K. Rothbart. 1977. Measuring Effects of Incongruity and Resolution in Children's Humour. *In* It's a Funny Thing, Humour, Antony J. Chapman and Hugh C. Foot, eds. New York: Pergamon. Pp. 211–13.

Pike, K. L. 1945. Tone Puns in Mixteco. International Journal of American Linguistics 11:129–39.

———. 1946. Another Mixteco Tone Pun. International Journal of American Linguistics 12:22–24.

———. 1954. Language in Relation to a Unified Theory of the Structure of Human Behavior. Pt. 1. Glendale: Summer Institute of Linguistics.

Pilcher, W. W. 1972. The Portland Longshoremen: A Dispersed Urban Community. New York: Holt, Rinehart & Winston.

Pittenger, R., C. Hockett, and H. Danehy. 1960. The First Five Minutes. Ithaca: Martineau.

Plessner, H. 1950. Lachen und Weinen. Bern: Francke.

———. 1953. Zwischen Philosophie und Gesellschaft. Bern: Francke.

Podair, S. 1956. Language and Prejudice toward Negroes. Phylon 17:390–94.

Porter, K. 1965. Racism in Children's Rhymes and Sayings: Central Kansas, 1910–1918. Western Folklore 24:191–96.

Potter, S. 1954. The Sense of Humour. Harmondsworth, England: Penguin.

Prange, A. J., and M. M. Vitols. 1963. Jokes among Southern Negroes: The Revelation of Conflict. Journal of Nervous and Mental Diseases 136.162–67.

Price, R., and S. Price. 1976. Secret Play Languages in Saramaka: Linguistic Disguise in a Caribbean Creole. *In* Speech Play, Barbara Kirshenblatt-Gimblett, ed. Philadelphia: University of Pennsylvania Press. Pp. 37–50.

Quinn, N. 1977. Anthropological Studies on Women's Status. Annual Review of Anthropolgy 6:181–225.

Quirk, R. 1951. Puns to Sell. Studia Neophilologica 23:81–86.

Radcliffe-Brown, A. R. 1940. On Joking Relationships. Africa 13:195–210. (Reprinted in Radcliffe-Brown 1952/1965:90–104.)

——. 1949. A Further Note on Joking Relationships. Africa 19:133–40. (Reprinted in Radcliffe-Brown 1952/1965:105–16.)

——. 1965. Structure and Function in Primitive Society. New York: Free Press. (Originally published in 1952.)

Radin, P. 1914. Religion of the North American Indians. Journal of American Folklore 27:335–73.

——. 1969. The Trickster. New York: Greenwood. (Originally published in 1956.)

——, ed. 1937. African Folktales and Sculpture. New York: Bollingen Foundation.

Raglan, Lord. 1949. The Hero: A Study in Tradition, Myth, and Drama. London: Watts. (Originally published in 1936.)

Rapp, A. 1947. Toward an Eclectic and Multilateral Theory of Laughter and Humor. Journal of General Psychology 36:207–19.

——. 1949. A Phylogenetic Theory of Wit and Humor. Journal of Social Psychology 30:81–96.

Rasmussen, K. 1931. The Netsilik Eskimos: Social Life and Spiritual Culture. Copenhagen: Report of the Fifth Thule Expedition 1921–1924, 8(1–2).

Rath, R., and N. C. Sircar. 1960. The Mental Pictures of Six Hindu Caste Groups about Each Other as Reflected in Verbal Stereotypes. Journal of Social Psychology 51:277–93.

Rattray, Robert S. 1930. Akan–Ashanti Folktales. Oxford: Oxford University Press.

Ray, V. F. 1945. The Contrary Behavior Pattern in American Ceremonialism. Southwestern Journal of Anthropology 1:75–113.

Reynolds, V. 1958. Joking Relationships in Africa. Man 58:29–30.

Richards, A. I. 1937. Reciprocal Clan Relationships among the Bemba of N. E. Rhodesia. Man 37:188–93.

Richards, C. E. 1969. Presumed Behavior: Modification of the Ideal-Real Dichotomy. American Anthropologist 71:1115–17.

Ricketts, M. L. 1964. The Structure and Religious Significance of the Trickster-Transformer-Culture Hero in the Mythology of the North American Indians. Doctoral dissertation, University of Chicago.

——. 1966.The North American Trickster. History of Religions 5:327–50.

Rigby, P. 1968. Joking Relationships, Kin Categories, and Clanship among the GoGo. Africa 38:133–55.

Rinder, I. D. 1965. A Note on Humor as an Index of Minority Group Morale. Phylon 26:117–21.

Risley, Sir H. 1915. The People of India. London: W. Thacker.

Roback, A. A. 1944. A Dictionary of International Slurs (Ethnophaulisms). Cambridge: Sci-Art.

Robbins, R. H. 1967. The Warden's Wordplay: Toward a Redefinition of the Spoonerism. Dalhousie Review 46:457–65.

Roberts, J. M., M. J. Arth, and R. R. Bush. 1959. Games in Culture. American Anthropologist 61:597–605.

Roberts, J. M., and B. Sutton-Smith. 1962. Child Training and Game Involvement. Ethnology 1:166–85.

Rogers, S. C. 1975. Female Forms of Power and the Myth of Male Dominance: A Model of Female/Male Interaction in Peasant Society. American Ethnologist 2(4):727–55.

Rosaldo, M. Z., and L. Lamphere, eds. 1974. Women, Culture, and Society. Stanford: Stanford University Press.

Rosenberg, B., and G. Shapiro. 1959. Marginality and Jewish Humor. Midstream 4:70–80.

Rosenthal, F. 1956. Humor in Early Islam. Philadelphia: University of Pennsylvania Press.

Rosten, L. (Leonard Q. Ross). 1937. The Education of H*Y*M*A*N* K*A*P*L*A*N*. New York: Harcourt, Brace.

——. 1959. The Return of Hyman Kaplan. New York: Harper.

——. 1972. Rome Wasn't Burned in a Day. Garden City: Doubleday.

Rovit, E. 1966–67. Jewish Humor and American Life. American Scholar 36:237–45.

Rubin, J. 1968. National Bilingualism in Paraguay. The Hague: Mouton.

Sacks, H. 1974. An Analysis of the Course of a Joke's Telling in Conversation. In Explorations in the Ethnography of Speaking, Richard Bauman and Joel Sherzer, eds. New York: Cambridge University Press. Pp. 337–53.

Salinas, J. 1975. On the Clan of Anthropologists. In The Human Way, H. Russell Bernard, ed. New York: Macmillan. Pp. 71–77.

Salter, M. A., ed. 1978. Play: Anthropological Perspectives. 1977 Proceedings of the Association for the Anthropological Study of Play. West Point: Leisure.

Samarin, W. 1969. The Art of Gbeya Insults. International Journal of American Linguistics 35:323–29.

Sanches, M., and B. Kirschenblatt-Gimblett. 1976. Children's Traditional Speech Play and Child Language. In Speech Play, Barbara Kirshenblatt-

Gimblett, ed. Philadelphia: University of Pennsylvania Press. Pp. 65–110.

Sanday, P. R. 1974. Female Status in the Public Domain. *In* Women, Culture, and Society, M. Rosaldo and L. Lamphere, eds. Stanford University Press. Pp. 189–206.

Sapir, E. 1932. Two Navaho Puns. Language 8:217–19.

Scherer, K. R. 1972. Judging Personality from Voice: A Cross-cultural Approach to an Old Issue in Interpersonal Perception. Journal of Personality 40:191–210.

Schermerhorn, R. A. 1970. Comparative Ethnic Relations. Chicago: University of Chicago Press.

Scheub, H. 1975. The Xhosa Ntsomi, London: Oxford University Press.

Schiffman, H. 1978. Diglossia and Purity/Pollution in Tamil. *In* Language and Civilizational Change in South Asia, Clarence Maloney, ed. Contributions to Asian Studies, 11. Leiden: Brill. Pp. 98–110.

Schlegel, A. 1972. Male Dominance and Female Autonomy. New Haven: HRAF Press.

——, ed. 1977. Sexual Stratification: A Cross-cultural View. New York: Columbia University Press.

Schmerler, H. 1931. Trickster Marries His Daughter. Journal of American Folklore 44:196–207.

Schneider, D. M. 1961. Introduction. *In* Matrilineal Kinship, D. M. Schneider and K. Gough, eds. Berkeley: University of California Press. Pp. 1–29.

Schusky, E. L. 1972. Manual for Kinship Analysis. New York: Holt, Rinehart & Winston.

Schwartzman, H. B. 1976. The Anthropological Study of Children's Play. Annual Review of Anthropology 5:289–328.

——, ed. 1980. Play and Culture. 1978 Proceedings of the Association for the Anthropological Study of Play. West Point: Leisure.

Schwartzman, H. B., and L. Barbera. 1976. Children's Play in Africa and South America: A Review of the Ethnographic Literature. *In* The Anthropological Study of Play: Problems and Prespects, David F. Lancy and B. Allan Tindall, eds. Cornwall, N.Y.: Leisure. Pp. 11–21.

Secord, P. F., W. Bevan, Jr., and B. Katz. 1956. The Negro Stereotype and Perceptual Accentuation. Journal of Abnormal and Social Psychology 53:78–83.

Seligman, C. G., and B. Z. Seligman. 1950. Pagan Tribes of the Nilotic Sudan. New York: Humanities Press.

Shah, I. 1972. The Exploits of the Incomparable Mulla Nasruddin. New York: Dutton.

Sharman, A. 1969. "Joking" in Padhola: Categorical Relationships, Choice, and Social Control. Man, n.s., 4:103–17.

Sherzer, J. 1970. Talking Backwards in Cuna: The Sociological Reality of Phonological Descriptions. Southwestern Journal of Anthropology 26:343–53.

References

——. 1973. Verbal and Nonverbal Deixis: The Pointed Lip Gesture among the San Blas Cuna. Language in Society 2:117–31.

——. 1976. Play Languages: Implications for (Socio) Linguistics. *In* Speech Play, Barbara Kirshenblatt–Gimblett, ed. Philadelphia: University of Pennsylvania Press. Pp. 19–36.

Shibutani, T., and K. Kwan. 1965. Ethnic Stratification: A Comparative Approach. New York: Macmillan.

Shonek, R. 1974. Personal communicaton.

Shultz, T. R. 1972. The Role of Incongruity and Resolution in Children's Appreciation of Cartoon Humor. Journal of Experimental Child Psychology 13:456–77.

——. 1976. A Cognitive-Developmental Analysis of Humour. *In* Humour and Laughter: Theory, Research and Applicatons, Antony J. Chapman and Hugh C. Foot, eds. New York: Wiley. Pp. 11-36.

Shultz, T. R., and F. Horide. 1974. Development of the Appreciation of Verbal Jokes. Developmental Psychology 10:13–20.

Sidis, B. 1913. The Psychology of Laughter. New York: Appleton.

Simmons, D. C. 1963. Protest Humor: Folkloristic Reaction to Prejudice. American Journal of Psychiatry 120:567–70.

——. 1966. Anti-Italian-American Riddles in New England. Journal of American Folklore 79:475–78.

Simmons, W. W. 1971. Eyes of the Night: Witchcraft among a Senegalese People. Boston: Little, Brown.

Siskind, J. 1973. To Hunt in the Morning. New York: Oxford University Press.

Skeels, D. 1954. A Classification of Humor in Nez Percé Mythology. Journal of American Folklore 67:57–63.

Smith, E. O., ed. 1978. Social Play in Primates. New York: Academic.

Speck, F. G. 1949. Midwinter Rites of the Cayuga Long House. Philadelphia: University of Pennsylvania Press.

Spencer, H. 1860. Physiology of Laughter. Macmillan's Magazine 1:395–402.

Sperling, S. J. 1953. On the Psychodynamics of Teasing. Journal of the American Psychoanalytic Association 1:458–83.

Spicer, E. H. 1940. Pascua, a Yaqui Village in Arizona. Chicago: University of Chicago Press.

——. 1954. Potam, A Yaqui village in Sonora. Memoir 77. Menasha: American Anthropological Association.

Spies, E. 1943. Observations on *Utani* Customs among the Ngoni of Songea District. Tanganyika Notes and Records 16:49–53.

Spitz, R. A, and K. M. Wolf. 1946. The Smiling Response: A Contribution to the Ontogenesis of Social Relations. Genetic Psychology Monographs 34:57–125.

Spradley, J. P., ed. 1972. Culture and Cognition: Rules, Maps, and Plans. San Francisco: Chandler.

Spradley, J. P., and D. W. McCurdy. 1974. Conformity and Conflict: Readings in Cultural Anthropology. Boston: Little, Brown.

Stefaniszyn, B. 1950. Funeral Friendship in Central Africa. Africa 20:290–306.

Stephenson, R. M. 1950–51. Conflict and Control Functions of Humor. American Journal of Sociology 56:569–74.

Stern, T. 1953. The Trickster in Klamath Mythology. Western Folklore 12:158–74.

Stevens, P., Jr. 1977a. Laying the Groundwork for an Anthropology of Play. In Studies in the Anthropology of Play, Phillip Stevens, Jr., ed. West Point: Leisure. Pp. 237–49.

——, ed. 1977b. Studies in the Anthropology of Play: Papers in Memory of B. Allan Tindall. Proceedings from the Second Annual Meeting of the Association for the Anthropological Study of Play. West Point: Leisure.

——. 1978. Bachama Joking Categories: Toward New Perspectives in the Study of Joking Relationships. Journal of Anthropological Research 34:47–69.

Steward, J. 1931. The Ceremonial Buffoon of the American Indian. Papers of the Michigan Academy of Science, Arts, and Letters 14:187–207.

Stirling, M. W. 1942. Origin Myths of Acoma and Other Records. Bulletin 135. Washington, D.C.: Bureau of American Ethnology.

Stone, L. J., and J. Church. 1957. Childhood and Adolescence. New York: Random House.

Strachey, J., ed. 1960. Jokes and Their Relation to the Unconscious, by S. Freud. Newly translated from the German. New York: Norton.

Street, B. V. 1972. The Trickster Theme: Winnebago and Azande. In Zande Themes, André Singer and B. V. Street, eds. Oxford: Blackwell. Pp. 82–104.

Suls, Jerry M. 1983. Cognitive Processes in Humor Appreciation. In Handbook of Humor Research, Paul E. McGhee and J. H. Goldstein, eds. New York: Springer. Pp. 39–57.

Sumner, W. G. 1906. Folkways. New York: Ginn.

Susman, A. 1941. Word Play in Winnebago. Language 17:342–44.

Sutton-Smith, B. 1959. The Kissing Games of Adolescents in Ohio. Midwest Folklore 9:189–211.

——. 1968. The Folk Games of the Children. In Our Living Traditions: An Introduction to American Folklore, Tristram P. Coffin, ed. New York: Basic Books. Pp. 179–91.

——. 1972. The Folk-games of Children. Austin: University of Texas Press.

Sutton-Smith, B., and J. M. Roberts, eds. 1972. The Cross-cultural and Psychological Study of Games. In The Folkgames of Children, Brian Sutton-Smith, ed. Bibliographical and Special Series, vol. 24. Austin: American Folklore Society. University of Texas Press. Pp. 331–40.

Suzuki, D. T. 1927. Essays in Zen Buddhism: First Series. London: Luzac.

Suzuki, P. 1977. Japanese [hs:], American English [hm:], and Dutch [X] as Expressive and Intercultural Communication. Anthropological Linguistics 19:420–30.

Swain, B. 1932. Fools and Folly during the Middle Ages and the Renaissance. New York: Columbia University Press.

Swartz, M. J. 1961. Negative Ethnocentrism. Journal of Conflict Resolution 5:75–81.

Sykes, A. J. M. 1966. Joking Relationships in an Industrial Setting. American Anthropologist 68:188–93.

Tatje, T. A. 1970. Problems of Concept Definition for Comparative Studies. *In* A Handbook of Method in Cultural Anthropology, R. Naroll and R. Cohen, eds. New York: Columbia University Press. Pp. 689-96.

Tax, S. 1955. Some Problems of Social Organization. *In* Social Anthropology of the North American Tribes, F. Eggan, ed. Chicago: University of Chicago Press. Pp. 3–32.

Taylor, A. 1962. The Proverb and an Index to the Proverb. Hatboro, Pa.: Folklore Associates. (Originally published in 1931.)

Tew, M. 1951. A Further Note on Funeral Friendship. Africa 21:122–24.

Thomson, D. F. 1935. The Joking Relationship and Organized Obscenity in North Queensland. American Anthropologist 37:460–90.

Thompson, J. 1941. Develpment of Facial Expression in Blind and Seeing Children. Archives of Psychology, no. 264:1–47.

Thompson, S. 1946. The Folktale. New York: Dryden Press.

——. 1955. Myths and Folktales. Journal of American Folklore 68:482–88.

——. 1966. Tales of the North American Indians. Bloomington: Indiana University Press. (Originally published in 1929.)

Thorpe, W. H. 1972. The Comparison of Vocal Communication in Animals and Man. *In* Non-verbal Communication, Robert A. Hinde, ed. New York: Cambridge University Press. Pp. 27–48.

Tiger, L. 1970. Men in Groups. New York: Vintage. (Originally published in 1969.)

Titiev, M. 1975. Some Aspects of Clowning among the Hopi Indians. *In* Themes in Culture, Mario D. Zamora, J. M. Mahar, and H. Orenstein, eds. Quezon City, Philippines: Kayumanggi. Pp. 326–36.

Towsen, J. H. 1976. Clowns. New York: Hawthorn.

Trager, G. 1958. Paralanguage: A First Approximation. Studies in Linguistics 13:1–12.

——. 1961. The Typology of Paralanguage. Anthropological Linguistics 3(1):17–21.

Trudgill, P. 1974. Sociolinguistics: An Introduction. Baltimore: Penguin.

Trueblood, E. 1964. The Humor of Christ. New York: Harper & Row.

Turnbull, C. M. 1961. The Forest People. New York: Simon & Schuster.

Turner, J. H., and A. Maryanski. 1979. Functionalism. Menlo Park: Cummings.

Turner, V. W. 1957. Schism and Continuity in an African Society: A Study of Ndembu Village Life. Manchester, England: Manchester University Press.

Tyler, S. A. ed. 1969. Cognitive Anthropology. New York: Rinehart & Winston.

Utley, F. L. 1961. Folk Literature: An Operational Definition. Journal of American Folklore 74:194–206.

Valentine, C. W. 1942. The Psychology of Early Childhood. London: Methuen.

Van den Berghe, P. L. 1963. Institutionalized Licence and Normative Stability. Cahiers d'études africaines 3:413–23.

Van Gennep, A. 1960. The Rites of Passage. Chicago: University of Chicago Press. (Originally published in French in 1909.)

Van Hooff, J. A. R. A. M. 1967. The Facial Displays of the Catarrhine Monkeys and Apes. In Primate Ethology, D. Morris, ed. London: Weidenfeld & Nicholson. Pp. 7–68.

———. 1972. A Comparative Approach to the Phylogeny of Laughter and Smile. In Non-verbal Communication, Robert A. Hinde, ed. New York: Cambridge University Press. Pp. 209–41.

Vatuk, V. P. 1968. Let's Dig Up Some Dirt: The Idea of Humor in Children's Folklore in India. In Proceedings, Eighth International Congress of Anthropological and Ethnological Sciences, vol. 2 (Ethnology). Tokyo: Science Council of Japan. Pp. 274–77.

Vinacke, W. E. 1949. Stereotyping among National-Racial Groups in Hawaii: A Study in Ethnocentrism. Journal of Social Psychology 30:265–91.

———. 1957. Stereotypes as Social Concepts. Journal of Social Psychology 46:229–43.

Voegelin, E. W. 1949. Trickster. In Funk & Wagnalls Standard Dictionary of Folklore, Mythology, and Legend, Maria Leach and Jerome Fried, eds. New York: Funk & Wagnalls. Pp. 1123–25.

Wallace, A. F. C. 1966. Religion: An Anthropological View. New York: Random House.

Wallace, A. F. C., and J. Atkins. 1960. The Meaning of Kinship Terms. American Anthropologist 62:58–80.

Wallace, W. J. 1953. The Role of Humor in the Hupa Indian Tribe. Journal of American Folklore 66:135–41.

Wallis, W. D. 1922. Why Do We Laugh? Scientific Monthly 15:343–47.

Washburn, R. W. 1929. A Study of Smiling and Laughing of Infants in the First Year of Life. Genetic Psychology Monographs 6:396–537.

Webster, G. 1960. Laughter in the Bible. St. Louis: Bethany.

Weitz, S.,ed. 1979. Nonverbal Communication: Readings with Commentary. 2d ed. New York: Oxford University Press.

Welsch, R. L. 1967. American Numskull Tales: The Polack Joke. Western Folklore 26:183–86.

Welsford, E. 1935. The Fool: His Social and Literary History. New York: Farrar & Rinehart.

West, J. 1945. Plainville, U.S.A. New York: Columbia University Press.

Westermarck, E. 1931. Wit and Wisdom of Morocco. New York: H. Liveright.

White, C. M. N. 1957. Joking Relationships in Central Africa. Man 246:187.

———. 1958. A Note on Luvale Joking Relationships. African Studies 17:28–33.

Whiting, B. B., ed. 1963. Six Cultures: Studies of Child Rearing. New York: Wiley.

Whiting, B. B., and C. P. Edwards. 1973. A Cross-cultural Analysis of Sex Differences in the Behavior of Children Aged Three through Eleven. Journal of Social Psychology 91:171–88.

Whiting, J. M. 1941. Becoming a Kwoma. New Haven: Yale University Press.

Whorf, B. L. 1964. Language, Thought, and Reality: Selected Writings of Benjamin Lee Whorf. Ed. and with an introduction by John B. Carroll. Cambridge: MIT Press. (Originally published in 1956.)

Wilde, L. 1973a. The Official Polish Joke Book. New York: Pinnacle.

———. 1973b. The Official Italian Joke Book. New York: Pinnacle.

Wilder, R., Jr. 1977. You All Spoken Here. Spring Hope: Gourd Hollow.

Willeford, W. 1969. The Fool and His Scepter. Evanston, Ill.: Northwestern University Press.

Williams, C. E., and K. N. Stevens. 1972. Emotions and Speech: Some Acoustical Correlates. Journal of the Acoustical Society of America 52:1238–50.

Williams, F. F. 1930. Orokaiva Society. London: Oxford Universtiy Press.

Williams, M. D. 1981. On the Street Where I Lived. New York: Holt, Rinehart & Winston.

Williamson, R. W. 1937. Religion and Social Organization in Central Polynesia. Cambridge: Cambridge University Press.

Wilson, M. 1957. Joking Relationships in Central Africa. Man 57:111–12.

———. 1971. Good Company: A Study of Nyakyusa Age-Villages. Boston: (Originally published in 1951.)

Winick, C. 1961. Space Jokes as Indication of Attitudes towards Space. Journal of Social Issues 17:43–49.

Wiser, W. H., and C. V. Wiser. 1965. Behind Mud Walls 1930–1960. Berkeley: University of California Press. (Originally published in 1930.)

Wolcott, H. F. 1967. A Kwakiutl Village and School. New York: Holt, Rinehart & Winston.

Wolfenstein, M. 1954. Children's Humor: A Psychological Analysis. Glendale: Free Press.

Wolff, H. A., C. E. Smith, and H. A. Murray. 1934. The Psychology of Humor: A Study of Responses to Race-Disparagement Jokes. Journal of Abnormal and Social Psychology 28:341–65.

Wolff, P. H. 1963. Observations on the Early Development of Smiling. In Determinants of Infant Behavior, vol. 2, B. M. Foss, ed. London: Methuen. Pp. 113–33.

———. 1966. The Causes, Controls, and Organization of Behavior in the Neonate. Psychological Issues 5(1, Whole No. 17):1–99.

———. 1969. The Natural History of Crying and Other Vocalizations in Early Infancy. *In* Determinants of Infant Behavior, vol. 4, B. M. Foss, ed. London: Methuen. Pp. 81–109.

Zenner,W. P. 1970. Joking and Ethnic Stereotyping. Anthropological Quarterly 43:93–113.

Zigler, E., J. Levine, and L. Gould. 1966a. The Humor Response of Normal, Institutionalized Retarded, and Non-institutionalized Retarded Children. American Journal of Mental Deficiency 71:472–80.

———. 1966b. Cognitive Processes in the Development of Children's Appreciation of Humor. Child Development 37:507–18.

———. 1967. Cognitive Challenge as a Factor in Children's Humor Appreciation. Journal of Personality and Social Psychology 6:332–36.

Zucker, W. M. 1967. The Clown as the Lord of Disorder. Theology Today 24:306–17.

Index of Cultures, Ethnic Groups, Geographical Areas, Languages, and Religions

Index of Cultures

Subject Index

LIBRARY OF CONGRESS CATALOGING IN PUBLICATION DATA

Apte, Mahadev L.
  Humor and laughter.

  Bibliography: p.
  Includes index.
  1. Wit and humor—Cross-cultural studies. I. Title.
GN454.55.A68 1985   306'.48   84-15618
ISBN 0-8014-1720-1 (alk. paper)